Searching for Peace

Searching
for
Peace

A MEMOIR OF ISRAEL

EHUD OLMERT

BROOKINGS INSTITUTION PRESS
Washington, D.C.

The Brookings Institution is a private nonprofit organization devoted to research, education, and publication on important issues of domestic and foreign policy. Its principal purpose is to bring the highest quality independent research and analysis to bear on current and emerging policy problems. Interpretations or conclusions in Brookings publications should be understood to be solely those of the authors.

Library of Congress Control Number: 2021950365

ISBN 9780815738923 (hc)
ISBN 9780815738930 (ebook)

9 8 7 6 5 4 3 2 1

Typeset in Calluna

Composition by Elliott Beard

Contents

Contents

Searching for Peace

The View from Cellblock 10

The Sabbath. I sit in the rec room of Cellblock 10 at the Maasiyahu Penitentiary, halfway between the cities of Lod and Ramla in central Israel. Around me, silence.

A few of the other inmates are tucked away in their cells, reading or praying. The rec room is not large, and there is an old television set off to the side that, in the evening, will be turned on to show a European soccer match to the inmates. A window opens to our little courtyard, where one of the inmates has planted a small vegetable garden. I sit at a small desk and write, longhand, on a legal pad.

Most of the inmates here were convicted in the case known as the Holyland Hotel Affair. I live with them, even though that particular scandal—in which dozens of officials, including myself, were accused of bribery and money laundering, an affair that captured the country's imagination for several years and made me the subject of countless commentaries and personal attacks—saw me acquitted by four justices of Israel's Supreme Court.

Holyland was one of my many vindications in court. After years of rumors, investigations, trials, and appeals—literally dozens of different cases—I successfully cleared my name in all but a small number of tangential and minor charges. None of the big cases you may have heard of ended in conviction on the central charge that justified the entire prosecutorial and political spectacle surrounding them. Most of these, indeed, amounted to nothing: closed investigations, decisions not to indict, acquittals in court, acquittals on appeal.

A small number of them, however, did end in conviction on charges that included bribery and obstruction. I ended up with a prison sentence that began in February 2016 and ended sixteen months later.

I wrote the majority of this book during that time.

Like all the other accusations against me, my two convictions were not just, as I will explain in some detail later on. They were, rather, the product of a prolonged campaign that began immediately after I entered the Prime Minister's Office in January 2006 and ended only after I was behind bars.

I have never been a criminal. To the contrary, every office I held was seen by everyone who dealt with it as a model not only of efficiency and effective decisionmaking, but also of probity. My convictions were not in any way related to the original indictments that led to my resignation as prime minister in 2008, or to anything I allegedly did while holding the nation's highest elected office. They were based on highly questionable evidence stemming from my earlier terms as mayor of Jerusalem or as minister of industry and trade—evidence that, I am convinced, would never have stood up in court if I had been an ordinary citizen.

But I went to prison anyway, left only to try and figure out what it meant.

Today, more than ever, I am convinced that things did not happen by chance. Rather, a tremendous array of forces, based not only in Israel but also in the United States, came to the conclusion early on that the government I led threatened something they held dear.

As we will see, my political opponents on the right, who believed that any territorial compromise in the pursuit of a peace deal with the Palestinians was tantamount to treason, enjoyed endless financing from abroad, as well as the feverish cooperation of certain elements in the local legal establishment. Erasing me from the political map became their highest priority, one that justified unprecedented acts, even for a country that had known its share of bloody political battles.

———

On February 15, 2016, I surrendered myself to prison authorities. Weeks earlier, Israel's Supreme Court had cut four and a half years off a six-year sentence that had been handed down by Judge David Rosen of the District Court in Tel Aviv. I was left with eighteen months—which, after more legal additions and subtractions, became sixteen.

For years, my wife, Aliza, and I had talked about the possibility that I would go to prison. She had, of course, followed every twist of the plot: The days and nights before each interrogation, the police questioning, the reports in the media, the slander, the distortions, the bile. She had always told me there was nothing to see here, just a mixture of coincidences and the ordinary perils of public life.

Slowly, however, she grew to understand that I was being actively pursued by people who wanted to see me fail and fall, and not just my political opponents, but also key members of the legal establishment who, through a process that was complex yet unmistakable, wanted to remove me from public life, and then to punish me in a way that would retroactively justify the effort.

Aliza never thought I deserved special treatment. She simply could not accept that the things I was accused of, detached from reality as they were, would lead to such an end.

The ruling of the District Court was a wake-up call.

It wasn't just the conviction, or even the long sentence Rosen handed down, as much as the justification he gave. Rosen, an imperious man with an insatiable appetite for media exposure and an unfortunate tendency to have his rulings overturned on appeal, concluded that I had knowingly allowed the transfer of half a million shekels, or about $150,000, to relieve the debts of my brother Yossi, and that this was, effectively, a bribe that I had accepted.

I had been out of touch with Yossi for years.

Yossi had given up a successful academic career for an ill-considered attempt at politics. His political adventures, including his futile run for mayor of the city of Ra'anana, had brought him to financial ruin, and, consequently, into black-market loans and debts he could not repay. He fled the country, divorced his lovely wife, Linda, cut himself off from his three daughters, and has not been back to Israel since. My other brothers, Ami and Yermi, kept in touch with him on occasion. He always needed money. But none of us had any idea how deep a hole he had dug. When we found out, we tried to help him as best we could, but we never crossed the line into anything illegal. Nobody knows this better than Yossi.

According to Rosen, however, the idea that a respectable scholar and man of letters like Yossi could come into that kind of money without telling his brother about it was unthinkable. Yossi's testimony, in which he admitted his own wrongdoing, didn't undermine Rosen's confidence. He ignored the evidence before him and decided it was "impossible" that Yossi would receive the money—which was never proven to have been received at all, or even to have existed—without telling me.

Naturally, I appealed to the Supreme Court. In their ruling, the justices apparently thought they were handing me a lifeline. They said they had cleared me of the "main charge." Aliza and I saw it differently. Yes, eighteen months was better than six years. But it should have been clear that the same reasoning that cleared me of charges in the Holyland case should have exonerated me in this case, as well: Both accusations lacked any concrete documentary evidence and were based on the testimony of the same man, a confessed criminal named Shmuel Dachner, who claimed he had given Yossi the money.

After the final ruling, I had forty-five days to get ready for prison.

Members of my security detail who had protected me for years now briefed me on my incarceration. As a former prime minister, I continued to have security even after leaving office, as I still do today. Maasiyahu Penitentiary, they explained, was spending $1.5 million to create a special wing, Cellblock 10, which could hold about 15 prisoners. They had visited the prison and inspected the cellblock but had no influence over anything. Prison conditions are decided by the Prison Authority. I saw photos, including of the individual cells, taken by Shin Bet, Israel's internal security agency that is also charged with protecting senior officials. I was asked whether I wanted to live alone or with cellmates.

I had no idea who the other prisoners in the block would be, and I said I preferred my own cell. I planned on spending a lot of time writing and wanted to be free of social obligations.

Soon afterwards they informed me that having my own cell wasn't an option after all. I was given the names of two convicts vetted by Shin Bet, and I was asked what I thought about them.

The first was Danny Dankner, a former senior banking executive serving time in connection with the Holyland affair. We had known each other for years, though we were never close. I immediately said yes. The second was the former city planner for Jerusalem, Uri Sheetrit, who had been convicted in the same affair, for allegedly taking bribes. Uri had been my right-hand man in many of the development projects we had done when I was mayor. We were friendlier than was normal for a mayor and his subordinate. Delighted, I agreed. Looking back, I know I made the right choice. Danny, Uri, and I became close.

Danny proved to be an impressive human being: Sweet, warm, determined, curious, an avid reader who felt a sense of responsibility for the entire cellblock. He was also a fantastic cook. The food delivered to the cellblock three times a day was a weird mix of formerly frozen food, long-chilled raw vegetables, and other staples. No Michelin stars for prison mess halls. But once Danny did his magic, it was not bad at all.

Twice a month we were allowed to place orders through the prison canteen, at our own expense. Danny, along with Uri and Eliezer Simchaioff, who had been my deputy in the municipality and was also convicted in the Holyland affair, decided what we needed to make our food palatable.

Danny was a significant figure, and not just in the kitchen. He kept us organized, scheduling our chores and acting as manager of the cellblock by mutual consent. He also planted a small garden in the yard, growing vegetables and herbs.

Uri was no less important in his role. An internationally renowned architect, Uri had graduated *magna cum laude* from Harvard, spoke fluent English and French, was a classical music aficionado, a crossword puzzle genius, and a student of history and literature. In his spare time, he gave the other inmates English lessons. All in all, my two cellmates had a lot to teach me, and were wonderful companions.

———

At 8:30 a.m. on February 15, 2016, I left my home in Motza. Aliza and I said goodbye as I left the house, as on an ordinary day. A warm hug, a gracious smile from this incredible woman whom I was blessed to meet half a century before.

Our family has never stood on ceremony. I felt awful for the suffering I was causing her, but I knew she would be surrounded by friends, both hers and mine.

I would miss her deeply in prison. She made sure to visit whenever she was allowed, which would lift my sprits to no end. Our children supported her. Sometimes I called her in the evening, and she let out a sigh of relief. "Finally I have some time to myself," she said. "All day long it's just friends and grandchildren."

My security detail, after careful preparation, managed to avoid the many reporters and camera crews who had gathered at the prison by bringing me in through a side entrance.

I walked twenty feet in, surrounded by men taller and younger than myself, and was swallowed into the facility. My detail stayed behind. From that moment on, I was an inmate.

I looked at the prison guards. They looked at me. Looks of surprise. Like they couldn't believe I actually showed up. My bags were opened and thoroughly checked. My aftershave, my fitness watch, my DVDs, other unimportant things—they couldn't come in with me. My jeans and t-shirts apparently weren't a problem.

A few more steps accompanied by an officer, and I was in Cellblock 10. The block commander, whom we'll call Esther, waited for me.

She smiled and introduced herself. I did the same. Handshake? No, we don't shake hands with inmates. This was my first lesson about life behind bars. My biggest problem, it seemed, would be the fear that somebody would interpret any words and gestures toward me as violating the norms concerning inmates. Everyone was equal, and I might even be less so. Nobody on earth cared what an ordinary inmate complained about and why the authorities accepted or rejected his request. When it came to this particular inmate, anything I said or did could end up on the news.

The wardens held me to account for any reports that appeared in the media. When it did happen, I knew they were the ones who had leaked. When I was in politics, I had a lot of experience with the police, the prosecutor's office, and the courts. They, too, always blamed me for leaks. From the details of the news items, however, I knew it was them. It could not have been anyone else. I gave up on that argument a long time ago.

———

I don't want to compare our conditions with those of inmates at other Israeli prisons. Without question, this small, intimate cellblock, with its calm and warm relationships, was much better off than others. The guards, who rotated in shifts every day, were friendly. The fact that their prisoners included a former prime minister, a former CEO of the country's biggest bank, and a few others who had held top positions in different areas sparked their curiosity and gave them a sense of importance.

Their work was also a lot easier than that of their colleagues at other prisons. From day one, all the inmates in our block, without even bothering to coordinate, followed every rule and showed uncompromising respect for the guards and wardens. It was not easy or fun. None of us wanted to be there, but we all wanted to get through it as smoothly as possible.

The cellblock locked down at 8:30 p.m, and we couldn't even go out into our little courtyard after that. The individual cells were bolted at 10:00 p.m. and didn't reopen until 6:00 a.m. We were stuck in our rooms. Three of us, together, with our books and newspapers.

Again, we did have a television in the rec room. At first, most of the channels were in Arabic or Russian. Only three channels in Hebrew. No sports, at least at first. This particularly annoyed me. I'm a big sports fan. No movie channels either, except for one in Arabic.

It was only natural that inmates turned to me for help. They knew the cellblock had been built for me in order to create proper conditions for a former prime minister, and they expected me to take up their issues with the wardens. I didn't really care for the role, but it was unavoidable: Not just the wardens but also top officials of the Prison Authority always wanted to chat with me. They sought my advice as well as insight on issues of the day, and it became a perfect opportunity to pass along the inmates' complaints. Senior officials would come to the prison, spend no more than three minutes inspecting it, and then summon me for a private talk.

And so, almost daily I had the opportunity to raise our problems. Why couldn't the inmates bring aftershave from home? Aftershave, I was told, had alcohol, and somebody might drink it. I asked whether Cellblock 10 inmates seemed like the type of people who would drink aftershave. The answer was always the same: "Those are the rules."

They said we could purchase aftershave in the prison canteen. So I did. It said on the bottle that the aftershave contained alcohol. I asked whether that meant I was allowed to drink the aftershave, so long as I had bought it at the canteen, which was of course more expensive than stores on the outside.

Another example. My fitness watch was confiscated when I went in. I never understood why. They told me that maybe it had a concealed thumb drive, and I'd be able to pass documents. But my fitness watch didn't have a concealed thumb drive.

In general, whatever prisoners took with them to prison on the first day was all they got to keep with them the entire sentence. If they read all their books and wanted new ones, they had wait until a furlough and then take home the same number as they wanted to bring in.

The same was true for shirts, pants, underwear, and socks. There's probably a logic to these rules, but inmates did not usually understand it. I certainly didn't. I expected the Prison Authority to show a measure of flexibility and judgment, to distinguish among different inmates depending on the crimes they committed, how dangerous they were, or what they were capable of understanding. Not to blindly apply the same rules to every inmate.

And so, we weren't allowed to bring in movies on DVD, because the discs might also have data burned on them. We could only purchase movies from the canteen. My son Shaul brought me 160 DVDs filled with my favorite TV shows. I asked whether they could inspect the discs before letting them in. At first the warden said I could bring in thirty at a time, swapping them out for another thirty when I was done with them. Then they told me thirty was too many, and I would need to make do with just fifteen. Then they told me I couldn't bring in any. I asked why. They told me that the original permission was only for home movies like weddings or other personal events, not TV shows.

I asked: How many home movies could anyone possibly have? Who would bring thirty of them to prison and then swap them out for another thirty? "Those are the rules," I was told. But we could buy DVDs at the canteen. The selection was meager, and the prices were double what they were outside.

———

Who else was in Cellblock 10?

Aside from Danny and Uri, we also had Igor, whose Russian was still better than his Hebrew. Igor was my exercise partner, and he was younger and stronger than I. When I bench-pressed 110 pounds, or pulled 190, he would add a few dozen more pounds for himself and just enjoy the look on my face. Igor was serving time for larceny and would be released before long. In the meantime, he was willing to do whatever work was given him. He never questioned it. He was a determined fellow, with a strong work ethic and impressive discipline at the gym.

Eliezer Simchaioff, my former deputy at the mayor's office, was a father of nine and had a rapidly growing brood of grandchildren. He added two more in the month we were together. He and Meir Rabin, a real estate developer, were the Orthodox Jews of the block, and they were smart enough not to have high expectations.

A third Orthodox Jew was Tomer Sigron. About age 30, he had been married for just two weeks when he was sent to prison for a fatal car accident he had caused five years earlier. Tomer was, and remains, a good friend. I loved him, and basically adopted him as my own son. He legally added my last name to his own.

Meir Rabin lived deep inside the world of the Torah.

From morning till night, taking breaks only for meals and chores, he sat in the corner of the prison synagogue and studied or prayed. I asked him how many more holy books we'd need to buy so that he wouldn't be left without something to read. He smiled and went back to his books.

Meir was a man of faith to the bottom of his soul. Nothing about him was fake. He wasn't trying to impress anyone.

In civilian life, he had had some business dealings. He was convicted on a charge that nobody had ever in Israeli history been convicted on—he and Danny Dankner, the bank executive. It was called "conspiracy to commit bribery" in the Holyland case. They didn't actually bribe anyone. Nobody was convicted of taking a bribe from them. Yet they apparently conspired to get a public servant to break the law. But there wasn't any actual specific public servant who broke the law or public trust, or who received a bribe from them. I was left scratching my head. How exactly was this a crime under Israeli law?

Danny was actually the first person ever to be charged with this crime, after the same Judge David Rosen of the Tel Aviv District Court warned prosecutors that Danny would be acquitted if they went after him on actual bribery. Okay, they said, so it's not bribery. It's conspiracy to commit bribery. What's important is to put Meir and Danny behind bars. It was bizarre. It was also depressing.

Meir was sentenced to five years. He never complained or despaired. "The Lord delivers in the blink of an eye," he kept saying. Meanwhile he would pray, study, do chores, respect everyone around him—and everyone loved him in return. A special man. His sister and brothers were all lawyers. They, too, were Orthodox, but less steeped in the world of Torah.

When you read about people convicted of theft, bribery, and fraud, you probably imagine some pretty bad folks. People who have abandoned societal norms, people who victimize innocents. People to avoid.

But when circumstances are such that you actually spend time with these people, you sometimes find that they are sensitive human beings. Sometimes they are victims of circumstance—social, economic, or personal—that put them on a downward path. Sometimes they are good people, honest people, complete innocents who fell victim to unscrupulous prosecutors, people who simply didn't have enough money to defend themselves properly.

I know it may sound cynical. Some people will deride me for defending them. My life experience, however, gave me a very good eye for people. Meir Rabin was no criminal. True, he was convicted by Judge Rosen, and lost his appeal. But as he put it, "If I had not been a Mizrahi Jew, they would have seen me as a 'strategic consultant' rather than a *macher.* Nobody would have considered putting me on trial."

I'm not sure he was wrong about that.

———

Nati, thirty years old, joined us a few months after I arrived.

He was in prison for negligent homicide. He had caused a deadly traffic accident and accepted a plea deal. It didn't include an agreement about the sentence. The magistrate court gave him eight months. The prosecutor appealed the sentence (prosecutors can do that in Israel), saying that somebody was killed and Nati should pay a heavy price. He hadn't been smoking or talking on his phone or drinking or in any other way distracted from his driving. The appeal was heard by the Beersheba District Court.

A convict who appears in court has to wear a prison uniform. He is handcuffed and put in leg irons and then transferred to a local jail together with other shackled inmates. There they are loaded into a holding cell, like barrels of barley, the day before their court appearance. Nati spent the night with dozens of other inmates in the same cell, so that he could be on time for court the next morning.

Before entering the courtroom, they uncuffed his hands, but his feet remained shackled. That's how he appeared in court. The judged tacked on another four months. A year in all. The hearing ended at midday. He was taken out of the courtroom, cuffed again, and moved back into the holding cell and then overnight in a nearby prison. He was transferred back to Cellblock 10 the next day, in the late afternoon.

Why do you need to put someone who has no prior criminal record and no history of violence in chains? Why throw him into a truck that is barely fit for humans, without a shred of dignity? Why couldn't they take him to court and bring him back the same day?

Yes, those are the rules, and they apply to everyone. But shouldn't there be an enormous difference in the way inmates are treated depending on whether they're repeat offenders or those who obviously will never be back again? Isn't there a huge difference between a violent criminal and someone like Nati who's already paying an unfathomable price for an isolated, nonviolent lapse?

We had other inmates who were convicted in cases of terrible accidents.

One was Yaakov from Holon. He had no criminal record. He was driving an eighteen-wheeler when the trailer swerved out of the lane, hitting a bus, killing four passengers. When we sat in a group session and took turns sharing our experiences, Yaakov burst into tears. He was still living the nightmare of the lives he took, the families he destroyed. "I deserve my punishment," he said of his three-year sentence. He had not been drinking or texting as he drove. But he had caused the deaths of four people. The guilt never left him.

Being in prison helped Yaakov. It made him feel like he was somehow atoning for the suffering he had caused. Some people are like that. Not everyone plays the victim. It was really important having a man of his quality with us, and he also did a great job running the laundry room. We would bring him laundry twice a week, and he ran the machines and brought the clothes back to us clean. Pressing was not an option. But since we were mostly in jeans and t-shirts, it was the best we could hope for.

———

We took care of each other as well as we could.

Every man had his own needs. We had three Orthodox Jews, and their way of life was different from mine. They would wake up before six and by the time we got up they were still wrapped in prayer shawls in the synagogue room, with tefillin on their arms and foreheads. For them, praying in a *minyan*—a quorum of ten—was mission critical. For many of us it was utterly foreign, and certainly not important.

But we had to get through this together. For some of us, having access to sports broadcasts was important. We eventually got the channels that enabled us to watch soccer, basketball, tennis, the EuroCup. For the Orthodox, it was important that for half an hour every day we joined them in prayer to complete the necessary quorum of ten men. I convinced my friends to join them. All through the week there were successful *minyanim*, on Friday nights we would join them for Kabbalat Shabbat, and on Saturdays we would join them for prayers including a weekly Torah reading. We didn't suffer too much. We didn't feel it was forced on us. That was our way of creating an atmosphere of tolerance and mutual respect. Over the years I've learned that understanding begets understanding in return.

We got to sleep around 1:00 a.m. Danny would give us each a piece of dark chocolate before bed.

Sometimes I would stay up even later, if the writing was flowing and my hand still had strength. The guards woke us at six, checking in on us to make sure we hadn't escaped or died during the night. Most of us rolled over and went back to sleep, other than Danny who got up to smoke. By 8:30, we were all up, our beds made. Not as well as in a hotel. Not even as well as at home. But they looked neat enough, as did the cell.

Breakfast wasn't communal. Everyone took something out of the fridge in the kitchen. Danny, Uri, and I would make each other hot drinks, take some soft white cheese, crackers, and sardines in chili sauce, and by nine we were ready for the cellblock commander's inspection. She looked at the cells, asked a few questions, sometimes none at all. She smiled, or sometimes not. Usually not. She went on to the next cell.

By 9:05 we were getting on with our day. I read the paper, checked the obituaries to find out whom I'd have to call to offer condolences, and then walked around the cellblock sharing my experiences from the night before with my friends.

We took turns with chores. Danny was the boss. Early on he was picked to be the cellblock's "CEO." He denied having that role, but everyone gladly accepted his authority. If anyone came to me for help to appeal his decisions regarding duties in the kitchen, washing floors, cleaning the cells, he would get the same answer: Danny's authority is absolute. The result was that our block was clean and polished, and there was a pleasant atmosphere, full of activity.

When I had a job to do, I did it. When it was my turn to chop vegetables, I did my best. When the hallway floor needed washing and it was my turn, I washed it. Some of the inmates were aghast the first time they saw me with a squeegee in my hand. They ran up to me, ripped it away, and said, "Are you nuts? Our prime minister will not wash floors. Not a chance." I sat them down for a talk. Danny and Uri were even more assertive about this. They told them, "Ehud doesn't want to be any different from the rest of us. He feels like an equal and will be happier if you treat him that way."

In my own home, I washed dishes and floors. Why shouldn't I do the same in prison?

I tried to take advantage of the early-morning quiet to write a little more about my world around me. There wasn't much time before the lawyer visits, followed by an intense workout at the gym, then lunch, and then a group lecture by a social worker about what it was like to be in prison for the first time. Then a few hours of rest. I would write then, as well, and later turn on the sports channel. A little more writing and reading, and then summing up the day with my cellmates before bed.

In between all of that, a medic would show up with our daily pills. One inmate had back spasms, another had heartburn, another had high blood pressure, or needed blood thinners (that would be me), or a sleeping pill. Inmates weren't allowed to keep their own pills. Instead we would be given them by the medic, and he had to watch us take them.

The fear of inmate suicide is real. I don't really understand why it applied to us, however. All of us were first-timers, relaxed, disciplined. None of us had a massive axe to grind back home that weighed on our minds. But caution is the name of the game. Those were the rules.

————

It was only natural that my presence, along with that of a few other prominent inmates in this cellblock, would cause the guards and professional staff some confusion. On the one hand, the inmates spoke to them as equals. None of us ever talked down to them. We all lived simply, wore jeans or sweatpants and t-shirts. We all hung out by the communal telephone for hours, sharing experiences with friends and family. We were all, in many ways, just like them—so the guards told us—even though some of us were infamous, demonized on television.

On the other hand, these were convicts. Was it possible that men like these were wrongfully convicted? Maybe they didn't take bribes after all? Maybe they didn't commit fraud or break other laws? Was a prime minister jailed for no reason? The chairman of a big bank stripped of his assets and imprisoned unjustly?

How do you square that circle—the contrast between the kind of people in this cellblock with the crimes they were convicted of: this was the big question, and not just for the prison staff but also for many of our best friends on the outside, people who told us warmly, with compassion and friendship, that they just couldn't make sense of our sentencing. Like the staff, they might even have said to themselves: Is it possible that the Supreme Court of Israel made an error so grave that it would destroy a man's life, someone who had contributed so much? Could the judges not look past the unhinged anger of the prosecutors, journalists, and other puritans, and see the truth?

The answer is no, they often couldn't. It turns out that there are many people who carry the awful burden of false convictions. Judges make mistakes. Not out of malice. If a prime minister, an Israel Defense Forces chief of staff, an engineer, a doctor, a teacher or truck driver can all make mistakes—why can't a judge?

Of course they can. The only difference is that judges are immune to criticism. In Israel, anyone who dares suggest that a court ruled incorrectly gets tarred as an enemy of the rule of law. Judges are seen as a symbol of justice, humility, and honesty.

Sorry, but I'm not there. I have seen too much. I can't live with that illusion.

———

Losing your freedom is a heavy punishment.

Imprisonment shouldn't necessarily mean that someone who has already lost his freedom, even if he committed the crime, should also be crushed under heel, or be made to suffer unnecessary indignities. It makes no difference whether we're talking about repeat offenders—as most inmates, unfortunately, are—or people who are in prison for the first time. We need to find a smart way to turn prisons into a platform for rehabilitation, for healing, and for inculcating norms that can form the basis of a new life once they're out.

But that requires having people in charge of the system who are insightful, flexible, and progressive in their thinking—and I didn't see that during my time in prison. I spent my whole career making decisions that shaped the lives of individuals and families, offering them hope and sometimes disappointment. In some of my roles, these were life-and-death decisions. Even as an inmate, I didn't let myself sink into self-pity. I looked around and asked what could be improved.

Prisons, however, are the lowest priority in the national conversation.

Who talks about prison conditions? Who protests when a prisoner is brought into court in chains, or asks whether the man is actually dangerous, even as he's surrounded by guards? How many hearings has the Knesset held to discuss the quality of life for convicts? Who has ever demanded an increase in the budget of the prison system to have it meet international standards? I don't remember the subject ever coming up.

It will be argued: Why didn't I do something about it when I was prime minister? Good question. There were many things I didn't do anything about. A prime minister has to set priorities. There are many important issues that he simply can't deal with himself.

I am most disappointed in the leadership of the Prison Authority. It's no secret that I'm not a huge fan of the police and its top brass. Many of them behave unprofessionally, arrogantly, brutally. Only when I met the heads of the Prison Authority did I start asking myself harder questions. Who appoints them? Who trains them and gives them tools to deal with a population so diverse and problematic? Some of them were former local police chiefs who were sent over to the prisons because they weren't fit for promotion within the force. My meetings with them raised doubts about their abilities to wisely and compassionately manage so sensitive a system.

———

The second item on Channel 2's news hour one night was a report that I had received visits from no fewer than thirty-seven lawyers.

Many of these, the reporter said, were personal friends who took advantage of their law licenses to visit me. At no point had anyone from the prison said a word to me about the number of visits. But somebody was, apparently, keeping count.

First thing the next morning, we were told that there would be new rules about lawyer visits. They would be limited in number and could not last more than forty-five minutes. From the timing it was clear the head of the Prison Authority had prepared these rules before the story even broke. The legal term is *ad personam*—rules made with a specific individual in mind.

Lawyer visits were a pleasant diversion. It was flattering to discover how many people wanted to see me. Most of them were busy people, and coming to the prison involved traveling, waiting, meeting me, and traveling back. How many billable hours were they missing just to spend time with a fallen prime minister?

These meetings did not, ever, conflict with my prison obligations. On the contrary, I would reschedule them around any prison activity, even though I didn't have to. There was a sanctity around lawyer visits—they took priority above all else, even above meetings with the prison commanders. Suddenly, that sanctity was gone.

The leak, the rule change, the time limits—these were all a needless provocation. They were obviously motivated by a desire to get the attention of a couple of journalists and "enlightened" purists, to get the head of the Prison Authority a few moments of TV fame through cheap populism. I even wondered whether she had been given instructions by somebody above her, or whether she was acting to please her superiors.

Whatever the motivation, she ended up walking it back. She informed me later on that the thirty-seven attorneys who had previously visited could keep coming to see me. I replied, in a letter, that I have taken note that I am allowed to meet with thirty-seven attorneys.

One day, an attorney came to advise me on some tax issues surrounding a company I owned. They didn't let him in. "He's not on your list of thirty-seven," they said.

"I don't have a list of thirty-seven," I said. "That's your list, not mine."

"The fact is," they said, "you wrote in your letter that you are aware that you are allowed to meet with the thirty-seven attorneys that you had previously met."

"That's true," I said, "but where does it say I can't meet any others? This lawyer is dealing with important legal matters for me."

The Prison Authority always had answers. "The policy right now," I was told, "is that anyone who appears on the list of thirty-seven attorneys who previously visited you, even if they are not coming on legal business, may visit. Anyone who's not on the list, even if he is dealing with your legal affairs, will be denied entry."

In the meantime I got the lawyers union to file suit with the Supreme Court against the new rules, especially concerning the time limits. Lawyers often meet with convicts for hours on end, preparing testimony in court. Time limits were a clear violation of their rights.

In response, the State Attorney's office, acting in the name of the Legal Adviser to the Prison Authority, responded with a flat denial that such limitations had ever been imposed. Other lawyers, representing inmates, presented sworn depositions from attorneys claiming that their client meetings had been cut short by prison guards, who told them that their forty-five minutes were up and they had to leave.

In other words, the Prison Authority lied to the court.

They had good reasons to be terrified the lie would come to light, so the time limits suddenly disappeared. The other limits were lifted, as well, as long as the last meeting of the day ended by 4:45 p.m. All this just proves that the entire affair was a publicity stunt meant to give the Prison Authority head her fifteen minutes of fame and a seal of approval from the puritans of the legal establishment.

———

At first glance, Cellblock 10 was just like any other at the Maasiyahu Penitentiary, which housed hundreds of inmates. In reality it was very different. There were cameras everywhere. At the entrance, opposite Esther's office, there was a control room, where a guard sat in front of the screens all day, studying the camera feeds. Two of the cells had cameras as well. One was mine. The other was empty.

The control room usually had a few additional guards. When I sat in the rec room and wrote, or watched TV, a guard showed up every few minutes to make sure I was still there. I asked one of the wardens why we were so closely watched. It was not like any of us were likely to escape. He said that the concern in our case was not a breakout as much as a break-in. I couldn't tell if he was joking, but it sounded idiotic.

I once asked the prison warden whether, given the intense scrutiny we were all under, it wasn't possible to leave our cell doors unlocked at night. He said, in all seriousness, that there was no reason to give us special treatment. I pointed out that in other cellblocks, ten inmates weren't being watched by four guards around the clock, and there weren't cameras in their cells.

Our guards also took turns writing things down in some kind of journal. I tried once to find out what exactly they were writing. It turned out that they were logging everything we did. When I was in my cell, when I slept, when I was in the rec room, when I watched TV. Why? No idea. My life had never been so closely scrutinized—and that is saying a lot.

Esther would show up at work before 8:00 a.m. When I emerged from my cell and made myself tea, I would see her closely reading the journal, getting up to speed on what had happened in the cellblock overnight. Sometimes, she would summon one of the inmates for a reprimand over something a guard had written down.

I, too, was summoned.

My fellow inmates wanted me to give a talk once a week about current events, and also about things I had been directly involved in as prime minister. I agreed, of course. Despite the intense curiosity, I never revealed any classified information. There were plenty of great stories without it.

One of the inmates posted a notice on the bulletin board, inviting everyone to a talk with me one evening. It read: "Our friend Ehud Olmert, the once and future Prime Minister, will speak on such and such a day and time."

Esther hauled me into her office and asked me what the notice was supposed to mean.

I asked her what, exactly, was troubling her.

She said, "Why does the notice say 'once *and future* Prime Minister'?"

I laughed. I hadn't actually seen it, and certainly hadn't written it. "Someone was trying to flatter me, I guess. Is that a problem?"

Esther answered that political activity was strictly prohibited in prison.

I don't suppose they choose cellblock commanders based on their sense of humor. At any rate, I went to the bulletin board and crossed out "and future," to make her happy. I decided it would be a waste of time to explain to her just how long the road was from Maasiyahu Penitentiary back to the Prime Minister's Office, and that it did not seem well paved for me.

———

At lunch and dinner, we ate together.

Over dinner, all the differences we brought with us into prison vanished. We would talk about the little things of life in prison for a few hours before the doors locked and we were relegated to our cells. Before the guards did the head count for the millionth time, in case anyone had escaped, even though they knew full well that everyone was there and nobody had left or could leave.

My friends asked me how I kept my spirits up.

I don't have a good answer for why some things happened to other people and not to me. Why I felt good, happy, optimistic. The years before my incarceration were extremely hard—all the insults, the public humiliation—and I never lost my sense of self. This wasn't new with me. My whole life, even during wartime, even when meeting with families that had just buried their loved ones, meetings that were nothing short of heartbreaking, or even at times when I was accused and verbally assaulted, or when making decisions that would mean death for many and would bring military reprisals against us—I don't remember a single occasion when I lost my bearings or reacted out of emotion. I learned over the years how to keep my cool. All the more so in prison.

Maybe this fact disappointed some people, but there was no chance I would fall into depression. On the contrary, I felt I had a duty to make a show, for the other inmates, of the joie de vivre, the self-confidence, determination, and inner peace I truly felt. If I could do it, so could they. If, after the injustice I had endured, I could be at peace—so could they. And if we were all at peace, we could get through this unpleasant experience relatively easily. The strategy proved itself.

My daughter Michal brought me a gift. A black t-shirt with the words "mega-optimist" emblazoned in white. Her neighbor had printed it for me. I saw it as a message to the wardens. Do whatever you want, make up new rules, constrain us, take away our belts, our aftershave—nothing will break my spirit. I really hoped nobody would want to test my resolve. But if they did, I would overcome.

I planned on leaving prison stronger than when I went in, happy even when sad, hoping for the best even in the middle of a storm.

———

Everyone brought books to prison.

Mystery novels were the most common, especially Harlan Coben. Books were passed around. Daniel Silva, too, was well represented. He's a pro-Israel Jew, whom I've met in person. He wrote a whole series of fascinating books about Israel's fight against Islamic terror. The lead character is Gabriel Allon, a veteran Mossad agent, one of Israel's secret heroes. He is fictional, of course, but Silva manages to make him complex and compelling, a restorer of old paintings whose reputation precedes him. He's also a cold-blooded killer.

Silva lives in Washington, D.C., but his books are filled with the jargon of our own intelligence services. He clearly has friends in the Mossad, in Military Intelligence, in Shin Bet—but the reality he describes bears little resemblance to the real world of spies. I told him once that even though I know a thing or two about intelligence operations, I'm an avid reader of his books, and I especially love the fact that the good guys—us, that is—always win.

For some reason my own reading kept going back to World War II and the years that led up to it, and especially the Holocaust. William Shirer, author of *The Rise and Fall of the Third Reich*, also wrote a series called *Twentieth Century Journal*. We are used to reading history books written on the basis of scholarly and archival research and older firsthand accounts. Shirer, however, was there. He met socially with Ernest Hemingway, James Joyce, T. S. Elliot, Gertrude Stein, Sinclair Lewis, Thornton Wilder—he shares all his conversations with them. This is very different from historiography. Intimate conversations with figures still early in their careers, before they became famous—it's fascinating. Shirer's books kept me awake late into the night.

I know there will be some who say: "You see? It's not so bad in prison." It's a good joke. I would prefer to read books at home.

———

In 2016, the state comptroller issued a report about the travel agency used by the family of the prime minister, Benjamin Netanyahu.

This was actually the hardest thing I endured in prison. I thought I would explode. I, a man who can withstand even the most vile affronts, thought I was going to lose it.

For years they went after me about my trips abroad. The attorney general and the police leaked every last detail about the investigation against me in the Rishon Tours affair, and did so even before the investigators were done questioning me. The affair, in which it was claimed that I had double-billed my travel expenses to multiple charities that had flown me abroad to help their fundraising efforts, was handed to the media on a silver platter. Photographs of travel receipts appeared in *Haaretz*. They made me out to be a thief, saying I had stolen from my favorite charitable organizations. Days, nights, crazy flights, little sleep—all of these were the price of my boundless commitment to these charities. What becomes the headline? That my kids flew abroad on the nonprofit's dime, that I had used technical trickery in the payments. I stress—these charges all ended in acquittal. Not I, not my wife, and not my kids had taken a penny for ourselves. But the avalanche of slander never stopped coming. It tortures me to this day.

Now it turned out that Benjamin Netanyahu was being accused of much worse. According to the report, when he flew to a conference hosted by the British-Israel Public Affairs Committee—BIPAC, a now-defunct British group modeled after the American-Israel Public Affairs Committee, or AIPAC—he stayed at one of the most luxurious hotels in the world, the kind I never dared set foot in, and asked the organization to foot the bill. Mrs. Netanyahu flew first class with her husband. The costs of those flights were covered by Israel Bonds, a state-owned entity under the authority of the Finance Ministry, even though he wasn't flying on their behalf, and at a time when Netanyahu himself was the finance minister.

If these charges were true, it would constitute misdirecting public funds for personal use.

Maybe they were not true. Not everything that appears in such a report is true, even if it's written by the state comptroller. Netanyahu, too, gets the presumption of innocence. But how is it possible that the attorney general refrained from even opening an investigation? We're talking about tens of thousands of dollars' worth of illicit benefits. The police and state attorney's office covered it up. Only because of the courage of a single journalist, Raviv Drucker from Channel 10, did these things come to light and force an inquiry by the state comptroller.

These were things I couldn't get out of my mind.

Despite all my optimism, I couldn't get over my anger, my sense of injustice, my sense that the authorities had conspired against me. I would never let it rest.

————

It is the common practice in Israel that prisoners get a third off their sentence for good behavior. In addition to having to show remorse—a problem for those who maintained their innocence—prisoners looking to get their sentence reduced were required to present the parole board with a letter confirming they had participated for at least six months in a "rehab group."

Some of the inmates were nearing the point of six months before their potential release date, but no rehab groups had been set up by the warden. He was, apparently, in no hurry. They kept telling us "it'll work out." Prime Minister Yitzhak Rabin used to say that the Hebrew expression *yiyeh b'seder*—it'll work out—is a clear signal of sloppiness, shallowness, and negligence. The fact is, for most people who are refused a reduced sentence, it's on the grounds that they didn't spend a full six months in a rehab group.

After two months of discussions, our cellblock finally launched a group dedicated to rehabilitation. The delay came from causes with which I was quite familiar.

In government you often enter a meeting in which everyone in the room knows everything they need to make a decision. The pluses and minuses, the risks and rewards—everything is known, and the decision just requires the ability to overcome obstacles and be flexible. In the case of the rehab group, the best answer required deviating a little from the regulations, taking into account the specific character of our cellblock and its unusual human mix. Nothing would be gained by delaying the decision. And yet, the same empty ritual kept repeating itself. They would summarize the previous discussion, start a new one, summarize that one, and go through it all over again without arriving at a decision, which would be pushed off until the next meeting.

I once heard members of the Likud Party say that their government was unusually "serious." As proof, they cited the number of meetings held on a given issue—ten meetings, each one lasting hours. But I don't call that serious. I see it as a horrible waste of time. Rarely does anything change from one meeting to the next. In the vast majority of cases, a decision made after seven hours of discussion is no better than one made after two. The extra five hours are filled with people repeating things that have already been said, or else the facts, which were known before the meeting started, are ground into fine dust. The only thing that keeps the meeting going is the fear of making a decision.

I often wonder why anyone would want to take a job that requires skills they don't possess.

Making decisions requires a certain mental readiness. It's true in any context or position, in any field of responsibility. The harder or more complex the job, the more decisions that need to be made more frequently, the more difficult it is.

I held a position that required making fateful decisions on a daily basis. Decisions never scared me. I always drove straight to the decision point. Very early in the process, I would say to myself, based on my experience, that every decision requires a risk of failure or conflict—but not making a decision is itself a decision. Here, too, there was a risk. Here, too, people could get hurt. You need to live with the uncertainty—and to decide. And if you go with your conscience, you'll sleep well at night.

Leadership requires certain qualities of character. You need to be determined, stubborn, and sometimes harsh. Yes, a level of unpleasantness, some might call it callousness, is required to make fateful choices without blinking. You have to keep in your heart a vision of the future for your people and your country—and to make decisions that further that vision. To know how to speak with rivals and allies alike. To know how to impose your will, but also how to listen. To keep a cool head when you send people into dangerous situations. How to do battle with your rivals but also how to disappoint your allies. How to dash the hopes of people who were loyal to you, whenever those hopes can't be realized.

It's a strange combination of qualities, which sometimes work together and sometimes clash. But life isn't built in an orderly fashion. Things don't line up. You have to be nice and nasty, callous and generous, calm and pleasant but also unyielding, uncompromising, and unforgiving.

And after all of it, you have to know how to forgive, to think about the future without forgetting the past, to look for joy, to offer hope, and to love.

If you can do all of that, then you'll be ready for the challenges of leadership.

––––––

In the public eye, at least in Israel, I am often seen through the lens of my incarceration—as the first prime minister to have ended up in prison. But sixteen months is a brief period of time, and when I look back on a career spanning five decades, I know that I have been blessed to take part in the history of my country.

From the time I first appeared as an upstart student activist in the 1960s calling for Menachem Begin's resignation as leader of the Herut Party, to my election to Knesset in 1973 in the wake of the Yom Kippur War, to my work leading the Likud electoral campaigns and developing a working relationship with Prime Minister Yitzhak Shamir in the 1980s, to a decade as mayor of Jerusalem in the 1990s, to my close relationship with Prime Minister Ariel Sharon as his deputy in the early 2000s, and finally to the role of prime minister in the wake of Sharon's stroke in early 2006—I have been witness to many of the most fateful decisions made by the leaders of Israel in the last half century.

It was more than just a ringside seat. In a wide range of areas, from the development of trade and health policy to the municipal life of the most important and controversial city on earth, I was given the opportunity to make a real impact through decisions that rested on my own shoulders. As prime minister, I led my country in the Second Lebanon War in 2006, which, though controversial at the time, has given our northern communities a decade and a half of peace. I directed a successful military strike in 2007 to eliminate the possibility of Syria having a nuclear weapon—which would have affected not just Israel but the entire world, especially after Syria later descended into an unthinkable chaos.

In the story that follows, I will also delve into the circumstances of my legal downfall—the forces behind it, which included major players not just in Israel but also in the United States; the deluge of cases that suddenly appeared when I became prime minister but none of which pertained to anything I allegedly did while in that office; and the long-term implications of how money and ideology can distort the democratic process, not just in Israel but around the world.

And most important perhaps, I led the most serious, ambitious effort to reach a final peace agreement with the Palestinians—to fulfill the deepest and most urgent aspirations of both the Israeli and the Palestinian people. This effort came within a hair's breadth of resolving the world's most vexing conflict and changing the fate of both our peoples.

But to understand any of it, it's important to first take a look at the world in which I was born, in the years before the founding of Israel, when the land was still ruled by the British, and the State of Israel was itself still a dream.

We need to go back to the beginning.

ONE

In the Beginning

On the morning of September 30, 1945, my mother lay alone in the maternity ward of Hadassah Hospital in Tel Aviv. She had gone there, on her own, the day before. My father and two brothers, Ami and Yermi, had stayed behind in Shuni, where we lived. Today, without traffic, this would be a one-hour drive straight down the coastal highway. Back then, however, getting to Tel Aviv required effort. There were no regular buses, and very few people had cars. The trains didn't run yet, though the tracks had been laid from Tel Aviv to Haifa. Of course, nobody had telephones.

Late that afternoon, a truck rolled up into Shuni, on its way up to Zichron Yaakov. The driver yelled out of his open window. "Who's Olmert?"

"Hang on," two locals answered. "We'll go get him."

My father ran up to the truck. "It's a boy," the driver told him. "Your wife says he weighs nine and a half pounds."

My father was beside himself. He already had two boys, but he started running in circles in the yard, shouting, "I have a son! I have a son!"

I am that son. My Hebrew birthday, 23 Tishrei 5705, was the day after the holiday of Simchat Torah. Thirteen years later, I would celebrate my Bar Mitzvah on the day that the reading of the Torah in the synagogues restarted its annual cycle: *Bereishit*. "In the Beginning."

I lived in Shuni for the first eighteen months of my life. I don't remember it, other than a vague snapshot of our move to the nearby commune of Nahalat Jabotinsky in Binyamina, on the back of a horse-drawn cart. Yermi and I were tossed around among the boxes and luggage.

Today, every Israeli has heard of Shuni. Some of the country's biggest music festivals are held there at its ancient Roman amphitheater. Back in the day, however, when I told people I where I was born, nobody knew about Shuni, its amphitheater, its Crusader fortress, or its other archeological treasures.

When we lived there, before the State of Israel was established, when the British ruled and the Jews defended themselves through secretive paramilitary forces, Shuni served as little more than a base for the underground militia known as the IZL, or *irgun tzva'i leumi*—the National Military Organization—which most of us just called "the Irgun" ("the Organization"). There were twenty-eight families. They had been deployed during the days of Operation Wall and Tower, a series of moves in the late 1930s and early 1940s to establish dozens of new Jewish settlements on hilltops across the country in response to Arab assaults on the Jewish population. In 1939 they created the commune of Tel Tzur, which later changed its name to Nahalat Jabotinsky. Two years later, they came to build Shuni.

There was no running water or electricity. Even by the standards of the 1940s, the Jews who went to settle places like Shuni, Tel Tzur, and the other settlements, far from the bustle of Tel Aviv or Haifa, were roughing it. They had very limited access to modern midcentury comforts, from telephones to cars to penicillin. My parents, like the others, spent their days in the Mediterranean sun, clearing rocks from what would one day be one of the most beautiful parks in the country. Some five hundred yards away were the barracks of British soldiers.

My parents, Bella and Mordechai, came to Palestine twelve years before I was born, from the city of Harbin, in northeastern China.

In China my father had headed up the local branch of the Beitar youth movement, a role that earned him a permit to travel to what it referred to as "Palestine, the Land of Israel." He and my mother had been about to get married, but the arrival of the permit threw a wrench in their plans. There was permission to go—for one of them. They agreed that my father would go on ahead, and that my mother would come along in due course, and they would get married once she got to Palestine.

Eventually another permit arrived. This one was intended for the second-in-command of the Harbin branch of Beitar, Eliyahu Lankin, who would later become the commander of the ill-fated ship *Altalena*. Unlike my father's, however, this permit was for a couple. The Beitar people suggested that he take along his classmate Bella Wagman. All they had to do was get married. So Eliyahu and Bella officially tied the knot and set sail for Jaffa, where my father waited for her at the dock.

When my parents finally wanted to get married in Palestine, they discovered that my mother was still registered as married to Lankin. He was, at the time, conducting operations for the Irgun up north in the Galilee, and my parents sent him a telegram asking him to come immediately to Petach Tikva in order to divorce my mother. Eliyahu sent back a telegram asking for twelve piasters to cover his bus fare. The money was wired, the bus came, they divorced, and my parents were wed.

———

The group that had come to Palestine from Harbin made a real contribution to the struggle against British rule. And they were also involved in one of the most dramatic episodes in the Jewish state's independence.

Late in 1947, the Irgun's chief, Menachem Begin, who would become Israel's prime minister three decades later, sent my father to back to China to raise funds from the Jewish community there to support the fight against the British. He flew to Paris, where the Irgun had built a hub for its European operatives. Lankin was there, as was Natan "Niko" Germant. Niko, too, was from Harbin.

From Paris my father traveled to New York, and then on to San Francisco, where he stayed with Lankin's older brother, who had moved to the United States decades before. From San Francisco he then set sail for China, a trip that took more than a month.

He was received with excitement. The local Beitar group set up meetings for him with Jewish communal leaders in Harbin, Shanghai, Tianjin, and Beijing.

I cannot say how much money he raised for the Irgun, but it was considerable. The battle for Palestine deeply energized the Jews of China. Women came to parlor meetings with fine jewelry in hand and gave it to him in lieu of cash.

On his way back to Israel, my father stopped again in Paris. He delivered the money and jewelry to Niko Germant, who was running guns for the Irgun. Most of the weapons purchased with the funds were loaded onto the *Altalena*, a repurposed American cargo ship commanded by Lankin. Three young men who had come all the way from Harbin, dedicated and courageous Zionists meeting up in Paris to deliver independence to the Jews of Palestine.

My father returned to Israel ahead of the *Altalena*'s scheduled arrival. It was June 1948, just weeks after Israel declared independence and was assaulted by Arab forces from all sides. This would be the ship's final journey. Before docking in Jaffa, the ship was fired upon and sunk by the newly formed Israel Defense Forces (IDF), on the orders of David Ben-Gurion, Israel's first prime minister, who refused to allow the arming of independent militias like the Irgun. Almost all the crew made it to shore alive, but the weapons ended up at the bottom of the sea.

My father was eventually appointed head of the settlement division of Herut, the political party that succeeded the Irgun after statehood. He represented Herut as a member of Israel's parliament, the Knesset. Eliyahu Lankin became a member of the first Knesset, and later an attorney and ambassador. Niko Germant went on to become the CEO of the Vita corporation, and the author of children's books and poems. For years, Lankin remained close with our family. When I relocated to Jerusalem in 1965 as a student, he told me that my parents had asked him to look after me. And he did.

———

On the day I was sworn in as prime minister in 2006, I thought of my parents.

I thought of the long path, one they couldn't even dream of, that led from a small city in northeastern China to the Prime Minister's Office in Jerusalem, the capital of the Jewish state. It was an impossible fantasy. But that is the story of the Jewish people. That is the story of the resurrection of a nation unlike any other story in human history.

What would my parents have thought if they'd been able to sit in the visitors' gallery of the Knesset and watch their son being sworn in as prime minister of the Jewish state? Would they have shed a tear? Would they have held onto each other, as they did all their lives, shaking with disbelief?

I was close to tears. Not for myself, but for them. For what they had achieved. For their courage, to come to a hot wasteland, ruled by the British and clouded by uncertainty. Because of their courage, and that of their whole generation, of our neighbors, of the people I grew up with, of my friends who would be friends for life, who were with me in the Beitar youth club in Binyamina—because of all the Jews who fought to raise Jewish sovereignty from the ashes in our only homeland. Because of all of these comrades in arms who didn't live to see the redemption.

Until that moment, on May 4, 2006, when I stood on the dais in the Knesset and set my eyes on an endless horizon, on everything that had been and everything that would need to happen to ensure the future of this nation, more than sixty years of my life had passed. From Shuni to Balfour Street in Jerusalem.

———

When I finished high school, I wanted more than anything to enlist in the IDF's prestigious Golani brigade.

I also wanted to follow the example of my brother Ami and serve in Golani's special forces unit, Sayeret Golani. When the time came, I got into the Golani infantry brigade, but not into the special forces. I started basic training at the Ben Ami base near Acre. I was assigned to Regiment 13. My friends and I were then sent to the Pilon base near Rosh Pina, close to the Syrian border, to finish boot camp. Golani soldiers were going to take up positions on the front line along the base of the Golan Heights, at a time when tensions with Syria were at their highest.

The year was 1964. Most of the Golani soldiers had grown up on kibbutzim in the north, as well as a few kids from cities or the suburbs like myself. We lived in tents. The discipline was rigorous.

A few months after I got to Pilon Base, I started feeling severe pains in my left arm and left leg. I was sent to Rambam Hospital in Haifa, where they discovered two old fractures that had never properly healed. The physical stress of military service had made them flare up. I was transferred to a desk job on a different base, and I suddenly had two years of dead time ahead of me.

I started looking for other options. I quickly came to the conclusion that the only way out was to ask for a service deferment, to go home until my injuries healed properly, and then rejoin a combat unit later on.

My request was approved. At the clinic, they put casts on my left leg and left arm. I looked ridiculous. The story started going around that I had been wounded in a commando raid deep behind enemy lines in Syria. But I was really just the victim of bad luck. In November 1963, when I had enlisted, I'd been pumped for the challenge and wanted to fight in the special forces. By May 1964, I was a civilian again, and I couldn't walk. Being left-handed, I couldn't really write either.

———

My connection to politics didn't come out of nowhere.

Menachem Begin, the leader of the Irgun and founder of the Herut Party that followed it, understood after the War of Independence that the settlement enterprise, embodied by the kibbutz and moshav movements and their affiliated youth groups, was the source of the left's political power. He wanted to imitate it, and my father—a founder of Nahalat Jabotinsky—was the natural candidate to put this idea of Beitar settlements into practice.

My father started touring the land, recruiting settlers and finding appropriate locations to build, all with the aim of creating a parallel infrastructure, but one that wasn't socialist. They arranged for him to have a car—a tiny Nash—but he couldn't drive, so they gave him a driver as well.

My father worked day and night. He drove up north and down south. He rebuilt Mishmar Hayarden in the northern Galilee, a town that had been destroyed during the War of Independence. He built Hosen, in the western Galilee, on the ruins of an Arab village called Suhmata that had been abandoned in the same war. He helped start the village of Nordia in the Sharon and Misgav Dov near Gadera, named after Dov Gruner, the Irgun hero who was hanged by the British.

My father wanted to build a town near the Jordanian border just south of Jerusalem in the Judean hills. He asked for help from Levi Eshkol, who at the time was the head of the settlement division of the Jewish Agency and later would become prime minister after Ben-Gurion. Eshkol laughed at him. He said that he "would grow hairs on the palms of his hands" if my father could get people to move there, just a few hundred yards from a hostile border. But Mevo Beitar was founded and became a thriving community.

One of the settlers was a young man from the United States. In 1940 he had been at the Beitar summer camp in upstate New York. That summer, Zev Jabotinsky, the visionary who had founded Beitar as well as the Revisionist political movement that served as a more liberal-nationalist alternative to the Labor Zionism of David Ben-Gurion, had died of a heart attack while visiting the campers and counselors. The young man's name was Moshe Arens.

Arens served in the U.S. Army Corps of Engineers during World War II and moved to Israel immediately after independence in 1948. He went back to the United States after a few years to study aeronautical engineering at MIT and Caltech, and then returned to Israel, taught at the Technion, received tenure, and became the chief engineer of Israel Aircraft Industries. He never went back to Mevo Beitar, but he eventually became a senior Likud leader, ambassador to the United States, and then defense and foreign minister.

For our family, however, my father's work made things especially difficult. While he roamed the country, there was no way to call him, to find out how he was faring or share news with him, to know when he was coming back or where he was. Fedayeen militias often crossed the border from Jordan and butchered people at night, and I very clearly remember my mother walking the streets at three in the morning, terrified, until the Nash with my father in it would ramble up the road.

———

My father built towns. Not "settlements."

It's hard to talk about the Beitar enterprise, and my father's decisive role in it, without also speaking about the most divisive topic after the Six-Day War in 1967: The settlements of the West Bank. But there is no relation between the two. Those settlements are not normal towns, but rather a political statement. That's what they were from day one, and it's not surprising that it wasn't people from Herut who initiated and agitated for their creation.

Unlike the kibbutzim of the left, Beitar was not an agricultural movement. It wasn't about working the land, growing produce, having chicken coops and barns and cows. And yet, Nahalat Jabotinsky, Nordia, Mevo Beitar, Aviel, Amikam and all the rest were still meant to follow the strategy pioneered by the Labor movement—a strategy of building a new way of life for Jews in their homeland.

By contrast, the West Bank settlements were, and continue to be, nothing more than a political statement. Their entire purpose was to seize control, one step at a time, of the biblical Jewish lands of Judea and Samaria, and to turn them into an integral part of the State of Israel and thereby prevent the creation of a Palestinian state. It's no coincidence that most of the settlements are nonagricultural, scattered, with large houses and red roofs and a suburban way of life.

Many people have asked me over the years if my father wouldn't have been appalled at my support for dismantling these settlements. My answer is simple: I have no doubt that he would agree with me. My father was a hawk, but a humble man of the land, who wouldn't have countenanced the idea of emptying our coffers to build fancy villas on the pretext of redeeming our ancient homeland.

———

My father was not good at handling people—and without knowing how to handle people, political life turns into a series of traffic accidents. At a certain point, Begin asked him to take upon himself the task of rebuilding the Beitar branch in Haifa. Three days a week he was there. In the following elections, Herut's representation spiked in a city known as Red Haifa, dominated as it was by the socialist Mapai party.

But despite my father's successes, Begin didn't like him. After two terms in the Knesset, he was pushed down to the twentieth spot on the party list, and didn't get into the fifth Knesset. Begin claimed he was not involved in the decision. For years afterward, Begin told me that he never acted against my father. My father didn't believe it. Begin crafted an image of the soft-hearted Jewish noble, but he could be cruel and vindictive as well.

I ran into this tendency a few times during the years I worked closely with him. Begin knew how to make his rivals pay for confronting him. His term in office may not have been an unambiguous success, but from the perspective of Jewish history there's no doubt he was one of the most important personalities of the last few centuries. Jabotinsky was a prophet. Begin was a leader.

Between the two of them, Begin's contribution was, in my view, infinitely more important. Begin, despite his flaws, led the underground during the prewar period. It was he who said the famous words: "Civil war—never." During the horrible *Saison*, when Ben-Gurion's Haganah forces hunted down fighters from the Irgun as well as from Lehi, another paramilitary group, and through the sinking of the *Altalena*, Begin was the real democrat. A humble man, honest, humane, sentimental, ascetic, depressive—the one who made peace with Egypt, and above all someone who contributed to the unity of our people and gave a sense of belonging for the first time to the Mizrahi community, the huge numbers of Jews who came to Israel from North Africa and the Middle East.

No one else came close to him in these areas, and he deserves eternal praise.

———

I returned to my parents' house, my service deferred, but all my friends were in the army. With the fall semester at the university still six months away, I was bored. I filled the time by teaching fourth graders at the local elementary school. In October 1965, I finally left home and moved to Jerusalem to begin my studies.

A new world opened before me. In Jerusalem I felt like a stranger in a strange land.

I had applied for the psychology and philosophy programs, but the Hebrew University's psychology department, the best in the country, was in high demand. Acceptance into the program required a psychometric exam. More than 800 young people were invited to take the test, and only 80 passed it. Somehow I managed to be among those 80.

When I got to Jerusalem, I encountered many representatives of the elite, ambitious class, the future leaders of Israel, who had attended all the prestigious high schools, like Gymnasia Herzliya in Tel Aviv or Liyada in Jerusalem. Compared to them, I felt like a kid from the sticks.

Campus life was wonderful.

The central meeting place was the cafeteria on the ground floor of the National Library. A lot of couples met there for the first time. Anyone who wanted to be part of the action on campus had to spend hours there. Gradually I blazed a path by moving from chair to chair, from table to table.

Ours was the generation of the "flower children," and there were echoes of that on our campus as well. We had heard all about what was happening at colleges in the United States. Freedom and liberalism were in the air for us as well. Sexual liberation replaced puritanism, and the campus became a hotbed of sexual innovation. New winds blew through the campus, and I was filled with expectation.

Dramatic events took place in May 1967, toward the end of my second year in university.

The government decided to have the military parade on Independence Day take place in a limited fashion, mostly at the university stadium in Jerusalem, to avoid provoking the neighboring Arab states. Yitzhak Rabin was the IDF chief of staff. Levi Eshkol was the prime minister. A big stage was set up in the stadium. Tanks rolled. Thousands of soldiers marched.

But immediately after the parade, clouds gathered. Egyptian President Gamal Abdel Nasser ordered his forces to pour into the Sinai Peninsula, which had been demilitarized since the 1956 war, and they started moving toward Israel. Syria, too, deployed heavy weapons and issued threats. Within hours, festivity had turned into foreboding. It seemed we were on the brink of war.

The rest of the story is well known, and it changed our lives forever. The terror of the "Waiting Period" of May 1967 turned into a stunning victory by the Israeli military in six days over the combined forces of Egypt, Syria, and Jordan in early June. But what looked like a world-historical redemption—the Jewish people had miraculously returned, for the first time in two millennia, to Jerusalem's Old City and to the biblical heartland of Judea and Samaria—eventually turned into a new threat to our survival, as the occupation of territory taken in that war gradually transformed from a strategic asset in any future negotiation to an unbearable moral, military, economic, and diplomatic burden.

But who can forget the sense of relief at the time, after weeks of existential terror? The pride, the joy, the hope, and also the power-drunkenness that victory brought in its wake? Moshe Dayan, a military hero and defense minister at the time, went to the Wailing Wall, just days after it was captured, and declared: "We have returned to our holiest sites, and we will never leave them."

The country had changed forever.

When the war erupted, I was called up by the army as part of a group of undergrads to a base at Yesud Hamaalah, along the base of the Golan Heights. We were bombarded with Syrian shells. Fellow student-soldiers were wounded. Some were killed. The horrific images are burned in my memory.

I didn't exactly fight, though. Because of my deferment, I was no longer in Golani but instead had been reassigned to the IDF's academic division. I didn't charge up the Golan Heights. The IDF didn't respond to the bombardments for four long days. Only on Friday, after the Gaza Strip and Sinai Peninsula had been captured to the south, and after the whole West Bank and Jerusalem's Old City were in our hands, did the assault on the Golan begin. By Saturday night it was over. The Golan had been captured, as well, at the cost of many dead and wounded.

It was not long before we returned to normal—but nothing was normal.

———

Aliza Richter was a student in the School of Social Work at Hebrew University. Her statistics professor was Mina Tzemach, who would later become Israel's most famous political pollster. I had taken the same statistics course the year before. Toward the end of the school year I bumped into Mina. She told me she couldn't be there to monitor the final exam for the semester and asked if I'd be willing to fill in. I readily agreed.

Aliza was there. We didn't know each other, but something about her took hold of me and didn't let go. She was beautiful, but more important, she had something special, different. I told myself that we would, at some point, connect.

Our paths crossed from time to time. In the summer of 1969, I had completed my coursework and started preparing for the grueling exams for the degree. One day, I was sitting on the lawn near the Kaplan building with some friends and I saw Aliza walk by. I went up to her and got to the point. I told her I would call her when the exams were over. She said, "Okay."

It took me a few months. In the spring of 1970, I spent an evening at the Savion Restaurant on the corner of Gaza and Ben Maimon streets in the Rechavia neighborhood of Jerusalem. This restaurant would later change its name to Moment, where a horrific suicide bombing would, in 2002, take the lives of eleven customers.

But that evening in 1970, one of the restaurant's owners told me that Aliza Richter, who worked there as a waitress, was interning at the psychiatric ward of Hadassah Hospital. I have no idea why he felt the need to tell me this, but now I knew where to find her.

I called the hospital and asked to speak with her. I reminded her of my promise to call her, and the time seemed right. She said she hadn't taken it as a real promise, but if I wanted to meet, she had no objection. We set a time to meet a few days later.

———

I arrived, in sandals and a faded shirt, at Aliza's apartment at 20 Carmon Street in the Beit Hakerem neighborhood. The walls of her apartment were covered with works of art, including some batik tapestries. I wondered who had made them all. She told me it was a hobby of hers. I told her that I greatly admired creative people. She took that as a compliment.

We spent the evening at a coffee shop in the center of town, and then went for a stroll in the Old City. Back then you could walk down the narrow alleys feeling completely safe. During our walk, my sandal broke, and I had to hobble on one bare foot until I found a rock and a little nail, and I fixed the sandal. My resourcefulness impressed Aliza, although to the best of my knowledge it was both the first and last time I demonstrated it. But on that evening, in the alleys of the Old City, I impressed her.

Independence Day fell at the end of that week. Aliza suggested we go to Eilat, down south on the shore of the Red Sea, together with another couple. I couldn't have imagined anything better. We took the bus, and only when we arrived did we realize we hadn't arranged for a place to stay. Fortunately I had a friend, Shmuel Meltzer, who was from Eilat and worked in tourism. Meltzer offered us an apartment of his that was still being built. "There's no electricity," he said, "but there's running water and gas, and I'll give you some blankets."

That suited us just fine. Aliza and I felt like we were made for each other. When we got back to Jerusalem, she told me it would be nice if I asked her mother, Genia, for permission to marry. Aliza's father, Yosef, had died of a heart attack a few months before.

Fortunately Genia Richter accepted my proposal.

The following weekend I called my parents and told them I was coming home for the weekend with my new girlfriend whom I had decided to marry. My mother sighed in relief. "I was afraid you would grow old as a bachelor," she said. I was not yet 25.

My parents liked Aliza from the moment they met her. After a month and a half, early in July 1970, we were married in the Sokolov House in Tel Aviv.

We had no money. Neither did my parents. Aliza's mother lived in an apartment in Holon, with Aliza's sister Neta, who was ten years younger. I was the third son in my family, and my parents had not been able to help out the first two. It was clear we would have to build our new lives on our own.

By this time I had no intention of becoming a psychologist, and I applied to law school. Psychology didn't match my temperament, and I wanted something more dynamic. I already knew at that point that I was bound for politics, and law school felt like a good fit.

———

Yes, politics.

The political bug started tickling me early in my studies. I successfully ran for student council and quickly found myself in the thick of campus life. During my freshman year, I joined the Gahal student group.

In Israel at the time, before the 1967 war and its territorial conquests, one's political affiliation wasn't so much a matter of carefully considered ideology as it was an almost tribal affair. You grew up with like-minded people, you involved yourself according to your family's traditions and connections. Your affiliation began at a relatively young age, through the different youth groups run by the political movements. To the extent there were ideological differences, they surrounded questions of national pride, Jewish tradition, and the role of the state in private life. Herut, led by Begin, was a liberal-hawkish party, steeped in the teachings of Jabotinsky with an added reverence for the sentiments of classical Judaism. Herut was locked in permanent opposition to the dominant Mapai-Labor party, led at first by David Ben-Gurion, which believed in centralized decision-making, a command economy, and a more secular-universalist approach with an emphasis on worker's rights.

Following the lead of the national party, Herut's campus branch had merged with the Liberal party, and together created Gahal, a Hebrew acronym that stood for the "Herut-Liberal Bloc." Together with me was David Kulitz, who came from a traditional home and wore a knitted kippa. He was tall, strong, good-looking, and worshipped by many young women. David's family lived on King George Street opposite the Frumin House, where the Knesset originally met. They were very close with the Begin family. Every evening after the parliamentary work was done, Begin would cross King George Street and drink tea with David's parents and other friends, and they would talk into the night.

Our student group also included Moni Altman, later Ben-Ari. His father, Aryeh Altman, was the head of the Revisionist movement in Palestine before statehood. Because Begin had led the Irgun, he had more of a natural right to leadership than Altman. With independence in 1948, Begin launched Herut ("Freedom"), a political party that automatically pushed aside the Revisionists as heirs to Jabotinsky's legacy.

For his whole life, Begin spoke of Jabotinsky with an air of reverence. In Begin's eyes, Jabotinsky had been his rabbi. The infallible authority.

And indeed, Jabotinsky's writings became sacred texts for the nationalist movement—and not just for them. His idea of the Iron Wall, coined before the Holocaust, as an existential requirement for Jewish independence in the land of Israel, became the country's security doctrine under the leadership of Jabotinsky's nemesis, David Ben-Gurion. He said, in short, that the Zionist movement would succeed in realizing the rights of the Jewish people, without dependence on the graces of the Arabs, only if we possessed our own independent military power. Only then would the Arab population realize the benefits of coexistence and peace.

As opposed to Begin, who never publicly desecrated the Sabbath, who observed the commandments and showed respect not just for Orthodox Jews but also for their political parties, Jabotinsky had been a secular liberal in every respect. "Only then will they live together in prosperity, the Arab son, the Nazarene son, and my son," he wrote about the future Jewish state. He envisioned, in other words, a Jewish state that non-Jews could see as their own, as well, with full equality. The prime minister would be a Jew, he proposed, and his deputy a Muslim.

So even though Begin always spoke about Jabotinsky with total reverence, in fact he chose a different path. Even the decision to launch Herut can only be understood as creating a separate political structure, independent of the one Jabotinsky had left behind, free from many of the basic principles of the political worldview of his revered mentor.

To take the most glaring example: the principle of the "Greater Land of Israel," as Begin coined it, was much sharper and more obligating than that of Jabotinsky. The Irgun's logo had a map that covered not just the biblical lands of Judea and Samaria (the "West Bank") but also the east bank of the Jordan River—including all of what is today the Kingdom of Jordan—as the land promised not just by God but, in his view, also by the Balfour Declaration and the League of Nations mandate.

This is not what Jabotinsky had in mind.

He had never wanted a rigid Orthodox-Jewish approach, which Begin clung to until his dying day. Begin claimed Jabotinsky's legacy, but he ran his own show. His ability to project a Jabotinskyite illusion on the face of the Herut movement was one of his many impressive political feats.

With historical perspective, Jabotinsky deserves his place in history as the prophet and visionary, while Begin put that vision into practice. He managed to take a paramilitary group—one that made a huge contribution to ending British rule—and reinvent it after Independence as a powerful political party in an independent state. I was more enamored with Jabotinsky than with Begin. Like many of us of a certain generation who were born into Revisionist families, I found Begin's rhetoric alienating for years before I would say so publicly.

Among major political figures on the right, it was, rather, the vision of "Israeliness" of Shmuel Tamir that spoke to me much more powerfully.

———

Tamir was a native of the Land of Israel. His parents belonged to the General Zionist movement, and his mother Batsheva Katznelson was a member of the Second Knesset. Tamir was a talented man, articulate, dynamic, and charismatic, but above all a man overwhelmed by his own sense of importance.

Tamir was a commander in the Irgun. This was not in line with the rest of his family, and especially its most famous member, Berl Katznelson, visionary of the Labor movement and editor of the workers' daily *Davar* before statehood. The family had come to Palestine from the Ukrainian city of Bobruisk, but Tamir had been born in Jerusalem, and saw himself from an early age as destined to lead his people. He would tell people he had been the commander of the Irgun in Jerusalem, though this was inaccurate. He had filled a number of roles, but was never made commander. Nor was he involved in any of the group's most important military operations.

From the very beginning, Tamir understood that Begin, ten years his elder, would never make room for him at the top of the movement's leadership. From Herut's early days, Tamir connected himself to Samuel Merlin and Hillel Kook (also known as Peter Bergson), the American leaders of the Committee for a Jewish Army of Stateless and Palestinian Jews. You could say this was the first Zionist lobby, aggressive and determined, that functioned in the American political arena to work against the continued British rule of Palestine. They, along with Jabotinsky's son, Eri, as well as other frustrated former Irgun members who didn't make it in Herut, felt a need to band together.

Kook, Merlin, and the younger Jabotinsky were members of the first Knesset on behalf of the Herut Party, together with the renowned poet Uri Tzvi Greenberg. But they quickly fell out with Begin. They became bitter rivals. Tamir's connections with them paved his political path. He moved away from Herut and put his energies into his law practice. He returned to the public eye in 1954, with the Kastner trial—a pivotal moment of the first decade of Israeli history.

Rudolph Israel Kastner was a member of the Aid and Rescue Committee of Hungarian Jews prior to and during the Second World War. He ran a series of negotiations with senior Nazi officials, including Hitler confidant Adolph Eichmann, and arranged for a train that evacuated 1,684 Jews to Switzerland.

It was later claimed, however, that many of these were Kastner's own friends and family, and that he could have saved many more. In the early 1950s, a man in Jerusalem by the name of Malchiel Gruenwald published a series of letters attacking Kastner in a newsletter that Gruenwald published and handed out in synagogues. He accused Kastner of abandoning Hungarian Jews and collaborating with the Nazis. Kastner at the time was the spokesman for the Ministry of Industry and Trade. The attorney general decided to file charges against Gruenwald for slander against a public official.

Tamir, filled with ambition and lacking inhibitions, represented Gruenwald in court. He clearly saw this as an opportunity to transform himself from just another lawyer into a leader.

The Kastner trial turned into one of the greatest legal dramas in the history of the country, and Tamir was the star. He talked about Kastner, but his barbs were really aimed at Ben-Gurion and those by his side, who were responsible, in his view, for the abandonment of European

Jewry. The country reeled—this was less than a decade after the end of the Holocaust—and Tamir was the living force behind the storm.

In the end, the district court judge, Benjamin Halevy, ruled that Kastner indeed had lent a hand to the abandonment of Hungary's Jews, and to the death of the famous poet Hannah Szenes, who parachuted into Hungary and was arrested, tortured, and executed. Halevy went so far as to write in his ruling that Kastner "sold his soul to the Devil."

Kastner was subsequently murdered in front of his home in Tel Aviv, just as the Supreme Court was considering his appeal of the lower court's ruling. Three extremist youths were arrested in connection with the murder, convicted, and sent to prison. Kastner never lived to hear the Supreme Court overturn almost all his convictions.

The murder didn't stop Tamir's momentum. For many years I considered his behavior obscene and brutish, but the Kastner trial had turned him into a national hero. In his mind, the doors of the Prime Minister's Office had opened wide and were just waiting for him to walk through.

———

The 1965 elections saw the rise of a new political bloc. Gahal was built of an alliance of Herut and the Liberal Party, which itself had been formed of a merger between General Zionists and the Progressive Party in 1961. The new list had Begin at the top spot and Yosef Sapir, leader of the General Zionists, in the second position. Tamir held the fifth seat on the list, representing Herut.

Begin had good reasons to include Tamir on the Herut list. He knew that Tamir wanted to replace him. But he preferred, as Michael Corleone put it, to keep his enemies closer.

Tamir didn't hide his disgust for Begin. When he came to Jerusalem after the election, he immediately went to work expanding his local base.

I was in my first year of college. I and other students looked forward to Tamir's arrival on campus. We told him that the nationalist movement needed new leadership. Begin was out of touch, his actions reflected the past and offered no future. In short, we fit Tamir like a glove. He wanted to surround himself with a young cadre—the future leaders of the movement. We especially suited him because we were all children of Jabotinsky's followers, of Revisionist leaders. We were born into the heart of the movement. On the other hand, because we were young, we didn't carry the baggage of the movement's past.

In June 1966, we started preparing for the eighth national conference of the Herut movement. Tamir worked behind the scenes to build himself a large group of young people who would back him in any clash with Begin. The party granted students at Hebrew University two delegates, and Moni Ben-Ari and David Kulitz were chosen in formal elections. But Kulitz backed out at the last minute, and I was chosen to take his place.

Moni and I talked at length. We talked about the inevitable clash that would have to erupt on the first working day of the conference. The night before the conference was reserved for a speech by the undisputed leader of the movement. When we thought about what Begin would say, we realized there would have to be a forceful response, demanding changes in the way the movement was run and some of its core policy positions.

———

On the conference's opening night, Begin delivered a powerful speech opposing Labor's rule of the country.

He was a world-class orator, like a premier actor on a stage. But no playwright had written his part. He played himself, bringing out his complicated, stormy, fantastical inner fire. The political establishment did not like his speeches, and many of his rivals tried to dismiss him. In truth, they were terrified. The verbal explosiveness, the gestures of his hands and his body language—all these reflected his theatrical prowess. But the content, the essence of what he said, reflected a deep inner truth. He gave voice to the emotions that many felt, and he knew how to channel them and to set his audience on fire.

The next morning, the public debate began. The chair of the conference was Avraham Shekhterman, the deputy mayor of Tel Aviv who would later become a member of Knesset (MK) in the 1970s. He called the conference to order and declared, in a festive tone, that the movement wanted to rejuvenate the discussions, and therefore they would call up, as the first speaker, a representative of the students, a second-generation member of the movement: Ehud Olmert.

I was surprised. So was the audience. But I was ready.

Members of Knesset, led by Begin, sat on the stage. I knew what I wanted to say, and I knew that my words would set off a storm. At least, I hoped they would. The conference was held at the Kfar Maccabiah Hotel just outside Tel Aviv. The hall was packed with delegates. Perhaps a thousand people, not yet exhausted from the speeches and slogans to come.

I took the microphone. All my life I had prepared for this moment. I was only twenty-one, but I had rehearsed my speech until it flowed naturally. I spoke of the failure in the previous elections the year before. The creation of the bloc, I declared, had not proved itself. Gahal had garnered only 26 seats, compared with the 34 that the Herut and Liberal parties had combined to earn when they ran separately in the previous election. The election, I said, did nothing to bring the dramatic change that the country needed. The movement had ossified, and there was no choice but to take a revolutionary step: Begin would have to give up the leadership.

A long, deathly silence followed. And then the dam burst. People shouted. People cried. They yelled and threatened. I particularly remember Yehoshua Matza, a member of the Jerusalem City Council who later would serve as minister of health, running toward the stage, hysterical. "Get him off!" he shouted. Aryeh Naor, who would later become government secretary and whose wife Miriam would one day become the chief justice of Israel's Supreme Court, also rushed the stage, shouting, "*Take off thy shoes*, you brat!"—referring, I suppose, to Moses at the Burning Bush and the holy ground that I was, apparently, desecrating. It seemed like we were on the brink of a riot.

Something had to be done, and Begin knew it.

Begin strode confidently to the front of the stage, raised his hands above his head like the biblical Joshua bringing the sun to a halt, and then said just one word. "Quiet."

There was silence.

"Friends," he said. "I ask you all to sit down and calm down. If you do not, I will leave the conference and go home."

People cried out, "No! No!" But something very serious had happened. Begin was fifty-one years old. More than twenty years younger than I am today. At the time, he struck me as an old man. Six times he had stood for election as leader of Herut or Gahal, and six times he had failed to topple the regime of Labor and Ben-Gurion. In my mind, enough was enough. I never thought that calling for Begin's resignation was outlandish, but even I, who was born into the movement and a part of the family, never imagined the depth of the reverence felt for this man.

He wasn't finished. "Ehud Olmert," he declared, "is among the finest of our young people. Born in Shuni, raised in Nahalat Jabotinsky, from the Beitar youth movement, child of founders of the movement and veterans of the Irgun. No one will raise their voice to him. I am proud of you, Ehud my son. Continue speaking. Nobody will interrupt you."

Only Begin could have pulled this off. The crowd went silent. The microphone was in my hand, but Begin had won. Whatever else I may have said in my speech, I can no longer remember.

Immediately after I got off the stage, Begin asked me to join a meeting in a side room together with the leadership of the party.

Tamir was troubled. He feared, with good reason, that Begin would blame him for organizing the call for his resignation. But Begin was one step ahead. He assumed that Tamir had arranged for other young people to voice similar opinions, and before it could turn out there was broad opposition to him at the conference, he announced his intention to resign as chairman of the party.

The leaders were shocked. Tamir dispatched one of his aides to get up on the stage and announce that my words had represented only my opinions and not Tamir's. Of course, everything I said perfectly reflected Tamir's own conversations with students. But I hadn't given him any heads-up about the speech. He may have wanted to replace Begin, but he hadn't asked me to speak out against him publicly.

But what was done was done. Israel's political history had been knocked off its course.

———

On the second day of the conference, the party leadership wanted to choose a standing committee in the wake of Begin's resignation. The unstated aim was to begin the process of destroying Tamir, so they gave Begin's loyalists a majority on the committee. Every few days the leadership met in its various committees, and in every meeting there was a clash between Begin's people and Tamir's—even as Begin himself remained in the shadows.

The drama reached its peak, as it often does, around something esoteric. In the thick of all these battles, a letter to the editor appeared in *Haaretz* by an angry reader who viciously attacked Begin and his people. Yohanan Badar, Begin's economic adviser and the number two on the Herut list, was curious. Who was this correspondent who went by the name of S. Rosenbaum? Something didn't smell right.

Badar was a special man. He had never been a member of the Irgun, but he was a Revisionist from the early days and he carried a certain bourgeois gravitas inside Herut. Originally from Poland, he still spoke with a thick accent even after many years in Israel.

Educated in a variety of fields, Badar's curiosity knew no bounds. Somehow he got his hands on the original handwritten letter to the editor. After a little detective work—he was also a graphologist—he concluded it had been written by Haim Amsterdam, a member of the Herut central committee. He was one of Tamir's most vocal supporters. Tamir must have been behind the letter.

Tamir and Amsterdam were sent to a party tribunal. They were charged with conspiring against the party and defaming it. The court suspended Tamir from the party. Begin stayed behind the scenes, but everybody knew the decision had his approval.

Tamir's two top loyalists in the Knesset, Eliezer Shostak and Avraham Tiar, declared that if he was out, they would quit the party as well. The crisis ended with the three of them breaking away from Herut and creating a new faction called the Free Center. With Tamir out and the opposition neutralized, the path was clear for Begin to return to the leadership of Herut.

———

I wasn't involved in this scandal.

I was torn. I felt that Begin's people were prepared to do anything to prevent new winds from blowing. But Tamir was arrogant, provocative, careless. I begged him not to divide the movement. I told him that Herut would one day be his to lead, and quitting the party would ruin him. He didn't care to listen.

Tamir invited me to join his new party. I knew the whole thing was a mistake, and that the Free Center would become a marginal force in Israeli politics. Still, I couldn't walk back what I had said in my speech. Yes, Begin had to resign, but the story couldn't end with Tamir being kicked out of the movement. I told him I would join, but that he couldn't count on me to rubber-stamp everything he did.

The Free Center was launched in March 1967, just a few months before the Six Day War. When the war came, the Free Center remained on the outside of the Israeli political discussion. Begin and Gahal, on the other hand, were suddenly in the limelight.

David Ben-Gurion had been forced out of the leadership of the Labor movement in the wake of a scandal known as the Lavon Affair and resigned from government and the party in 1963. Levi Eshkol, the former Jewish Agency bigwig who had questioned my father's ability to build Mevo Beitar, took over as prime minister. Ben-Gurion was not finished with politics, however. He started a new party called Rafi, together with Shimon Peres, Moshe Dayan, and others, which won only 10 seats in the 1965 election and did not join the government.

As war approached in early June 1967, the nail-biting weeks before it broke out, the fear that gripped the nation, Eshkol's lack of public confidence, and the sudden launch of the war itself on June 5—all these combined to bring about the establishment, on the first day of the war, of a national unity government that included both Rafi and Gahal.

Moshe Dayan was appointed defense minister, and in less than a week the war had been won. Later there would be endless arguments over his contribution. Did he really make a difference at the level of policy or military strategy? Probably not. But Dayan, suddenly the most famous general on earth, the confident face, the universally recognized eye-patch—all of these blew a new spirit into the country.

The unity government and the war transformed Begin's career no less than Dayan's. Begin was named minister without portfolio. More important, Herut and the national movement were no longer considered radioactive by the Labor-led political mainstream. "The man who sits next to MK Badar," as Ben-Gurion had disparagingly called Begin, was now a minister.

But now, Ben-Gurion was out: Eighty years old, he had no interest in playing second fiddle to Eshkol, and remained on the sidelines as Dayan became defense minister. Begin was in: He was saved from the internal mess of his camp and became, for the first time, a government minister.

Shmuel Tamir, on the other hand, was left behind. He wanted so badly to join the unity government and become a minister, but nobody thought he, of all people, could do anything to help unify the country.

And yet, I was fully committed to Tamir and the Free Center, at least for the time being.

At some point late in 1968, Akiva Nof came to see me. Nof was a special man, driven to a career in politics, but whose talents lay elsewhere. He was extremely gifted in music. He wrote a number of popular songs including "Water for King David" and "Jezebel," and made headlines when he interviewed John Lennon and Yoko Ono in their famous anti-war Bed-in protest in Amsterdam in 1969. Akiva got into the bed with them, had Lennon sing a song he'd written in Hebrew about Jerusalem, became famous around the world, and was happy. I have no idea why he ever wanted to be a politician.

When he first started out in the Free Center, Tamir asked Nof to be secretary of the faction. But now Nof had had enough and turned to other pursuits, and Tamir wanted to replace him. Nof was offering me his job.

Suddenly I found myself working in the Knesset, and I loved it. The work was fascinating. I sat in the famous cafeteria, within arm's length of the leaders of the nation. I had finally arrived.

I worked hard. Tamir found in me a good fit for his infinite energy, and I threw everything I had into parliamentary work. In the process, I developed a broad network of my own, included working relationships with all the central players in the arena. I knew all the reporters, spoke with ministers and heads of state—whether in hallway conversations or working meetings. In effect, I did the work of a member of Knesset without actually being one. I was the one who drafted the documents, agendas, formal letters, in every field. I initiated parliamentary actions, which other members of my caucus learned about often just from the news reports. I was given free rein, and I took full advantage. I enjoyed the work, and climbed the political ladder in terms of stature, recognizability, and opportunities, much faster than I ever would have if I had taken any other path. For that I am forever grateful.

I was swept up by Tamir's magic for a long time.

But as time went on, I grew increasingly aware that he was all smoke and mirrors. Aliza understood this well before I did. She didn't think he was dishonest or involved in anything illegal. She just felt that behind his inflated pose there was something shallow, arrogant, out of control.

The sanctity that people projected on him was a harmful, distorting thing. I felt like I was getting sucked into a cult of personality, for a man who didn't deserve it.

————

In June 1973, Major General Ariel Sharon retired from the IDF and began working with Begin on a new alliance of parties that would change the face of Israeli politics.

Sharon was a legendary general who had served in all of Israel's wars and was known among military strategists around the world for his creativity and boldness. He started out in the Liberal Party and pushed for a merger together with Herut and the Free Center, as well as the National List led by Yigal Horovitz and the Movement for Greater Israel led by the author Moshe Shamir and former general Avraham Yaffe. This new confederation of independent parties launched under the name Likud—meaning "confederation"—and ran for Knesset as a single list.

Tamir put me fourth on the list of Free Center representatives. He had promised me the number-three spot, but decided to put Akiva Nof, who had come back to politics, ahead of me. Though I kept it to myself, I was furious. It meant that as part of the overall Likud list, I was now 36th instead of 28th. In other words, my election to the Knesset suddenly seemed far from certain.

But then the Yom Kippur War erupted on October 6, 1973. Massive forces invaded from Egypt and Syria in a surprise attack on the holiest day of the Jewish calendar, while most soldiers were in synagogues, fasting. The first two weeks of the war saw enormous casualties on our side, before we turned things around.

The elections were pushed off from October 30 to December 31. Because of the debacle of the war, as well as Sharon's battlefield triumphs—he was brought back into the IDF and played a decisive role in Israel's counterattack in Sinai—Likud went up in the polls. We ended up with 39 seats, second only to Labor's 51.

On the last day of 1973, one of the most difficult years in our nation's history, I was finally elected to the Knesset.

TWO

From the Backbenches
to the Front Page

"The Youngest MK Has a Platform of His Own."
This was the headline of an interview I gave *Haaretz* soon after the election. The piece was short and buried on an inner page, but at eight o'clock that morning I received a call from Tamir. He was furious. "Where did you get a platform of your own? Get over here. Now."

After the election, parliamentary work had become the main focus of my life. I was doing committee work, speaking in the plenum, initiating legislation, meeting dignitaries from abroad and representatives from groups around the country.

From the moment I was elected, however, the tension between me and Shmuel Tamir had hung in the air, flowing from his broken promise about my place on the list. The blow-up was just a matter of time, and it came sooner than expected.

I told him I'd head out from Jerusalem within minutes. When I arrived at his home in Herzliya, he was fuming. "Who gave you permission to interview?" he asked. "Since when do you have a platform of your own? Why didn't you ask permission?"

I was taken aback. For years I had flooded the media with the minutiae of Tamir's initiatives, which were often really my own initiatives. I had never needed his permission to publish or interview. Because I was only 28, my election had caught the media's attention. Yossi Sarid, the Knesset member closest to me in age, was five years older.

"What permission?" I asked. "Since when do I need approval to talk to a journalist? I've been doing it for years, and you never complained."

Tamir told me that from then on, not only could I no longer interview, but I would need his approval on any parliamentary questions I wanted to submit. I asked him, sarcastically, whether that included those I submitted in his name.

I had a serious problem. Tamir was extremely paranoid.

Back then, members of Knesset didn't get their own offices or any technical support. There were no parliamentary aides or personal assistants. Tamir solved his Olmert problem by telling the secretary of the faction not to type up any of my correspondence, initiatives, parliamentary questions, or agenda items. I was being shut down.

But I wasn't a novice. There were other typists in the Knesset, including those from other parties, who were happy to help. But this couldn't go on for long. As far as Tamir was concerned, I was now a threat. He was powerless against Begin, so he put me in his sights instead. The idea that someone who wanted to overthrow Menachem Begin and lead the country would put his energies into crushing a young freshman legislator, a former aide from his own faction, struck me as absurd.

Things with Tamir went from bad to worse. My relations with other Free Center MKs suffered as well. Tamir was always looking over his shoulder, thinking Begin was trying to undermine him. We were part of Likud, and Begin was our leader—but Tamir couldn't accept it. He saw Begin as a mortal enemy, and anyone who undermined his absolute authority was suspected of collaborating with him.

I was in a different place. I wanted to succeed as an active member of parliament. I didn't have crazy ambitions. I cared about good policy, about legislation, about proving myself through parliamentary achievement. All I wanted was for Tamir to let me get on with my work.

He was deranged, though. In June 1974 President Richard Nixon came to Israel—the first visit ever by a sitting U.S. president. Nixon was deep into the Watergate scandal, just weeks before he ended up resigning, and was trying to divert attention with a trip abroad. Yitzhak Rabin had replaced Golda Meir as prime minister just a few weeks before. He welcomed Nixon with a festive dinner in Jerusalem, and he invited Begin, as leader of the opposition, to join. He was the only representative from Likud.

Tamir went crazy. He called Rabin and told him that leaving him out of the dinner was a "despicable" move. He then convened the leaders of the Free Center and insisted on releasing a letter of protest. Begin, he said, was behind Tamir's being left out, and now Nixon wouldn't have the historic opportunity to meet Shmuel Tamir. If they had gotten to meet, the letter said, the world would have been a better place.

Tamir's final years were particularly sad. After endless clashes with Begin and other Likud leaders, including myself and Shostak, Tamir left Likud and worked his way, together with Akiva Nof, into a new party called Dash—the Democratic Movement for Change—launched by the renowned general and archaeologist Yigael Yadin. After the elections of 1977, which Likud won, Tamir even managed to get Dash into the governing coalition, and, for the first time in his life, was named a minister in the new government led by his nemesis Begin. But even in his new role as minister of justice, Tamir used the opportunity to sow discord. Dash fell apart, not just because of him, and Tamir left the government before the next election.

Begin did everything—with good reason—to keep Tamir's sun from rising as justice minister. He turned the attorney general, Aharon Barak, into his personal justice minister, invited Barak to all cabinet meetings, which had no precedent, and brought Barak, rather than Tamir, to Camp David for peace talks with Egyptian President Anwar Sadat in 1978. Begin, in other words, treated Tamir with disdain, and effectively neutralized him.

Tamir died a few years later, in 1986. A talented man, with so much potential, whose appetites clouded his wisdom. He could have made a huge mark on history. But his flaws torpedoed his career, and he ended up barely a footnote in Israeli history, and almost completely unknown outside the country.

During my second term in the Knesset, which began in 1977, I was completely free of any obligations to Tamir. Shostak and I set up, together with longtime Ben-Gurion stalwarts Yigal Hurvitz and Zalman Shoval, a party called La'am, a combination of refugees from the Free Center, which had fallen apart, and from the National List, which had been built on the ruins of Rafi. We stayed in Likud and ran for Knesset as part of its list.

Those were the elections, in 1977, that brought the political revolution.

For decades, Labor had dominated Israel's electoral landscape, taking credit for founding the country and winning election after election. But by the mid-1970s, a lot of chickens had come home to roost. Ben-Gurion, out of the Labor Party for a decade, passed away in 1973. The failures of the 1973 war had turned into a national trauma, and the Labor Party was largely blamed. Golda Meir saw her career ended by it. The man who replaced her as prime minister, Yitzhak Rabin, endured a scandal involving illicit foreign bank accounts that forced his resignation as well. Meanwhile, the inefficiencies of the state-run economy had led to a crisis that included an inflation rate of more than 30 percent.

But perhaps most important, the country's enormous population of immigrants from Arab lands had matured into a significant political force, frustrated at decades of neglect by the Labor leadership. Menachem Begin's Likud, which shared the immigrants' respect for Jewish tradition and knew how to channel their resentments, resonated with them in a way no political leader ever had.

As a result, for the first time in the country's history, Labor lost, earning only 32 seats, to Likud's 43. Begin was tapped to create the new government. From within La'am, Hurvitz became minister of industry, trade and tourism, and then after two years would rotate into the position of finance minister. Shostak became minister of health.

Halfway through the Knesset's term, I received a call from the defense minister, Ezer Weizman.

More than fifteen years have now passed since Weizman's death, and something about his special charm, so practical—what we call *dugri*—

and so typically Israeli, that no-nonsense, don't-think-twice approach, has disappeared from the Israeli landscape. Yet neither his pedestrian wit nor his occasional lapses in judgment can take anything away from the enormous contribution he made to making Israel's air force into the finest in the world.

We Israelis are proud of our military, but I've known personally our own military leaders and those of other countries over generations, and nothing compares to the commitment, expertise, professionalism, and overall commitment to excellence of Israel's air force. And nobody played a greater role in making the air force what it is today than Weizman.

In the 1977 elections, Ezer Weizman managed our campaign. He asked me to join the small team in charge of it. We grew close.

Ezer was personable. A hugger. Now he invited me to his office. "Is it true," he asked, "that you never took an officer training course in the army?" I nodded. "Well, I'd like you to take one."

It was true that Israeli politicians benefited from having military credentials beyond the minimal three-year enlistment that everyone went through. Still, I was surprised. "I'm a member of Knesset, and I have a law firm. You want me to go back into the army and become an officer?"

"Well," he said, "David Kulitz is your age, and he just finished an officer course. Now it's your turn."

Doing this would require Aliza's approval. It was 1980, and by this point we had three small children at home with a fourth on the way. Taking the course would require my going to Mitzpeh Ramon, in the middle of the Negev desert, for five months. It sounded crazy. Aliza may or may not have thought it was crazy, but she gave her blessing nonetheless. My law partners would have no choice but to deal with it.

The course started at the end of the summer. I asked to take it together with the young recruits. "You nuts?" Ezer laughed. You're almost 35. You can't keep up with them."

I told him I would take my chances. I secured the approval of my Knesset faction, bid farewell to my colleagues and family, and went south, into the desert.

———

On the first day, I found myself at the assembly grounds on Training Base 1.

I stood at the edge of the grounds watching a group of soldiers huddling together, talking in hushed tones. Eventually a few of them walked toward me. "Excuse me," one said. "Is it really you?"

"Meaning what?" I asked.

"Are you Ehud Olmert? What are you doing here?"

"I'm doing the officer's course with you."

A pause. One of them said, "But you're old."

"Don't worry," I answered. "You won't notice."

We were processed, we put on field uniforms, and they drove us to another base, about half an hour north. Our company commander was Yoav Margalit. We got off the bus, and he started shouting, "Let's Go! Run!"

I was in excellent shape. In Jerusalem, I would run seven miles every morning in the Beit Hakerem neighborhood. So I wasn't worried. Young cadets were panting and heaving. I kept my pace. We ran about five miles. Yoav, a charming young religious guy, kept his eye on me the whole time but said nothing.

At the end of the first week, we had briefings with our commanders. "I was waiting for you to break," Yoav said. "You surprised me. You're in great shape."

I told him that I didn't know how I would fit in, or whether I'd be able to meet all the requirements of the course, but my physical condition wouldn't be a problem. I just had one unusual request. Because my wife was expecting, and because I was required to be available for urgent Knesset affairs, and because I had a law firm—I needed permission to have a car of my own at the base. I would leave it in the parking lot outside the main gate, and barring any emergencies I'd take the same leaves as anyone else, but I really couldn't handle needing to hitchhike or take multiple buses in case of an emergency.

It was approved.

One day, when we were on a field exercise, the jeep of the officer training school's commander, Colonel Yoram Yair ("Ya-Ya" as he was famously known) suddenly roared toward us. His driver was alone in the car. "Where's Olmert?" he shouted. "Ya-Ya needs him now."

I sat in the jeep and we sped back to base. The commander told me that the prime minister had called Lieutenant General Rafael Eitan, known as "Raful," and told him I was needed for a no-confidence vote that evening in the Knesset. Raful called Ya-Ya. "I want Olmert, dead or alive," he said, "in the Knesset tonight."

It was a four-hour drive. I got in my car and showed up in the Knesset, in dusty military fatigues, fifteen minutes before the vote. I cast my vote against the measure and drove all the way back. I nearly fell asleep at the wheel.

When the time came for fitness tests on the obstacle course, I had a sprained ankle and couldn't run. This was the day before the end of the officer's course, and Ya-Ya told me that if I didn't complete the test within the set time limit, I wouldn't get my officer's pin. I asked to take it the same day. I overcame the pain, ran like a madman, and finished it with the second-best time in the battalion. Fellow cadets cheered me on the whole way.

It was a great feeling.

Two weeks earlier, I had participated in the famous "march." We started off early in the morning from Gush Etzion, hiked to Jerusalem, and then in the city we marched three abreast through the streets, company by company, battalion by battalion, regiment by regiment. For some reason, our company commander put me up front. The media recognized me, and photographers started scrambling. The pictures made the front page the next morning. I was left having to explain to my commanding officers that it wasn't my decision and that I hadn't sought out media coverage.

I entered the course as an oddity and came out an officer. When I got home, I called Ezer Weizman and told him I'd finished. "Yes, I got a report," he said. "You were okay. They were impressed with your fitness."

This was, again, the first time that Likud was in power.

When we look at it from a historical perspective, we can see the enormity of the change that Menachem Begin brought. In the four and a half decades that have passed since 1977, the national camp has been in power for the great majority of the time, especially if you count the years I was prime minister as leader of the Kadima Party. But the reality is that other than the three years of Rabin's second term as prime minister in the 1990s, the six months Peres replaced him until the 1996 elections, and the year and a half that Ehud Barak was prime minister between 1999 and 2000, the nationalist parties, inheritors of the Herut movement, have been central to all the coalitions.

But Begin and the party that he led were completely different from the Likud that arose after him, and especially after Yitzhak Shamir.

Begin and Shamir were forged out of the horrific memories of the Holocaust.

Each in his own way felt the unbearable tension between the destruction of their families and their people, the cruelty that had no precedent in human history, on the one hand, and their mission as prime ministers of the Jewish state, on the other. Both of them, in their essence and values and understanding of the limits of power, were at heart humble men, restrained, honest, lacking in personal interest, dedicated with every fiber of their being to the task that destiny had given them: the security and prosperity of the Jewish homeland.

The Likud that emerged later was completely different. We can't absolve Begin and Shamir of responsibility for this. The seeds of it were planted in the Camp David agreements of 1978–1979. The peace treaty with Egypt was certainly the proper and unavoidable thing to do. It was incredible. I have admitted my own failure to see its importance at the time, and I apologized to Begin before he died for voting against it. But Begin could not accept that the inevitable next step, after giving up the Sinai Peninsula as the price of peace, would have to include giving up on the West Bank as well. His failure to understand this sowed the seeds of unending conflict. Our spiritual servitude to the idea of the Greater Land of Israel proved catastrophic.

To be clear, I believe in the Greater Land of Israel with all my heart. I hold every single speck of soil between the Mediterranean Sea and the Jordan River, and even some places beyond the Jordan, to be an irrevocable part of Jewish history. Everything buried beneath the ground, in every part of Judea and Samaria and some parts east of the river, is part of our past. The truth of the biblical stories is revealed anew with every archaeological discovery. There is no reference there to Arafat, to Palestinians, or to any Arab or Muslim tribe that would justify their claim to the land.

But if we are ever to end the state of perpetual war, we still have to give up the territories we captured from Jordan in 1967. Most of them. Almost all of them.

If Begin had had the wisdom to see this in 1978, he could have used his moral and political authority to finish the job. His inability to do so brought about the strengthening of the settlement movement, which like Frankenstein's monster arose to rebel against its creator and also endanger the future of Israel as a Jewish state.

————

One man who understood this was Moshe Dayan. There was never an Israeli leader whom I miss more than him.

Of all the people I met in politics, none was like him. I knew him up close, and I could have joined the chorus of detractors. The whirlwind of commentators, frustrated former army generals and disappointed rivals, destroying his legacy and belittling his contributions—sorry, but I'm not part of that.

He was unique. A child of Degania Alef, hero of the *kevutzot* and kibbutzim, who grew up in the aristocratic village of Nahalal, father of the *moshavim*, who joined the Palmach, fought, was wounded, lived with pain from his shot-out eye socket, courageous to a degree that can't be put into words, charismatic, charming, selfish, cruel, longing for solitude, alienated from many—including some in his own family— original, unusual, able to see with one eye what most people could never see with two or even six, lover of the land, attached to its past to the depths of his heart, who identified with its past heroes, tried to actually understand them, to touch with his bare hands whatever might be left of those who lay buried in its ground, soldier, fighter, leader, warrior and poet. What else can make a man special?

Leave aside what happened in the run-up to the Yom Kippur War, when as defense minister he oversaw the nation's most catastrophic intelligence failure. One thing is certain: He was appointed IDF chief of staff in 1953, for an army that had lost its fighting spirit, its boldness, its originality. He left behind in 1958 a winning army— bold, gutsy, dynamic—that never again would be what it had been before. Along the way, he was often totally unhinged, a wild man, sometimes immoral, without inhibitions.

In 1977, Begin asked Dayan to be his foreign minister.

I remember the anger among many in the Likud. After all those years we had waited to get into power, were we going to let a major figure from Labor run the country's foreign policy?

Begin was, no doubt, a little insecure about the challenges of governing, and he wanted someone experienced by his side. I think he also understood, even if he would never admit it even to himself, that as prime minister he would need to adjust his course from the one he had been on as leader of the opposition. Only one man seemed experienced enough, well-known enough, and carried himself with enough authority, to help him recalibrate.

For his part, Dayan had no problem leaving Labor to join the Begin government. True, he had grown up in the heart of the movement, and his father was also a Mapai (Labor) MK, but to him no political movement was nearly as important as what he believed he could get done in office. And he wanted to get things done.

His appointment made waves around the world. Even the harsh years after the Yom Kippur War, the loss of his prestige at home after he was named as one of the people responsible for the intelligence failures leading up to the surprise attack by the Arab alliance, even after the story went around that in the middle of the invasion he declared the "end of the Third Jewish Commonwealth"—none of this damaged his global prestige or the admiration of millions of people for this general with the eye-patch. Few people on earth were as famous as he was. Or as Begin put it, "When world leaders sit with my foreign minister, I want them to check the creases of their pants," to make sure they were fit to be in his company.

Dayan liked me. I don't know how our relationship developed, but it was clear, at least between us. When my son Shaul was born in 1975, I called him to let him know about the bris.

"I've heard all about it, and I'm coming," he said. Then he asked if he could be the godfather, and of course I agreed. I often remind Shaul that he has to remember to be a special person. After all, Moshe Dayan was his godfather.

Even though he wasn't a member of Likud, as foreign minister Dayan was invited to meetings of the Likud caucus in the Knesset to report on diplomatic developments. These meetings amused him. The dogmatism, the small-mindedness, the short-sightedness of many of the MKs made him uncomfortable. He would sometimes compose sonnets on little pieces of paper during the meetings and pass them to me. They poked fun at the faction, its members, and himself. He had no idea what he was doing there.

Dayan made a huge contribution to the peace treaty with Egypt. He got the negotiations started with a secret meeting with Hassan Tuhami, Egypt's deputy prime minister, in Morocco. He laid the groundwork for Egyptian President Anwar el-Sadat's historic visit to Israel in November 1977. And Dayan gave Begin the confidence to do something he didn't really want to do: To give back the Sinai peninsula in exchange for peace.

———

The Camp David talks, held at Camp David, Maryland in September 1978 together with Sadat and U.S. President Jimmy Carter, had nearly blown up toward the end, when all was ready to be signed.

In the final summary meeting in Begin's bungalow, Sadat suddenly raised the issue of the fate of Jerusalem. Jerusalem, the object of longing by Jews for thousands of years, the site of our historic Temple, had been fully restored to Jewish sovereignty only in 1967. Just over a decade later, Sadat was asking for it to be put back on the negotiation table. And President Carter was backing him up.

"I need ten minutes alone," Begin told them.

"What for?"

"If you insist on talking about Jerusalem," Begin said, "it'll take me that long to pack my things and go. I'm not even willing to talk about it."

Carter and Sadat were stunned.

"Let me tell you the story," Begin continued, "of Rabbi Amnon of Mayence. Rabbi Amnon of Mayence was the most honored Jew in the city. One day, the archbishop summoned him and said that if he was willing to convert to Christianity, he would receive anything he asked for. Rabbi Amnon said he wanted to think about it. Three days later he returned to the archbishop and said he would never convert, no matter what.

"The archbishop had him tortured, and when he could take it no longer, Amnon of Mayence, author of the Yom Kippur prayer *Unetaneh Tokef*, declared that he deserved his suffering because he had hesitated, and didn't reject the offer on the spot."

Sadat and Carter got the message. In the end, they found a phrasing that satisfied both sides: The Arabs could ask to discuss the fate of Jerusalem, but Israel was not obligated to agree to discuss it. The Camp David Accords were saved, and Carter and Sadat learned something about Begin's worldview.

I met Carter many times over the years, and we had long conversations. I think that neither he nor Sadat liked Begin very much, but there was something about the latter's old-world European style, his manner of speaking, that earned Carter's respect.

———

The second part of the Camp David Accord dealt with Judea and Samaria—the West Bank. Begin talked about autonomy for the Palestinians, but I'm convinced he never really believed in it. It was, after all, a non-starter, an illusion he managed to sell the other side. There was never any chance of reaching agreement with the Palestinians later on the basis of autonomy, because above all it would never solve the most basic problem: How do you stop ruling over another people? How do you stop depriving them of basic rights and going on as if nothing is wrong?

This game of pretend was born out of Begin's unwillingness, his spiritual and emotional inability, to accept the fact that there was no choice but to give up on land in Judea and Samaria, not just Sinai. Begin simply said to himself, in the manner of the ancient rabbis, "It is not for you to finish the job." He built for Sadat and Carter an imaginary structure, so that the fate of Judea and Samaria would be pushed off until after he was long out of office.

Dayan thought otherwise. He never stopped coming up with creative ideas. He came to Begin with an idea that was meant to square the circle: "Unilateral autonomy." We would declare it autonomy, he said, and we would start unilaterally withdrawing from the territories.

This was a historic opportunity. Most of the land was still empty of Jewish settlements. But Begin understood Dayan's true intentions, and spiked the idea. All their lofty rhetoric about the importance of a Jewish presence in Sinai had been forgotten, but when it came to the historic Land of Israel, Begin was not ready for compromise.

Would he have changed his mind later on? I seriously doubt it.

————

The Knesset deliberations over the Camp David Accords lasted days.

It was an extraordinary debate by any standard. Begin, in a typical gesture, asked that every Member of the Knesset speak, and he did not impose party discipline on the vote. It was riveting. People spoke from the heart. Those in favor, those who opposed, even those who planned on abstaining. I felt like I had to oppose it. I was born of the Beitar movement. All my life I had been taught that nothing was more important than establishing communities everywhere, and withdrawing from Sinai would mean dismantling settlements where more than 8,000 Israelis now lived. Begin himself had never stopped saying it. "Always build, never destroy." Yet here he was, destroying everything that had been built in Sinai.

Begin announced that he would not attempt to influence anyone's vote. Everyone was to vote his conscience. I was still in a different world. Before taking my turn to speak, I asked him if we could speak privately. "Come, Ehud my boy," he said. "Let's talk."

With his arm around me, we walked out to the wide corridor outside the plenum, between the stairs that descended to the parliamentary offices and the main entrance. I told him I was voting against the deal.

He was surprised. "You? You, too, want to be like those 'people of conscience'? So that's how it's going to be? I'm the one who divides the Land and you're the people of conscience?"

We argued for about forty-five minutes. People were staring at us—MKs, journalists, photographers. Nobody came near us. I explained my position, but he wasn't having any of it. In my case, he had decided to try and persuade me. He failed. To his credit, he never made me pay a price.

He was, of course, right. I was wrong. I should have supported it. Just to think that we might have been stuck in Sinai, for decades, with all the military reserve duty and billions of dollars spent, permanently worried about a war that could erupt on multiple fronts. Begin himself went back and forth about it a lot. But once he decided, he made history.

The ratification of the accord was not even a question. He had the votes. The only question was how many MKs would approve, how many would oppose. And especially, how many members of Likud would vote against a historic move of giving up territories, being led by none other than Menachem Begin. The measure was approved with eighty-four in favor, including the majority of the Labor Party. Thirteen opposed, including six Likud members other than myself.

Begin did not mention me in his speech. In his combative mood, I wouldn't have been surprised if he had thrown a political sucker punch at me. He didn't. I wasn't yet important enough, apparently.

———

Dayan left the government late in 1979. In his memoir, he wrote that Begin breathed a sigh of relief.

He felt politically isolated beforehand, but once Begin had rejected his idea of unilateral autonomy, he was even more so. I remember him sitting in the corner of the cafeteria in the Knesset, by himself. Members of Knesset, as a matter of habit, would usually take a seat, along with their guests, at tables where others were already dining, and join in the conversations. When someone asked Dayan if they could join him, he refused.

Except for me. I don't know why, but he would wave me over to join him.

In the Knesset cafeteria, there was a lot of talk that Dayan would run again.

He didn't care about polls. I told him that a list he headed would earn 16 to 18 seats. "In such a case," I said to him, "you could be kingmaker for the next government. You're more popular than you think."

"Young man," he chided me. "You know why I am so popular? Because I'm not running. As soon as I decide to run, I won't be popular." It turned out he was right. In the end, he decided to run in the June 1981 elections at the top of the Telem list, and his party won only two seats. He was beloved, but the burden he had carried since the Yom Kippur War remained a heavy one.

Four months later, Dayan passed away.

Before his death, Dayan submitted to the Knesset his proposal for unilateral autonomy. Likud unanimously voted against it—except for me. Begin called me into to his office. "You, of all people, you who voted against Camp David, support this?" He didn't yell. His voice was filled with disappointment. "You have some deep sentiments for Dayan?" he asked.

"It's true," I told him. "But I supported his proposal because I think he's right."

———

The 1981 election was, in some ways, even more important than that of 1977.

True, the revolution happened in 1977. But the question being decided in 1981 was whether Likud's victory was a flash in the pan or a real change in the country's direction. On the one hand, the peace treaty with Egypt had been a historic achievement. Also, Begin's major domestic achievement—"rehabilitating the urban neighborhoods"—reflected his determination to make good on his promise to the Mizrahi voters, whose massive support for Likud had brought him to power.

On the other hand, inflation was skyrocketing. The economic crisis had only gotten worse since Likud came to power, and created a sense of malaise that cost Begin support. It is often assumed by outsiders that Israelis only vote on issues of security. Terrorism, war, peace with the Palestinians, Iran, and so on. But it's really not true. Like anyone else, Israelis care about the quality of their lives, and vote on issues such as jobs and the cost of living. In times of significant economic distress, economic policy can often decide elections.

Shimon Peres was now leading the Labor Party. He and his team took every opportunity to press the economic issue. They attacked Begin's two finance ministers, first Simha Erlich and then Yigal Hurvitz, who couldn't get the truck out of the mud. Begin was at the peak of his abilities, doing a tour of electrifying appearances around the country, but polls showed the parties neck-and-neck, with a slight edge given to Labor.

Three weeks before the election, on June 7, the eve of the Shavuot holiday, Israeli warplanes bombed a nuclear reactor in Osirak, Iraq, destroying it. This operation was supposed to be kept secret, but two days later, the government publicly took responsibility. Israelis were thrilled.

It has been argued that destroying the Iraqi nuclear reactor was one of the most important military operations in Israel's history, and some even say it was just as important as the peace treaty with Egypt. I think this is an overstatement. It was the right thing to do, but Iraq was far from developing a real nuclear capability. Considering the distances involved, Iraq would need missiles capable of delivering a warhead far beyond anything available to Saddam Hussein at the time. He had no way of retaliating at all.

Begin's decision was a relatively low-risk affair—especially compared with our decision to strike the nuclear reactor in Syria in 2007, at a time when Syria had a full arsenal of missiles that could reach almost any point in Israel. True, most of the world's leaders condemned the strike in Iraq. U.S. Defense Secretary Caspar Weinberger was especially harsh. But in Israel there was only pride. The claim by Peres and the leadership of Labor that publicizing the operation had been a transparent electoral move was a childish one. Begin's motivation was nearly the opposite: He was afraid Peres wouldn't destroy the reactor if he won the election. And from a perspective of deterrence, it told the world that Israel's long arm could reach Iraq. Thanks to Begin, Israel was a force to contend with.

———

I was in charge of Likud's communications during the election campaign. I was responsible for messaging, slogans, media relations, and rapid response to both news events and the statements of opposing politicians.

The days when Likud was just a loose confederation of independent parties were coming to an end. In practice we worked as a single party. I had made myself useful to the party, and my place on the list was assured. The question was whether we could stay in power.

This was the stormiest campaign in our country's history. It was a tough battle, one that descended at times into violence. Peres was assaulted a number of times, and I distinctly remember one occasion in Beit Shemesh that triggered a series of clashes between Likud and Labor supporters. The widespread belief that the violence was being instigated by Likud supporters caused us a lot of damage. Hyperinflation and economic instability caused many to doubt Likud's ability to govern effectively.

On the last Saturday before election day, top campaign staff came together at the King David Hotel in Jerusalem. We had flown in a number of experts from the United States to help us, mainly with polling. The feeling was that we were about to lose. Ezer Weizman, who had been something of a star during the 1977 campaign, had left Likud and was unwilling to endorse us. We asked ourselves that morning what we could do to right the ship. Both parties had massive rallies planned that same night: Ours in Sacher Park in Jerusalem, where Begin would speak; and a parallel one for the Labor Party in Kings of Israel Square (known today as Rabin Square) in Tel Aviv, where Peres would speak.

That evening, in Sacher Park, Begin was on fire. The advisers warned we would lose the election, Ezer Weizman had written him off, but Begin was at war. He fired up the crowd. At the pinnacle of his speech, Begin baited the Syrian President, Hafez al-Assad. "Assad," he waved his hand, "Yanush and Raful are waiting for you!"

Raful was Lieutenant General Rafael Eitan, the IDF chief of staff. Yanush was Major General Avigdor Ben-Gal, the northern commander. Begin repeated the line a number of times, and the crowd roared. Later Begin was criticized for using the names of IDF generals at a campaign rally, but this was Begin at his very best. He rode the wave of his massive support, played the crowd, and repeated lines that set them ablaze.

Meanwhile, in Tel Aviv, at a Labor rally, one of the speakers was the comedian Dudu Topaz.

Topaz apparently forgot he wasn't doing a nightclub comedy routine.

He tried to compare Labor voters with Likud voters. "Who supports them?" he asked, and answered. "*Tchakhtchakhim!*" This was a derogatory term for Mizrahim.

With only three days to go, the campaign suddenly took on a racial tone. Voters were outraged, and the polls shifted. Labor leaders apologized. But Begin was riding high. Nothing would stop him.

The final campaign rally for Likud had been long planned for the following night, in the same location in Tel Aviv as the Labor rally of the night before. More than 100,000 supporters filled the enormous square. Begin now wanted to talk about *tchakhtchakhim*. "Are we *tchakhtchakhim?*" he hollered. "No!" the crowd roared back.

The way he enunciated the word—*tchakh-tcha-KHIM*—with his booming Ashkenazi accent, sounded like a battle cry.

———

Forty-eight hours later, we waited at Likud headquarters in Tel Aviv for the results of Channel 1's exit poll.

Even before the polls closed, I received information that Likud was now poised to win—but by just a single Knesset seat. I called Begin at home and told him. "If so, Ehud my boy," he said, "we will set up a government. The Orthodox have already agreed."

The final exit poll, however, gave a slight advantage to Labor. Israel Peleg, the Labor spokesman, stood on the stage at the Dan Hotel in Tel Aviv before hundreds of Labor activists. He didn't wait before calling up "the next prime minister, Mr. Peres." The crowd applauded. Peres looked satisfied. But, as happened to Peres more than once in his career, by the end of that tense night he was defeated.

Begin waited at his residence in Jerusalem. His experience had taught him that our biblical forebears were right when they said that a soldier on his way to battle should not praise himself like one who has returned victorious. So he waited to go to the Likud headquarters until very late in the night, after the final results were declared. When he finally arrived, he was basking in victory. We embraced, and he said, "You were right, my boy."

But this dramatic victory did not solve the country's problems. The challenges facing the new government were enormous, and foremost among them was still the economy.

I continued my parliamentary work. It would be my third term in the Knesset. I was now a recognizable figure, but I had no expectations of being appointed as a government minister—and, in fact, I wasn't. Not a deputy minister, either.

I was patient. I knew my time would come.

———

On June 6, 1982, the IDF launched Operation Peace for Galilee, and invaded Lebanon.

The day before, the government had green-lit the invasion in the wake of the shooting of Israel's ambassador to the United Kingdom, Shlomo Argov, by a Palestinian terrorist from a splinter organization headed by Abu Nidal. Argov was severely injured and would spend three months in a coma and the rest of his life, paralyzed but lucid, at Hadassah Hospital. More than twenty years would pass before he succumbed to his injuries.

The plan to strike the Palestine Liberation Organization (PLO), which had entrenched itself across southern Lebanon just across Israel's northern border, had long been discussed. It would require Israel to create a new order in our neighboring country. Up till that point, Begin had refused to give in to pressure to approve the plan. But the attempt on the life of our ambassador was a step too far. Begin decided it was time.

Months earlier, I had spoken with Begin in the prime minister's residence on Balfour Street in Jerusalem. He told me he was appointing Ariel Sharon as defense minister. In May 1980, when Ezer Weizman had quit the government, Begin had declined to choose a replacement at defense, and instead kept the role for himself. Sharon, who had expected the job, was furious and responded publicly, calling Begin "irresponsible." Begin nonetheless held off: He was concerned Sharon was unreliable, and that making him defense minister on the eve of the election could do more harm than good to the campaign.

After the elections, Begin considered it again. Simha Erlich, the leader of the Liberal Party, opposed the appointment. Many others did as well. Begin invited Sharon to his office, and later told me what he had said to him. He'd get the job, Begin told Sharon, but on one condition: "Nothing without my knowledge. Nothing without my agreement."

Sharon promised. Prior to the election, as minister of agriculture, Sharon had taken a car trip to Egypt, crossing the Sinai Peninsula on his way to Cairo, going by all the battlefields where he had fought over the years. The visit to Egypt was crowned a success. Sharon knew how to play the game, especially with people who respected him as a warrior. The Egyptians saw him as the most formidable of their enemies in war, but honored his courage and received him warmly.

Begin's concerns, however, did not abate. He didn't trust Sharon. About a month before the war in Lebanon, Begin told me that despite his misgivings, he had nothing to complain about when it came to Sharon's performance. He would later change his mind. He regretted that he never listened to all the warnings of friends and advisers about getting stuck in Lebanon, and later fell into a deep depression that did not leave him until the day he resigned as prime minister— in fact, not until his death.

———

Operation Peace for Galilee would later be known as the First Lebanon War, and when it was launched, it was widely believed that it would be a brief operation. Many asserted that the IDF wouldn't go more than 25 miles into Lebanese territory.

I was then a member of the Knesset Foreign Affairs and Defense Committee, as well as the subcommittee on Lebanon. We had three former IDF chiefs-of-staff on the committee: Yitzhak Rabin, Haim Bar Lev, and Motta Gur, as well as Shimon Peres, who, among his other achievements, had served as director-general of the Defense Ministry under Ben-Gurion. We were briefed by senior military and defense figures, and Sharon appeared before the committee a number of times during the first week of the war. He led us to believe that his target was the Beirut-Damascus highway, 50 miles deep into the country. It was clear that he didn't see himself limited to 25.

One didn't have to be a grand strategist to see where this was going.

Even senior Labor leaders knew it would not be a short war. Sharon told the committee, and I remember this as if it were yesterday, that even if a cease-fire were declared before the IDF reached the highway, it would almost certainly be broken, and the IDF would keep charging.

Despite this, the public got the impression that within a few days, a cease-fire would be declared and the IDF would halt its advance. When it didn't happen, opposition to the war began to grow.

There was silence from political leaders of both parties during the first week.

The opposition, and of course the government's coalition, followed the dictum of the journalist Amiram Nir, who wrote in *Yediot Aharonot*, "Quiet—we're shooting." But by the second week the mood had shifted, and the silence was broken. The number of casualties mounted, the public started turning against the war, and Begin was furious.

Israel became mired in Lebanon in 1982.

The truth is, we weren't ready for the kind of war we had launched. The IDF's comparative advantage, which had brought us impressive victories in previous wars, was based on the use of armor through quick adjustments, lightning strikes, and unexpected moves. The First Lebanon War didn't allow us to use these advantages. A significant part of the fighting took place on mountainous, rocky terrain, against small bands of fighters, moving relatively slowly.

We suffered heavy losses. A lot more than we were prepared to, given that this was our own initiative, against a smaller, weaker country. We took losses from ambushes and traps. I would look back on all of this as I was about to lead my country to war in Lebanon for a second time in 2006. I knew that I wouldn't let the IDF walk into the same trap it had taken us eighteen years to get out of. But we'll come back to this.

———

In August 1983, Begin announced, "I just can't do it any more."

Anyone who worked closely with him already knew that he could no longer lead the country. He had withdrawn deep into himself, was depressed and ridden with guilt. His wife, Aliza, had passed away in November 1982. So the depression could be explained. But what did he feel guilty about? We can only guess. Every commentator who has written about Begin after his retirement has offered explanations, whether they knew what they were talking about or not.

Did Begin really feel that Sharon had misled him and pulled the country into a tragic, impossible war that brought unsatisfying gains and incalculable losses?

I was involved in every detail of how that war developed, and you can count me among those convinced that Ariel Sharon never misled Begin. He definitely was secretive about his intentions, that he quite deliberately drove the country into a broad occupation of southern Lebanon, with the specific aim of toppling the regime and installing a friendly government that would make peace with Israel.

It's true that Sharon played loose with the facts.

In the thick of the fighting, I received a phone call from someone who identified himself as the grandson of the renowned scholar and Israel Prize laureate, Ephraim Urbach. He told me he had been pulled from the front line in Lebanon just as we were about to make our assault on the Beirut-Damascus highway. As he told it, his wife had just given birth, and he was being sent home to see his wife and newborn son. (I assume his commanders wanted to make sure that if he were to fall in battle, at least his wife and baby would have gotten to see him one last time.)

He said that something strange was happening in Lebanon. We were announcing through the media that there was a cease-fire, but in practice troops were getting orders to keep shooting and capture the highway at all costs. "Does anybody know about this?" He asked. "Are they lying to the nation? Does our government know what Sharon and the commanders are actually doing there?" He begged me to speak with the prime minister. I assured him I would.

Early the next morning I went in to see Begin. He was in a better mood than he had been recently. I told him about the call. Did he know, I asked, what was happening up at the Beirut-Damascus highway? Was it his decision that the highway be taken no matter the cost? And if so, why were we telling everyone, including our soldiers, that there was a cease-fire?

Begin answered me patiently. The highway was crucial in order to cut Lebanon off from Syria and prevent the resupplying of the PLO. There was no reason to declare our intentions and thereby tip off the enemy. Our troops had their orders, he said, and they should follow them. In just a few hours, he said, the objective would be reached.

Could anyone say Begin didn't know what was happening? Is it possible that he was somehow misled? I very much hoped that Urbach's great-grandson would never face the kind of experiences his father saw in Lebanon.

In November 1983, Begin announced his resignation.

I paid a visit to Begin at the Ichilov Hospital in Tel Aviv, years after his resignation. I imagine, though I can't prove it, that Begin never forgave himself for being careless, overconfident, that he had irresponsibly and naively believed that the goals of that war were achievable. The depression that shrouded the rest of his life was not the result of Sharon's deliberately misleading him.

Begin removed himself entirely from public life until his death in 1993.

––––––

In the wake of Begin's resignation in 1983, the Likud Central Committee met to choose a successor. The mood was somber. It was clear that an era had ended. There would never again be a leader like Begin. The man who created the Herut movement, led it through all its tribulations, brought it to power and brought down the rule of Labor, made peace with Egypt, and annexed the Golan Heights—this man had lost his will to fight. Nothing would ever be the same.

Yitzhak Shamir replaced Begin as prime minister, and would lead the Likud in the 1984 election campaign. The government had parted ways with its finance minister, Yoram Aridor, for his utterly failed plan to dollarize the economy. With my warm recommendation, Shamir picked Yigal Cohen-Orgad to take Aridor's place. Yigal was a good friend from back in the days of the Free Center, and I thought he was just the man to deal with a horrible economic crisis that included both hyperinflation and negative growth.

But this appointment didn't do the trick. Despite being a gifted economist and a good-hearted, wise man, Yigal lacked managerial experience. He wasn't able to calm the storm or the markets, and left as quickly as he came. I felt bad for him, but I think he understood that the task was too much for him to handle.

What were we supposed to do to keep Likud in power without Begin, with the lesser-known and much less charismatic Shamir at the helm?

———

Yitzhak Shamir was forged of steel. I never met anyone with the determination and mental strength of that man. But he didn't make a very good first impression.

He was not eloquent, and he cut the figure of an extremist—he had abstained in the vote on the peace treaty with Egypt, and if he hadn't been speaker of the Knesset I'm pretty sure he would have voted against it. And even though he had served for a bit as foreign minister, he hadn't shown any real ability to manage an international diplomatic campaign. It would later turn out that many of our fears were unfounded. Shamir was a responsible, restrained, and careful prime minister. His opinions may have been extreme, but his actions and words were controlled.

In the summer of 1984, the IDF was bleeding out in Lebanon, the shekel had collapsed, the banking stocks had crashed, the economy was paralyzed, inflation reached triple-digits, and our candidate, despite being the incumbent, was a tough sell. As the election approached, we needed to inspire hope, security and opportunity, and for this purpose a mini-cabinet was created. It included Roni Milo, who was one of Shamir's most loyal supporters and would later leave the Knesset to become mayor of Tel Aviv; Moshe Arens; Dan Meridor, a longtime liberal Likud figure about my age whose father was close with Begin in the Irgun; and myself. I suggested that we advocate, as a central campaign promise, the idea of a national unity government to be formed after the election. The polls were showing that this idea resonated well, and in a televised debate between Shamir and Shimon Peres, two days before the election, he floated the idea.

This time around, the electoral results were not as good as we would have liked, but not as bad as we had feared. It was 44 seats for Labor, 41 for Likud—close enough to be considered a tie. For weeks, neither party managed to form a coalition on its own, and the national unity government was created by default, with a rotation agreement between the two prime ministers: Peres for two years, then Shamir.

Shamir wanted to go second. He wanted to get to the next elections as the incumbent prime minister. This was a smart move. But Peres also preferred it this way: He wanted to go first in order to cement his leadership in his own party, where he had a bitter rivalry with Yitzhak Rabin. It was true that Labor had earned three more seats than Likud, but polls had given Labor a much bigger advantage. The fact that Peres failed to live up to expectations and couldn't form a government was seen as yet another in his growing list of political failures.

———

Going second, of course, entailed a certain risk. Would Peres actually keep his end of the deal? I was convinced that barring any unusual dramas, Peres would indeed leave office on schedule. At the same time, I knew Peres was very good at generating unusual dramas.

And indeed, just before the scheduled rotation, in October 1986, Peres demanded the firing of the finance minister, Yitzhak Modai, after Modai had publicly described him as our "flighty prime minister." A crisis ensued.

Some thought Likud would blow up the deal rather than accept the firing.

First of all, what Modai said was entirely true: Peres was indeed flighty, and had in fact flown to every corner of the earth. Second, according to the coalition agreement, Shamir had the sole right to decide who Likud's ministers in the government would be.

I saw the militant mood among the Likud members, and I did what I could to calm them.

We came together as a caucus in Shamir's office. It was unnerving to hear several of our MKs call for tearing up the coalition agreement and going to elections. I responded sharply. "Why should we play into his hands? What will we do three months from now if Shamir isn't prime minister? Instead of running the country, we'll be sitting in opposition, drafting parliamentary questions."

I offered a compromise. Moshe Nissim, who had originally come from the Liberal Party, would replace Modai as finance minister. Modai would stay on as a minister without portfolio. Modai was hurt, but the proposal was approved. Peres had no choice but to accept it as well. The main opponent of the plan was Nissim himself, who had no background in economics. I talked to his wife. Once I had secured her approval, he gave in.

To Nissim's credit, he was at least open about the fact that he didn't know anything about economics. As opposed to so many other politicians, who always make a show of knowing everything about everything, he agreed to listen to the professionals, and turned out to be a very responsible finance minister.

The coalition held. Peres kept his promise and rotated out. Shamir became prime minister. Likud was leading the country again.

I, meanwhile, continued in my roles in the most important Knesset committees, supporting the leadership of the party, and waiting patiently for my turn.

THREE

The Man of Steel

The 1988 campaign was a turning point in my career. I was appointed treasurer of the Likud, which meant I was in charge of fundraising in advance of the November election. For the first time in Israel's history, Likud raised more money than Labor in an electoral campaign, and I played a significant role in making that happen.

It was during that campaign that I came to know the renowned banker Edmond Safra.

His family came from Aleppo in Syria and moved to Beirut, where his father opened his first bank, and where Edmond was born. From Beirut the family moved to Switzerland, and eventually to South America. The business went with them and, with time, made the family extremely wealthy.

When I first met Safra, he was already one of the richest Jews in the world. The owner of the Trade Development Bank in Geneva, his clients included the wealthiest Arab businessmen from around the Persian Gulf as well as other countries that did not have relations with Israel. They all knew Safra was a pro-Israel, Orthodox Jew. But where their personal finances were concerned, the politics was irrelevant. The confidence these moguls had in him was absolute, and they entrusted him with billions.

In 1983, American Express offered to buy Safra's bank. He agreed, and became the largest shareholder of American Express and the chairman of its board. He had already been well regarded among American businessmen. Now he became a leading figure of American finance.

The CEO of American Express, James Robinson, was a tough-as-nails American, and the two didn't really get along. Safra had spent his whole life as a private, self-employed businessman, and suddenly he sat atop a gigantic public corporation. His management style didn't mesh with Robinson's. A rift emerged between the two. Safra sold his shares back to American Express for an enormous amount of money and signed a noncompete agreement for five years.

On the day the agreement expired in 1988, Safra reopened his bank in Geneva, under a different name but in the same building. Within a few months, he had rehired many of his senior staff, and soon after that, many of his biggest clients returned. They still preferred Safra.

After reestablishing himself in Switzerland, Safra built up the Republic National Bank of New York. It quickly became one of the largest private banks in America. Safra was again a leading figure—not as the chair of a public conglomerate, but as the master of his own private empire.

———

One day in 1988, Safra called me and asked if I'd meet at his office in Midtown Manhattan with Walter Weiner, the CEO of Safra's American bank and who was personally close with Safra. The office was located in the modern, luxurious executive wing of the bank's headquarters on Fifth Avenue. On another occasion, Safra had taken me to the front of the building and pointed out the enormous, beautiful *mezuza* designed especially for him, encased in thick protective glass. Safra pointed to it and said, "This is the only *mezuza* at the entrance to a big public building on Fifth Avenue." He was proud.

I met with Weiner, and he told a tale that took three hours. At the center of it stood a stream of nasty news stories about Safra appearing in papers across South America, Africa, and Europe. What they all had in common was the insinuation that Safra was an international criminal and that his bank was a money-laundering operation for mafia and drug cartels. If that wasn't bad enough, they also claimed he was illegally transferring, on a weekly basis, millions of dollars to the Soviet government.

Whoever was behind these stories knew exactly what they were doing. Safra was always afraid something would happen to him, fears that were not unfounded. A large part of his family lived in Brazil, where the kidnapping and ransoming of family members of wealthy people was commonplace. The publication of these stories upset him greatly, and he felt he had to get to the bottom of what looked like a coordinated assault, which came from different sources and surprising directions.

Weiner asked me what could be done. Safra, he said, was convinced that international anti-Semitic elements were behind the campaign.

I offered a different theory. It struck me that the campaign was likely coming from American Express, which was very hurt by Safra's quick reemergence and his ability to attract experienced senior executives and big-ticket clients. The corporate bosses knew that these kinds of insinuations would get under Safra's skin.

Weiner disagreed.

He walked me over to Safra's office. Safra's official role at the bank of which he was the principal shareholder was that of a consultant. To get to his office, we had to take the elevator down from the 29th floor to the lobby, exit out onto the street, walk around to the other entrance, and take a private elevator up to Safra's offices. Again, the elevator stopped on 29. But then we had to climb up two more flights of stairs and go through a number of secure entrances, almost all of which were guarded by former IDF special forces.

We finally sat with Safra, and I told him my theory. He agreed with Weiner. In his view, there was no way American Express was behind the campaign. It was a public company, and they had far too much to lose if their involvement became known. We shook hands and said goodbye.

A few weeks later, Safra called me. He was planning on coming to Israel on his private jet, and wanted me to set up a meeting with the prime minister. The meeting was set for a Friday, and I was asked to join.

—————

Yitzhak Shamir didn't know Safra, and this was their first and, I think, last meeting.

Safra spoke fluent English, French and Arabic. He liked to insert Arabic curses into his sentences, like *yihrab beito* ("may his house be destroyed"), and he spoke in a way that reminded me of Rabbi Ovadia Yosef, the spiritual leader of the Sephardic Shas Party. This style was foreign to Shamir, and I wondered whether the two could find a common language.

The meeting was riveting. Safra told him the whole story, and said he thought it was driven by anti-Semites on a global scale.

"What can we do to help?" Shamir asked him.

Safra asked if the Mossad would look into it.

Shamir turned to me and asked what I thought.

"If global anti-Semites are in fact behind a defamation campaign against a major Jewish financier," I said, "it should be of interest to the Mossad."

Shamir promised to think it over. He told me after the meeting that he was very impressed with Safra. "I could see the wheels spinning in his head," he said.

So I connected the Mossad with Edmond Safra. His people came to Israel, met with the relevant people, and presented documents. The Mossad looked into it for a few months and got back to him. Their investigation, they told him, had revealed that the campaign was being directed from inside the United States. But because the Mossad couldn't act on U.S. soil, they wouldn't be able to continue pursuing it, and suggested that he hire American investigators to take it from there.

Safra enlisted the help of detectives in the United States, and within a few months they got to the bottom of what turned into a major scandal. My instincts had been right. American Express was behind the campaign, and now Safra had proof.

One evening Safra called me. He told me the whole story, and said it would soon appear in *The Wall Street Journal*. His lawyer had put a proverbial smoking gun on the desk of the CEO of American Express, and the latter immediately confessed. The paper ran a large paid ad by the corporation apologizing to Safra, and announcing the board of directors' decision to donate millions of dollars to Jewish institutions, including the Anti-Defamation League.

It became a *cause célèbre*. A book came out called *Vendetta* by Bryan Burrough that told the whole story and became a best seller. My role, and that of the Mossad, was left out of what Safra had told the author and journalists, but from then on, he became a big fan of the Mossad. In turn, the Mossad was able to use the episode to their advantage in a number of sensitive cases.

———

Four years after the 1984 election had ended in a draw and forced the creation of a unity government, it happened again. This time, however, the edge was to Likud, which earned 40 seats to Labor's 39. Yitzhak Shamir was tapped to form a government, and six weeks later, on December 22, 1988, another unity government was formed.

The new government started out as an effort to show true cooperation between the two major parties. Labor had Yitzhak Rabin as defense minister and Shimon Peres as finance minister, while Likud had Shamir as prime minister, as well as Moshe Arens as foreign minister. For the first time, Likud also appointed a cadre of younger ministers, which signaled a generational shift: Dan Meridor as justice minister, Roni Milo as environment minister, and myself as a minister without portfolio in the Prime Minister's Office with a focus on minorities. We also had as transportation minister Moshe Katzav, the future president (and, after that, convicted rapist), who was our age and had served in the previous government.

Unlike the founding generation, who mostly immigrated from other countries and endured the horrors of the mid-twentieth century in Europe or in Arab lands, the members of the new generation of emerging political leaders—not just in Likud, but across the political landscape—were born in Israel, spoke Hebrew as their first language, and came of age in a country that had already won its independence.

These new Likud ministers were all around the age of forty. Shamir earned praise for grooming the next generation of party leaders. Moshe Arens, in the same spirit, chose Benjamin Netanyahu, our UN ambassador, to be his deputy foreign minister. He had been an adviser to Arens during the campaign and was rewarded for his skills and loyalty.

The new unity government was founded on an agreement to preserve the diplomatic status quo. Shamir was not prepared for major concessions to the Palestinians, if any at all. On the Palestinian side, Yassir Arafat, reviled in Israel as the father of modern terrorism, was still the uncontested leader of the Palestinian Liberation Organization, and the likelihood of dialogue between Israel and the Palestinians was slim.

At the same time, from the moment George H. W. Bush replaced Ronald Reagan as president of the United States in January 1989, things got messy.

Bush's secretary of state was James A. Baker III, a lawyer from Houston, a friend to big-oil, and a Bush loyalist. He was known as an aggressive actor, and soon after he took the post he decided to involve himself deeply in the Middle East. Baker didn't like Shamir's policies, and made that clear on many occasions.

Bush, for his part, was committed to Israel less than Reagan had been. He strongly opposed the government's settlement policies, or more precisely, the policies pushed by Ariel Sharon—both when he was minister of industry and trade, and especially once he was appointed minister of construction and housing in 1990. Shamir had to field criticism from Washington that became increasingly acerbic. The criticism was, however, warmly received by Shamir's coalition partners in the Labor Party, who also opposed Sharon's settlement efforts.

The American approach to Israeli policy, combined with the support it received from Labor, set the stage for one of the ugliest political episodes in our history.

———

In 1989, Secretary Baker launched a new diplomatic effort known as the "five-point plan," which focused on restarting negotiations with the Palestinians through a mechanism that involved both the American and Egyptian governments. It was developed in coordination with Egypt's president, Hosni Mubarak. The principles Baker presented added up to a major move away from Shamir's policy of zero concessions.

Shamir adamantly refused to join the effort. Moshe Arens, the foreign minister who had traditionally been seen as a hawk, along with Dan Meridor and myself, as well as Dan's brother Salai (an aide to Arens whom I would later appoint as ambassador to Washington), all thought there was no need to reject Baker's plan out of hand. We felt we should try to improve on it, and thereby put the burden on the Palestinians to show they were interested in compromise. Labor, on the other hand, wanted to accept the Baker plan as is.

Shamir wouldn't budge. Our efforts to soften him came up empty. Shamir generally wasn't the convincible type, certainly not as far as the Palestinian issue was concerned. He declared the Baker plan a nonstarter. In the end, the security cabinet voted an approval of the plan, but added a few conditions that were so constraining that it was tantamount to a rejection.

To this day I can't tell you whom Shamir trusted less: Arafat or Peres. He despised Arafat, but suspected Peres was somehow behind the American-Egyptian initiative. The fog would lift when, in March 1990, Shas—the Sephardic ultra-Orthodox party with little historical interest in foreign policy—suddenly demanded that Shamir accept the Baker plan. Now it was clear that behind what looked like a foreign policy disagreement was really a political coup attempt, driven by Labor.

Shamir didn't take kindly to threats. At a certain point, Shas insisted that Shamir meet with the party's spiritual leader, Rabbi Ovadia Yosef, to hear the rabbi's views on why Shamir should respond favorably to the initiative. Shamir wasn't willing to go to Yosef's house. Arens, Meridor, myself and a few others pressed him.

In the meantime, because Labor had gone behind Shamir's back to collude with Shas to try to force his hand, Shamir decided to fire Peres. He assumed that the rest of Labor's ministers would not be able to handle the sacking of their party's leader and would resign in sympathy. Shamir's reasoning was clear: If the government fell because of the crisis and there were new elections, it would become a caretaker government that couldn't take on new major diplomatic initiatives. Its hands would be tied, and it would be better to run an election campaign without Peres and Rabin as senior ministers in his government.

He fired Peres on March 11, 1990. The other Labor ministers quit, and Labor submitted a no-confidence resolution to the Knesset. Shas announced that if Shamir didn't accept the Baker plan, its members would vote no confidence as well.

Peres' chief rival in Labor, Yitzhak Rabin, famously called the episode the "stinky maneuver," a label that added to Peres' reputation as an underhanded politician, and which built Rabin's status in the party.

Shamir, finally, agreed to visit the rabbi at home. It was an extraordinary meeting.

No two people, it seemed, had as little in common as Rabbi Ovadia Yosef and Yitzhak Shamir.

Shamir detested all the pomp that surrounded rabbinic courts. This kind of pilgrimage was utterly foreign to him. He went as a man coerced, heard what the rabbi had to say, and responded: "I don't agree with a single word you are saying. I will do what is necessary, and you'll do whatever you want." Then he got up and left.

When Shamir arrived at the Knesset, the vote was held. For the first time in Israel's history, the government lost a no-confidence vote. The Shas members didn't show up, except for the party leader, Yitzhak Peretz, who voted against it. Shas blinked, but the motion passed.

On the face of it, the next step was simple: Chaim Herzog, Israel's president, would give Peres the mandate to form a new government, and Likud would go into opposition. But Israeli politics loves surprises.

———

The day after the no-confidence vote, Shamir convened the Likud ministers in his office. Naturally, the mood was grim. In the corridor outside, I had overheard people saying that maybe they should recommend to Herzog that he give Arens the mandate instead of Shamir. But nobody had the guts to suggest it out loud.

The meeting began. Shamir looked at the despondent ministers around him and pounded the table.

"What is going on?" he asked. "Why are you all in mourning? Nothing is decided yet. We will fight, and we'll hit back hard. Peres must not be allowed to form a government."

Unlike the rest of us, Shamir was in a fighting mood. He declared that Likud was going to launch a public campaign to keep Peres from forming a government. He said he was creating a committee to handle political outreach. Then he turned to me and said: "Ehud, I want you to lead the committee." I was surprised, but of course I agreed.

I asked to have Ariel Sharon, David Levy, and Yitzhak Modai on the committee.

These were the same three "troublemakers" who had, just a few months before, led a revolt against Shamir from the right when they thought he was going to waffle on the Baker plan. That crisis reached its peak at a meeting of the Likud Central Committee that included a moment when both Sharon and Shamir, each shouting into separate microphones, called on people simultaneously to raise their hands to vote on different measures. The meeting blew up, and Shamir eventually found himself cornered. Their efforts were largely responsible for his hard line on the Baker plan, and he was surprised that I, of all people, wanted them on the committee now.

He pounded the table. "No way on earth."

"Why?" I asked.

"Because I don't trust any of them," he fumed.

There was silence.

"Mr. Prime Minister," I said to Shamir. "If you appoint me to chair the committee, I will decide who's on it."

In the end, it took a week, but we managed to get the Shas Party to recommend to the president that Shamir, not Peres, form the next government. As though nothing had happened.

The old rabbi's courage had its limits. He had helped bring down Shamir's government, but the ultra-Orthodox community, and especially its Ashkenazic leadership, put enormous pressure on Yosef, and even threatened to excommunicate him. That was too much for him, and he gave the order to his party to support Shamir.

———

Peres, of course, had no intention of giving in. Herzog had asked him to form a government, and his six weeks of intensive efforts were met with counterefforts on our part, which included late nights, haggling with individual MKs looking for the best deal, and closing an agreement with Shas that was printed out, late at night, on my fifteen-year-old son's Commodore 64 home computer.

At one point, Peres even announced the successful formation of a government, but by the time the Knesset was set to vote on it the next day, two Ashkenazic ultra-Orthodox members of the Degel Hatorah Party had received instructions from their spiritual leader, Rabbi Menachem Mendel Schneerson, the Lubavitcher Rebbe, not to join any government that was planning on giving away biblical lands.

In the end, Peres failed. We won, and on June 11, 1990, Shamir formed a new government with no fewer than 11 parties—but without Labor.

Shamir saw me as largely responsible for the successful execution of the campaign. We were in power again—and I was the one who had delivered.

Ariel Sharon asked me what ministry he would be getting. Working on Shamir's behalf, I offered him Housing and Construction. He laughed. He had previously been defense minister and industry and trade minister, and now he would be building housing projects? I told him that in the next few months there would be an enormous wave of immigration from the collapsing Soviet Union, and we would need to build like never before. "It's a historic opportunity for you," I told him.

He agreed, on condition that he also got control of the Land Authority. I agreed. I reported back to Shamir. He reluctantly agreed.

"And what do you want for yourself?" Shamir asked me.

Immediately I answered, "Minister of Health."

"Really? Minister of Health?"

Nobody wants to be minister of health. It's usually left for the end, as a consolation prize for those who didn't get what they wanted.

I felt otherwise. I was convinced that the entire healthcare system needed to be overhauled.

A national commission of inquiry headed up by Supreme Court Justice Shoshana Netanyahu—Benjamin Netanyahu's aunt—was drafting a report that would recommend reform of the healthcare system. I didn't know her, but I knew well two other members of the commission. They each headed two of the biggest hospitals in Israel. They were both exceptionally talented people who could easily run the world's most prestigious medical centers. I was confident the report would form a good basis for the healthcare overhaul I wanted.

––––––

My tenure as minister of health was one of the most gratifying periods of my career.

A few weeks after I started, the Netanyahu Commission issued its report, and I submitted it to the government for approval. I asked Yoram Aridor, a former finance minister, to study it and propose a plan for its implementation. Then I set up a team to implement the reforms. I headed the team myself, and filled it with some of the best experts in healthcare, budgeting, and other relevant areas.

I decided to leave the Health Ministry's senior staff in place exactly as I received them. My intention was to take advantage of what little time we had until the next election, scheduled for November 1992, in order to push forward the reforms, which were desperately needed, and also to pass a new Health Insurance Act, which would transform hospitals into independent entities without the direct involvement of the government in their management. The Health Ministry would stop running healthcare providers, and instead be in charge of setting standards and oversight.

I was addicted to the job. For months I ran around, every night, all across the country, meeting with doctors and senior hospital management, to build support for the reform. My committee, meanwhile, worked hard on the draft legislation of the Health Insurance Act.

I don't think there was ever, before or since, so thorough an effort to reinvent Israel's healthcare system. The doctors were thrilled. The lifelong bureaucrats of the ministry—less so. But that's how it always is: Bureaucrats are suspicious of change. They were comfortable with what they had, even if it didn't meet the needs of a changing country.

––––––

The waiting times for different medical procedures were long and tortuous. Heart patients at high risk would wait months for an operation. In many cases, patients died before they could be operated on. I studied the problem. It turned out that hospitals had to fight just to get approval to be allowed to perform bypass operations. Having a department that did open-heart surgery added prestige to a hospital.

The same was true for in-vitro fertilization (IVF). Every head of gynecology wanted to be able to offer IVF. It made him more important and built up the hospital's reputation. Every week we would get a request from a different "friends-of" association asking for approval to create an IVF unit at the hospitals they were funding. Such departments, however, cost a lot in government support, and we needed to be careful with taxpayer money.

Our method of compensation was outdated. Hospitals back then could cover their expenses only according to the number of days a patient was hospitalized, regardless of the cost of treatment. If a patient had open-heart surgery and stayed six days, the hospital received the same payment as for another patient who was there to treat a viral infection. The inevitable result was that hospitals saw less-costly patients as more profitable. Some patients were admitted for no good reason, just to boost the hospital's income. Patients needing expensive procedures like open-heart surgery, on the other hand, were a major drain on the bottom line.

So the waiting times were horrific. Thousands waited, suffered, and often died. Senior hospital executives confided to me that the more heart surgery patients they got—which they had fought so hard to get—the hospitals' deficits only got worse. At a certain point hospitals started cutting back on the number of days that surgeries could be performed. Waiting times grew, and more people died.

I implemented a new method of compensation, called Diagnosis-Related Group (DRG) funding, which paid hospitals according to the costs of treatment. Suddenly hospitals received a lot more money for open-heart surgeries, IVF, and other costly procedures. It wasn't implemented across the board, but limited to specific, sensitive treatment areas that were endangering the institutions' financial viability.

The change was felt immediately: Waiting times plummeted within a few months, and lives were saved. Hospitals narrowed their losses, senior physicians came back to Israel, operating rooms were used more efficiently, and everybody benefited. To this day, the beneficial impact on Israeli hospitals of DRG funding continues to be felt.

———

Organ transplants were another serious problem.

Even back then, in 1990, we had heart and liver transplants being carried out in Israel. But the number of organs donated didn't come close to the number of patients who needed them. Israelis with means would travel to Belgium and stay for many months in hospitals that performed such procedures in accordance with the urgency of their situation rather than their place on the waiting list or what country they had come from. Others went to the United Kingdom, where they sought the services of the man considered the top transplant surgeon in the world, Sir Magdi Yacoub, who originally came from Egypt. His chief assistant was Dan Aravot, an Israeli who, with my help, would later come to the Beilinson Hospital in Petach Tikva as its chief of heart transplants.

During that time, the European Community changed its policy on transplants. There, too, a problem with waiting times had emerged, and it was decided that as of a certain date, European citizens would get preferential consideration regardless of their clinical status. This was horrible news for Israelis. Now they might have to wait years for a transplant. For many, it was a death sentence.

I got on a plane for London.

There I met with the British health secretary, Kenneth Clarke, who would later go on to serve as home secretary and chancellor of the exchequer and run, unsuccessfully, for leadership of the Conservative Party. We met at Westminster Palace and were joined by Nathan Meron, a senior diplomat at our embassy in the UK. We covered a range of topics—everything except for the actual purpose of my visit. I got the sense that Clarke was trying to avoid whatever it was I wanted to ask of him. He was, I felt, exceptionally full of himself.

At a certain point I rapped my knuckles on the table. "Mr. Secretary," I said. "Please, listen to me. I came here not to talk about international diplomacy, but people's lives." I explained to him the problem, about how the European decision meant a death sentence for thirty Israelis, some of whom had been hospitalized in British hospitals for more than a year. I knew that that changing a decision of the European Community would be an arduous process and anyway not within the authority of the health secretary of the United Kingdom. Therefore, all I asked was that they implement the decision only for patients who were admitted after the date that the new policy came into effect, but that those who were already hospitalized in Britain would receive organs according to their clinical need.

To my surprise, Clarke agreed. The next day I went to visit the hospital where many Israelis were waiting for organs, and I met with Doctors Yacoub and Aravot. I asked my friend Cyril Stein, owner of the bookmaking firm Ladbrokes and one of the wealthiest Jews in Great Britain, to accompany us.

We went from patient to patient, together with Cyril and the two senior doctors. We told them about the agreement we'd reached with Clarke. They were deeply grateful. For many, the extended hospitalization had completely upended their lives and those of their families. Whole families had relocated from Israel to Britain to be with their loved ones. Families had to sell everything they owned just to pay for it, and then had to wait without any guarantee their loved ones would survive.

It was heartbreaking, and I left with difficulty. I didn't know how many of these patients would live.

One in particular was a young man whom I will identify as A., who needed a heart-lung transplant. His parents had moved to London, near the hospital. His brothers and sisters visited often. The family's whole life now revolved around him.

Two months after my visit, my phone rang at four in the morning. On the other end, a woman was crying. She introduced herself as A.'s sister. They had found a match, and A. was on his way into his very risky surgery and had asked her to call me, so that I might pray for him. I was moved. I promised I would, and asked her to call me back after the surgery was over.

Twenty hours later, she called me back. "He's alive," she cried. The doctors were optimistic.

Two months after that, my secretary told me that A. was calling and wanted to talk to me. He was emotional. "Thank you," he said. "You saved my life." He later visited me at my office, and after that I attended his wedding.

Years later, when I was prime minister, I attended a graduation ceremony of the Shin Bet security service. As I arrived, a group of people emotionally waited for me together with Yuval Diskin, the head of Shin Bet. It was A., together with his sister and brothers. All of them now worked for Shin Bet.

———

Another major problem involved the enormous waves of immigrants who came to Israel from the former Soviet Union in the early 1990s. They included tens of thousands of doctors and other healthcare professionals. But what were we to do with doctors who had studied and worked in Russia, Ukraine, Georgia, or Khazakhstan? What was the level of their training? Could they be licensed in Israel?

The Soviet Union had not excelled in medicine. Its pharmaceuticals were not necessarily approved by the U.S. Food and Drug Administration (FDA) or similar bodies in Europe or Israel. Soviet medical technology was behind as well. Still, how could we prevent doctors, who had studied for years, worked for decades in hospitals and had built a lifetime of experience, from working in their trade, especially if we wanted them and their families to be successfully absorbed into the country?

The Israeli medical union demanded that immigrant doctors go through retraining and exams. It was not unreasonable. The head of the medical licensing board was Professor Yosef Shenkar, himself an immigrant from Russia, who was head of gynecology at Hadassah Hospital. As health minister, I spoke with him a few times, asking that the board find a way to license doctors rather than reject them. I didn't impose specific rules on him, but I stayed on top of them. I also met with new immigrant doctors to better understand their expectations and hear their complaints.

I only intervened in one case.

A doctor in his fifties came to me. For many years he had been in charge of internal medicine at a large hospital in Moscow. I did my homework and confirmed that this was a very serious person. He spoke to me with tears in his eyes. "I saved hundreds of lives," he said. "I was the director of a department that employed dozens of doctors. I'm a well-known professor in Russia. And they want to send me to a beginner's course?"

I promised to look into it. I summoned Shenkar, the head of the licensing board, and insisted that this doctor receive full licensing to practice his specialty. If, God forbid, it turned out I was wrong, I promised to take personal responsibility. The doctor got his license and started working, exactly as he had for decades before.

Years later, when I was prime minister, I visited Hadassah Hospital. A few doctors accompanied me, and I noticed that one of them was getting special deference from his colleagues. I don't remember what his specific job was, but it was clear that he was the most respected of them all. At the end of the tour, the doctor asked to speak with me one-on-one.

"I want to thank you again," he said. "You made sure I got my license."

———

My team drafted the National Health Insurance Act. The law would completely disconnect the Health Ministry from the management of hospitals and HMOs and set them up as independent bodies, competing for budgets based on the quality of their services and the healthcare choices made by individual patients. The Health Ministry would limit itself to its proper role of licensing, oversight and defining standards of medical care.

The vote in the Knesset was set for March 1, 1992—a stormy winter day. Jerusalem was snowed in, the city shuttered. I let everyone know that under no circumstances would I allow for a delay in the vote. The head of Israel's Histadrut labor union, MK Israel Keisar, who cared more about reducing the enormous deficits of the union-owned Clalit HMO than about the healthcare system as a whole, hiked up the mountain on foot from Shaar Hagay all the way to the Knesset just to vote against the reform. Out of respect, I agreed to hold off the vote until he made it. He arrived, voted against it, and his side lost. The law passed its first of three readings and went into committee.

I pushed the committee as hard as I could. I needed to get the law passed through second and third readings of the plenum before the election, which was coming up in eight months.

But politics got in my way. Three of our right-wing coalition partners pulled out of the government in protest over James Baker-led talks in Washington between Israel and a Jordanian-Palestinian delegation. The government fell, the Knesset was dissolved, and early elections were called for June 23. There was no chance my law would pass in time.

We lost the election badly. Labor, now led by Yitzhak Rabin, received 44 seats to Likud's 32. On July 13, 1992, Rabin formed a new government. We were out. On my last day on the job, I was still negotiating with the doctors' union about introducing reforms that would enable private practices to work out of the public hospitals. Minutes before the new members of the Knesset were sworn in, at a moment when I was technically still in office, we signed the agreement.

It didn't help. The new government took things in a direction very different from my own. Haim Ramon replaced me as health minister, and soon after that he was replaced by Efraim Sneh. Sneh eventually passed a healthcare law that looked little like the one I had pushed. Things improved, but not much.

———

On August 2, 1990, Iraq invaded Kuwait and triggered the crisis that brought about the First Gulf War.

President George H. W. Bush understood that if he sat back and did nothing, it would undermine the stability of the entire Middle East, especially in countries crucial to American interests in the region, including Egypt and Saudi Arabia. American supremacy in the Persian Gulf was being directly challenged.

Bush went to work building a broad coalition of nations for joint military action against Iraqi President Saddam Hussein. The most important partners were the Arab states: Egypt, Syria, Saudi Arabia, and the United Arab Emirates (UAE) all joined. Israel was both consulted and updated, but Bush didn't want us involved in the diplomatic or military action. He felt, justifiably from his end, that Israel's direct involvement in the coalition would make it much harder to keep the Arab partners on board.

On January 17, 1991, Operation Desert Storm was launched. By that point Israel no longer had a unity government, and I was minister of health.

Even though we weren't part of the operation, we were deeply concerned that Iraq would target Israel with its long-range SCUD missiles. The Americans made it clear that there was neither interest nor intention of involving Israel in the military response, and they promised to defend us. They also promised anything we might need, including medical supplies.

The biggest fear was of a chemical or biological weapons attack. These could claim hundreds of thousands of victims, and we needed to prepare, quickly, for a worst-case scenario.

I started issuing orders. All the hospitals in the country went to work. Hundreds of hospital beds were pulled out of wards and placed outside, to prepare for a massive influx of patients requiring triage. Equipment for treating victims was positioned outside the buildings as well. Medical staffs were given equipment to keep them safe from contagion. First responders were given protective gear, and antidotes to be administered on the scene of an attack were taken out of storage.

The most important thing in dealing with a chemical attack was ventilators for hospitals. Our intensive care units were equipped with very few automated ventilators. We had plenty of manual ventilators. But in a mass casualty event, we would need hundreds of automated ones. We couldn't use up all our hospital staff manually ventilating patients.

I looked for a donor and found one in S. Daniel Abraham, an American philanthropist and businessman who had spent time in Israel and was now based in Florida. I told him that I needed urgently about $1.5 million. He told me he would fly to Israel to meet.

Abraham landed in his private jet and was brought to a conference room at the airport where we waited for him. We made our presentation, and at the end he said: "The president of Israel, Chaim Herzog, used to be my lawyer. Even now that he's president, I won't make any major donation without consulting with him. Give me a day and I'll get back to you."

I took advantage of that day as well. I spoke to Herzog myself and told him I expected him to recommend the donation. He did, the money was deposited in the account of the Health Ministry's research fund within twenty-four hours, and the ventilators were purchased. We ended up not needing them for the war—when the SCUDs finally came, the warheads were conventional—but the hospitals benefited from them nonetheless.

A different donation caused me a bigger headache.

During the war, as SCUD missiles were landing in the center of Israel, I was walking into the King David Hotel in Jerusalem when I bumped into Pinky Green. Green, an Orthodox Jew, had been a partner of Mark Rich, and the two of them were among the wealthiest people on earth. Their trading company was one of the world's biggest private companies, but the two of them were also wanted by U.S. authorities on suspicion of illegally trading commodities, especially oil, without proper reporting to tax authorities. They fled to Switzerland, which wouldn't extradite them. Israel would let them visit the country in secret, but we were always afraid the Americans would find out and demand their extradition.

I asked Green what brought him to Jerusalem in the middle of a war.

"When my country is under attack," he said, "I have to be here."

I told him that what our country needed was a donation to buy medical equipment.

"I'll send you a few million," Green said. "But on one condition. Promise me that my name won't appear."

I promised. The money came, the purchases were made. At some point, however, the internal comptroller of the Health Ministry complained about it to the state comptroller, Miriam Ben-Porat. It was apparently a problem to accept anonymous gifts.

The donation, as well as the purchase of equipment, had been handled by the professional staff in the Health Ministry. I was not involved, but I was the only person who knew the identity of the donor. The state comptroller demanded to know who the donor was.

"What's the problem?" I asked. "The money arrived, and there's no obligation to give the donor anything in return. It's a donation to our healthcare system."

She didn't back down. Neither did I. I told her that I was going to seek counsel and get back to her.

I reached out to the attorney general, Yosef Harish, and spelled out the problem. In a fatherly tone, he explained to me that there is no greater act of Jewish generosity than to donate anonymously. I should keep my promise to the donor, he said.

When I got back to Ben-Porat, she was not impressed. "You can either give me his name," she said, "or I can involve the police."

I called Harish again. He told me that despite his fatherly advice, he would not be able to block a police inquiry.

I understood. I got back to Ben-Porat and told her I would reveal the name, but I insisted that she not pass it on to anyone.

The state comptroller's report was published, and, of course, his name appeared in it. Green was furious. I tried to explain what had happened. The state comptroller had had her way, and while there were no serious repercussions, my relationship with Pinky was never quite the same.

————

Two weeks into the war, Israel was hit by SCUD missiles launched from bases in western Iraq. On a Friday night and Saturday morning, four missiles hit the Tel Aviv area. The damage was not great, but there was panic. American Patriot anti-missile batteries had failed to intercept any of them. Shamir called a meeting in Tel Aviv of the ministerial committee on defense, in the historic conference room at defense ministry headquarters where David Ben-Gurion had once held his meetings.

Due to the life-or-death nature of the decisions that were being made, the Orthodox ministers, Moshe Nissim and Aryeh Deri, received a special rabbinic dispensation to drive to Tel Aviv from Jerusalem on the Sabbath.

The meeting was held at noon, and the mood was heavy. Even though there had been no casualties, the missiles carried a one-ton payload. If such a rocket hit an occupied apartment building, the carnage would be horrific. Could we really refrain from responding? And if we did retaliate, how could we reach the launch bases, which were hundreds of miles away, and take out the launchers, the locations of which were not exactly known?

Hard questions. The meeting began with an intelligence briefing as usual, followed by a diplomatic briefing. It turned out that the night before, a high-ranking emissary had arrived on behalf of U.S. General Norman Schwarzkopf, commander of the coalition forces. IDF generals told him that Israel was preparing to retaliate inside of Iraq. He asked when the strike would take place. The officers told him it would happen the following day. He was stunned.

After the diplomatic briefing, Defense Minister Moshe Arens presented the plan of attack. The commander of the Air Force, Avihu Bin-Nun, spoke next. He explained that the objective was to drop our most elite special forces, the Sayeret Matkal, near the launchers using helicopters, including a number of jeeps. The forces would seek out and destroy the launchers.

Ministers asked hard questions. What would their flight path be? They would, after all, have to fly over either Jordan or Saudi Arabia, both of which were enemies. Was there no risk that they would be taken out by air defenses of one of the countries? Helicopters were easy targets for anti-aircraft.

After the questions, the discussion began. The first to speak was Aryeh Deri, the interior minister, who spoke adamantly against any operation. In his view, the attack plan was not serious and had little chance of success. The Iraqi bases were huge, roughly the area of our whole country. How on earth would we find the launchers?

Other ministers were skeptical as well. Bin-Nun interrupted, saying it was crucial to come to a decision quickly, since the helicopters were already on the tarmac with soldiers aboard. Any delay would reduce the risk of success.

Suddenly there was a bang.

Shamir had slammed his hand on the table. "I ask for quiet. I would like to speak. I am very tired. I didn't sleep all night. I'm about to pass out in front of you and there won't be any point in the discussion.

"Last night, President Bush called me. He said he had heard that Israel was planning on attacking in Iraq, and that it was unacceptable to him. If Israel attacked, the United States would not prevent the Saudi Air Force from shooting down Israeli aircraft that flew in its airspace. The whole coalition, which includes many Arab states, will collapse. And all the blame will be on us."

If, however, Israel refrained from retaliating, Bush had told Shamir, the United States would do everything to help in terms of equipment, means, and money. Shamir summed it up: Israel would not attack. There was nothing to argue about. The meeting was over.

That was Shamir's style. No nonsense.

There is no doubt that Shamir's decision was the right one. He didn't like too much talking. One rap on the table and a sharp, clear decision that could not be challenged. Later on, the restraint that he showed would earn him accolades around the world, and in Israel as well. He earned them.

Sometimes, strength is knowing when to say "No." Shamir had that in spades.

————

When the Gulf War ended, U.S. Secretary of State Baker put his idea of a peace conference on the table.

Shamir's first reaction was dismissive. A gathering with Arafat and the Arab states was effectively an international conference, which went against one of his core principles—and not just his. Israel had always opposed, with good reason, international conferences for conducting negotiation with the Arabs, and especially with the Palestinians.

I think this is still the right policy. If we are going to give away parts of the Land of Israel—and we will have to do it—it has to be the result of our own choice, at our initiative, following direct negotiations. Making concessions through a public show of international pressure will deprive us of the key advantages we would gain from making them of our own free will in direct talks.

Shamir opposed the idea of a conference, but eventually came to understand that it was better to accept it, and sit through the offensive speeches, than to go head-to-head with James Baker.

The Madrid Conference of late October 1991 will be remembered mainly because of the televised speeches of the deputy foreign minister, Benjamin Netanyahu.

Shamir sat sullenly in the plenum. The conference, however, came and went. The speeches vanished into the ether. No actual peace negotiations happened. The only result of the conference was the resignation of David Levy as foreign minister, but this was part of the political infighting of late 1991.

Baker traveled to Israel a number of times, and each time he visited, another new settlement was announced during his visit. Bush was angry, and so was Baker.

Before one of his meetings with the secretary of state, Shamir asked me to join. Baker walked in, fuming. He pounded the table and excoriated Shamir. "The president and I are sick of hearing every time I come here that there's another new settlement Ariel Sharon has built. Cut it out. If you don't, we will respond."

Shamir lost his patience. Baker was, after all, just a secretary of state, and Shamir was the prime minister. He had no patience for that kind of dressing-down from the American secretary. He pounded the table himself and yelled, "Stop!"

The room was silent. It was Shamir's turn to speak. "I will not allow you to speak that way to the prime minister of Israel and the leader of the Jewish people. Do not ever talk to me that way again."

Baker bowed his head. "I apologize, Mr. Prime Minister."

I was proud of Shamir, even though I understood Baker's frustration. The announcement of a new settlement every time he came to town was a totally unnecessary provocation.

In the end, Baker gave up. He announced that he was no longer going to involve himself in the Middle East problem. ("When you're serious about peace," he said at one point, "call us." And then he left a phone number.) In the months that followed, Washington made its displeasure clear, culminating in the Bush administration's decision, in March 1992, to cancel $3 billion dollars' worth of loan guarantees Israel was supposed to receive to pay for absorbing a million immigrants from the Soviet Union. Those guarantees would have saved us hundreds of millions of dollars in interest. It was a hard slap, and it came just before our elections—no doubt contributing to Likud's defeat in 1992.

You can fight with the Americans, but there's a line you don't cross without paying a price. Likud paid for Shamir's intransigence.

I think today Shamir would have taken a much more flexible approach. He didn't trust Arafat, but I'm not sure he would have felt the same way about Arafat's successor, Mahmoud Abbas.

———

One afternoon, I received a call from Shamir. I was on my way to Tel Aviv. "Drop what you're doing," he said. "Come to my office in Jerusalem."

I told the driver to turn the car around and head for the Prime Minister's Office. Shamir asked everyone to clear the room so we could sit privately. The story he told me was, simply, incredible.

"Two hours ago," he said, "a man walked out of this room. He was a special emissary sent by Mikhail Gorbachev," the leader of the Soviet Union. At the time, we had no diplomatic relations with the Soviet Union. The Soviet president's emissary was the KGB bureau chief in Hungary, and one of Gorbachev's closest loyalists. He had been sent to Jerusalem on an urgent, top-secret visit.

"The Soviet Union," Shamir told me, "is on the verge of bankruptcy. It needs an immediate, massive infusion of funds. Gorbachev wants me to look at it as something of supreme importance. Israel's support will be greatly appreciated, and could bring about a complete change in relations between the two countries."

I asked him what kind of numbers we were talking about.

"Seventeen billion dollars," he said. "And they need it as soon as possible."

My head spun. The Soviet Union was asking Israel to bail it out?

I looked at Shamir. "You do realize that we don't have that kind of money. Not even a tenth of it."

"Of course we don't," Shamir said.

I think Gorbachev, like so many others, and not just our enemies, were convinced that there was some truth to the *Protocols of the Elders of Zion*. If Jews controlled the world and all its banks, after all, why not ask them to save the Soviet Union?

"You're asking my advice," I said, "not because you think it's possible to raise the money, but to help you figure out a way to make it look like we are doing everything we possibly can to help."

Shamir grinned. "Precisely. You need to come up with a fictitious plan."

I smiled too. "Let me think about it."

The next day I came back to see the prime minister. "Please call Mark Rich, Robert Maxwell, Edmond Safra, and Edgar Bronfman," I said to Shamir. "Arrange for me to meet with them next week. I will fly to them." These were some of the wealthiest individuals in the world.

"They're all your friends," Shamir said. "You always raise money from them. Why do you need me to call them?"

"For that reason exactly," I said. "If I call them, they'll think I'm asking for money. Tell them I am meeting them as your representative, about something of the greatest national importance."

Shamir agreed. We decided that the Sunday cabinet meeting would expressly authorize me to fly to a number of destinations in Europe. Embassies would get instructions to prepare a car for me with a driver, to meet me at the airport, along with a security detail. "Beyond that," I told Shamir, "the ambassadors and embassies will know nothing about the purpose of my visit."

On Monday I flew to Europe, going from city to city, making a show of the secrecy of my trip, reassuring our ambassadors in every country. Within days, I met with almost every "Elder of Zion" I could think of.

I made the same pitch every time. The Soviet Union needed money. If we could help, it would bring great benefit to the Jewish people. We would put a lien on Soviet property located around the Western world. Most of these properties were listed under the names of shell companies or thinly veiled state-owned entities. If it turned out that the Soviet Union was willing to put its properties up as collateral through a proper legal process, why not give them a line of credit?

Many were hesitant. The story sounded too outlandish, and they were worried that if the regime fell, the Soviets' legal obligations would vanish, along with their investment. Others were willing to take the idea seriously, but doubted whether the Soviet Union still owned properties that could be used. At the end of the day, I was able to pull together about two and a half billion dollars' worth of credit for the Soviet Union.

I came back to Jerusalem and reported to Shamir. He was disappointed. "Only two and a half billion? This won't impress the Soviets."

I disagreed. If they were so desperate that they turned to us for help, they would be happy with anything we had to offer. Might as well try.

Shamir acquiesced. I told him to bring back Gorbachev's man.

———

Two weeks later I got a call from Shabtai Shavit, the chief of the Mossad.

He told me that Gorbachev's KGB guy would be back in Israel within a week. Shavit's number-two, Efraim Halevy, would make sure I'd be included.

The meeting took place at the Dan Panorama Hotel in Jerusalem. We were given a lovely suite, and lunch was prepared. Halevy came with me. From the Russian side there was the KGB emissary, who was an older man who spoke only Russian, and also a young man in an expensive suit who spoke fluent English and introduced himself as the CEO of Exim, the bank that handled exports and imports for the USSR. He told us that he was Gorbachev's closest economic adviser.

The meeting began with the older KGB man raising his hand as if he wanted to say something. The younger fellow gave him a sharp look and said something in Russian, the gist of which I was able to make out, thanks to the Russian I learned in my parents' house when I was five years old and my grandmother came to visit from China and they spoke only Russian with each other. "Sit down and shut up," he said.

I was shocked. I looked at Halevy and he looked at me. We both understood the same thing: If a young adviser can talk that way to a KGB veteran, an old friend of Gorbachev, the Soviet Union was finished. We didn't say a word.

I made my presentation. I explained that if the Soviet Union had properties it owned in the West, if they were free of existing liens and could be liquidated, we could raise a significant amount of money. Seventeen billion dollars was too much even for a wealthy country like Israel, but we found a number of capital sources that would be willing to help under the terms I described. I shared the names of the individuals, and I said they would be happy to speak with them directly.

The visitors were satisfied. They thought it was a good start, and they could take advantage of these connections, with the blessing of the government of Israel, to raise the funds. The older man thanked me and then asked to speak with Shamir. He thanked Shamir, emotionally, and said he would report back to Gorbachev about our willingness to help. The Soviet leader would be very appreciative.

———

Three months later, Shamir was on an official state visit to the United Kingdom.

He called me from London and told me that Gorbachev's prime minister, Valentin Pavlov, wanted to meet him. Shamir asked if there had been any follow-up on the money. I told him I hadn't heard anything, and asked him to call me after the meeting. I was curious to find out whether our Elders-of-Zion bailout game had come to anything.

Shamir called me at midnight. "Pavlov thanked us for our help," he said, "and promised that he would work to reestablish diplomatic relations between our countries."

Soon after, however, Pavlov was named as one of the conspirators against Gorbachev in the August 1991 coup attempt that precipitated Gorbachev's downfall, helped put Boris Yeltzin in power, and accelerated the collapse of the Soviet Union.

Gorbachev eventually came to Israel for an informal visit. This was after the 1992 elections, and Rabin was now prime minister. Rabin hosted a luncheon in Gorbachev's honor at the King David Hotel and, to my surprise, I was invited. I was, at that moment, just an ordinary opposition MK. They seated me close to Gorbachev, who spent most of the time talking to Rabin and senior ministers. Suddenly he turned toward me and said "*Bolshoi speciba.*" Thank you very much. That was it.

Over the years, Gorbachev and I got together a number of times and even had an intimate dinner on the promenade in the Armon Hanatziv neighborhood in Jerusalem, overlooking the Old City. He never mentioned the story about the money. Neither did I. It seemed too crazy to bring it up.

FOUR

Mayor of the Eternally Divided City

On July 14, 1992, with the formation of the Labor government, I was suddenly once again a regular member of the Knesset. I had a lot of time on my hands now that I was in opposition. A number of top law firms reached out to offer me partnerships. But even though I often think like a lawyer, I turned them all down. The idea of immersing myself in the specific interests of a private person or corporation didn't appeal to me. Public life still fascinated me, and I was drawn to issues that affected the character of our country and the future of our citizens.

The municipal elections around the country were scheduled for November of the following year, and though I had never really been interested in local politics, the city of Jerusalem was another matter.

Being mayor of Jerusalem would not give me the same kind of opportunity to directly influence the great decisions affecting our country's future—whether on security, peace, the economy, or national industry—as being a government minister would. But it nonetheless was a much greater role than that of any other local-level position in the country. First, because of the size and complexity of the task: Jerusalem is twice as large in population as the second-largest municipality, Tel Aviv-Yafo. Its residents are divided into distinct neighborhoods—

secular, ultra-Orthodox, Arab—with different needs, cultures, and as-pirations. It is also an enormous source of international interest as well as tourism, with tens of thousands of Jewish, Christian, and Muslim visitors descending on the Holy City each year from almost every nation on earth. For Jews, it is the focus of thousands of years of longing. Being the mayor of Jerusalem offered both a tremendous responsibility and a global profile.

This is part of the reason the incumbent mayor, Teddy Kollek, man-aged to stay in office for more than two decades, since 1965. Kollek was masterful at building his own mythological status around the world.

But he was not a saint. Far from it. He was built of the stuff of Mapai—the workers' party that dominated the country's early years—and when he served as director general of the Prime Minister's Office, as the right-hand man of David Ben-Gurion, he had a role in some of the less worthy decisions in the country's history. He was Ben-Gurion's long arm in imposing ham-fisted censorship, politicization of the Israel Broadcasting Authority, and misuse of national resources for parti-san purposes. All the darker sides of the Mapai rule were connected to Kollek. If he hadn't become the mayor of Jerusalem, he would have gone down in history as a brutal political operative who served the govern-ment in its less seemly contexts. In today's terms, he would have been despised and rejected.

But he benefited from a miracle. In 1965, he ran for mayor on behalf of Ben-Gurion's Rafi Party, which he founded together with Ben-Gurion, Dayan, Peres and others. Just before the election, the Israel Museum was dedicated, and he was one of its biggest fundraisers. The creation of Israel's foremost museum was pivotal in building his reputa-tion as a cultural leader of the Jewish state.

With the conquest of Jordanian East Jerusalem in the 1967 war and the unification of the city, the return of the Jewish people to its holiest sites, the sudden rule over the holy sites of Islam and Christianity, from the Al-Aqsa mosque and the Dome of the Rock to the Via Dolorosa and the Church of the Holy Sepulchre—all of these made administration of the city into an immense challenge, unlike anything that came before.

I later discovered, to my amazement, that Kollek had never, over twenty-six years, translated the vision of a unified city into a master plan, one that would design the Jerusalem of the future and address, among other things, the spectrum of populations that lived in it, with all the gaps between them and their unique needs. The failure to make such a plan just shows, more than anything else, how impossible was the vision of a unified city. It was just a slogan we used to deceive ourselves and to make ourselves feel good—but we never really meant it.

Over the years, I had been asked to consider running for mayor against Kollek on behalf of Likud, but the timing hadn't been right. I was building a career in the Knesset, which I saw as the best path to government.

By 1992, I was in a different place. I had already been a government minister. I had been at the epicenter of major strategic decisions. I had tasted that life. I hoped I would later return to national leadership, but I didn't want to dismiss the idea of taking advantage of our time in opposition to take a break and focus on something no less critical and sensitive—just on a local scale.

It took me time to come around. But once the idea had been planted in my mind, the wheels never stopped turning. The days went by, the papers ran stories, people talked, planned, organized. At a certain point you have to make a decision. Early in 1993 I started floating the idea of running for mayor in conversations with friends and colleagues.

My relationship with Kollek had been cordial. We were on different paths that hadn't really crossed. But around this time, I was reminded of an interview that he had given to the *Maariv* newspaper the year before. Kollek had offered some harsh words about the future of the city and its relations with its Arab residents. He also said he wouldn't run for mayor again, since by the time of the election he would be eighty-two years old. Who would vote for such an old man? "Even I," he said, "wouldn't vote for me."

What really struck me about the interview, however, was how he adamantly "denied" claims that he had been too attentive to the needs of the Arab population in East Jerusalem. Such claims, he insisted, were "lies, lies, lies." In truth, he insisted, he hadn't done a thing for the Arabs of Jerusalem. He also didn't want to do anything for them.

The only exception was when the sewage in the Arab part of the Abu Tor neighborhood had been flowing freely on the sides of the road and had never been taken care of. Freely flowing sewage in the streets is a recipe for disease, and there had been an outbreak of cholera in the neighborhood. Nothing had been done, Kollek said, maybe even with a little pride, but then some of the more wealthy and powerful residents of the Jewish half of the neighborhood began complaining that neglecting the Arab part of the neighborhood would cause the cholera to spread to their part as well. So Kollek took care of it. "I had no choice," he said.

I read it and couldn't believe it. Did Jerusalem's mythological mayor really just say, proudly, that he had deliberately neglected the Arab residents of the city? Or was it just an empty statement, not a particularly clever one, from a man too old to take public responsibility for his own behavior?

Either way, something in his words caught my attention. More and more people were asking me about running.

––––––

I'm not the kind of person who tortures himself endlessly before making a decision.

I'm not rash, either. Really. But my life experience taught me that I could analyze the different options, weigh the circumstances, the costs and benefits, and get to a decision more quickly than most decision-makers can. Deep inside, I started getting used to the idea of running for mayor of Jerusalem. It wasn't clear whom I'd be running against, neither in the Likud primary nor in the general election.

I knew that Reuven "Ruvi" Rivlin, who would go on to become the speaker of the Knesset and president of Israel, wanted more than anything to be mayor of Jerusalem. Rivlin saw himself as the ultimate Jerusalemite. I was a newcomer. The very fact that I wanted to run for mayor angered him. He also resented the fact that I hadn't supported him in his earlier attempts to become the Likud's candidate for mayor.

I called a press conference and announced my candidacy.

I came into the mayoral race as a seasoned politician who had seen his share of electoral battles. And yet, all these had been on behalf of a party. I had been a senior campaigner for Likud in five election campaigns between 1977 and 1992. I knew every aspect of the national political arena. But nothing prepared me for the local battles, especially in a hyperenergetic city like Jerusalem.

The second step in my long path to City Hall was the primary elections within the Likud Party in Jerusalem. This battle drew the attention of both the national media and the other political parties; a feeling of change was in the air due to Kollek's age and long tenure.

Rivlin believed he was destined to be the first Jerusalem mayor from the national camp.

His father, Yoel Yosef Rivlin, had translated the Koran from Arabic to Hebrew and was one of the most important men of letters at the Hebrew University and in the country as a whole, and one of the great Rivlins over the generations. Ruvi believed he was the heir to his father's legacy, not just in academia but in leadership of the city. He and his brother Laizy, who had passed away a few years before, had sponsored the Beitar Jerusalem soccer team for many years, and they were beloved by tens of thousands of pro-Likud soccer fans.

In the end, Ruvi didn't pose a serious challenge. Ten thousand registered Likud members in Jerusalem were asked to decide between us. I won 75 percent of the vote.

Once the results were in, Ruvi and I sat down to meet. I told him that despite my victory in the primaries, I wasn't planning on running at the top of the Likud list. I had decided to run on a new list of my own, which would have heavy representation from Likud members—after all, I was still an MK for the Likud party—but I wanted to also include a few nonpoliticians in order to reach a broader audience.

I offered Rivlin the third spot on the list and promised him whatever job he wanted if we won, including deputy mayor.

Ruvi was, characteristically, both blunt and a bit nasty. He said he didn't think he was prepared to be my number two, much less number three.

This basically encapsulated our entire relationship, and it never changed. There were times when we worked together for the benefit of the Likud, but we were never allies. Instead I put the architect David Cassutto as number two, and the former deputy police chief, Meshulam Amit, as number three.

Now I had to prepare for the big battle against the aging lion.

The Labor Party couldn't find anyone who they thought had a better chance against me than Teddy Kollek. They pressed him, and Kollek agreed to run. If you win, his friends told him, you can resign soon after and hand the city over to someone else from the party who wouldn't have won on his own.

This battle was therefore mine to win, but also mine to lose. If I lost, it could easily have been the denouement of my political career. Teddy was a world-renowned fundraiser, and he would likely have unlimited resources for the campaign. It also didn't hurt Kollek that Yitzhak Rabin was prime minister and Shimon Peres was foreign minister—two of Kollek's comrades in arms from the time when they carried water for Ben-Gurion.

Early in the campaign, Rabin took a walking tour of the city along with Kollek and the famous violinist Isaac Stern to rally the street on Kollek's behalf. Stern stood on the pedestrian mall at Ben Yehuda Street, put his wide-brimmed fedora down on the pavement for people to donate money for the campaign, and performed. If I had walked by right then, even I would have tossed money into the hat. A few shekels for an Isaac Stern concert is not a bad deal.

But it became clear very quickly that Teddy's glory had faded. His campaign never took off. The street was indifferent. Jerusalem was in bad shape. The streets were horribly crowded. The noise and pollution were intolerable. The roads were filled with potholes. We didn't yet have a sewage treatment plant. And there weren't enough jobs. The ultra-Orthodox community was bitter and poor. In short, many people felt that an eighty-two-year-old man was not likely to succeed in a job that he had already been failing at for twenty-eight years.

My campaign looked very different. I thought I'd need a lot of money to prevail against his well-oiled fundraising machine, but actually the opposite happened. I went around the world and managed to raise a considerable sum, while Teddy failed to do so. He sent personal letters to all his regular donors and then complained that I raised more money than he did. One big donor wrote him back saying that after so many years of giving to his campaigns, he was now convinced that Teddy needed to step aside and let a younger man run the city—so he would be donating to mine instead.

But most didn't write back. They simply ignored his letters. There's a life lesson here: know when to fight on, and know when to retire.

————

Money is of course important in a long and exhausting political campaign. But something else ended up determining the outcome of this election: Young people. Hundreds of young men and women, lacking any political or municipal experience, volunteered for my campaign.

I also hired the services of the PR agency of David Fogel and Tzvika Levin from Tel Aviv. Fogel was an ardent leftist, full of ideas, and his firm was small, warm, friendly, and creative. He put together a team to work with me and it was a winning combination. The campaign slogan we went with was unusually blunt but accurate: "We love you Teddy, but we're voting for Ehud."

This drove Kollek's people insane. Their point of departure was that there was no chance anyone could defeat Teddy. From a certain perspective, they were actually right. When the campaign began, I commissioned a poll to see where I stood and to guide me in crafting the campaign and adopting the right kind of messaging. When respondents were asked to choose between Teddy and me, he received 63 percent; me, 7 percent.

Everybody told me I was headed for a disaster and would never recover. But I was optimistic, as usual. I believed I had a winning message. I made sure never to go negative on Teddy, never to offend him or impugn his integrity, because of both his age and his winning reputation. I smothered him in love, and gently, subtly, sent out the message that he was no longer relevant. A great man, a legendary mayor, but nothing is forever.

This approach worked. Fogel and his team worked efficiently, and also enlisted help from my political allies—Dan Meridor; Benny Begin, Menachem's son; and Tzachi Hanegbi, the son of the renowned former Lehi fighter and Likud MK Geula Cohen. One day, the four of us toured the pedestrian mall at Ben Yehuda Street. No violins this time. Benny

Begin marched up front with a megaphone. "Ladies and gentlemen," he cried, "the next mayor of Jerusalem!"

———

I kept it positive. But Teddy's team ran a brutal campaign. Every day, they put up posters showing a headline about me from fifteen years earlier in the weekly communist rag *Haolam Hazeh*, which had referred to me as a "gangster." Back then, I had been clashing with the former general Rechavam Zeevi, who was tight with the editor of the paper. Now Teddy's campaign was trying to make the word "gangster" stick.

As the elections drew near, it became clear that Kollek also had a clandestine team working for him, made up of former senior Shin Bet officers. They tried to get Arabs from East Jerusalem to come out en masse and vote for Kollek, to keep the "extreme right-wing fascist" Ehud Olmert from taking over the city. My team got together—Dan, Benny, Fogel and myself—to figure out what to do. Fogel suggested dedicating the final three days of the campaign to a sharp attack on Kollek, saying that he was "selling Jerusalem to the Arabs." Benny, Dan and I all rejected the idea. We would win without changing our strategy or indulging in Kollek-style sewer-talk. Later on, Benny told me how amazed he was that Fogel, the leftist, would propose an anti-Arab strategy, while the three right-wingers were the ones who opposed it.

In any case, the Arabs didn't take Kollek's bait. They didn't know what to think about me, but they knew Teddy hadn't lifted a finger for them, as he himself had boasted in that newspaper interview. The reality was that the election didn't interest them. Teddy never took advantage of the Arab voters, or even the Jewish voters. Turnout overall was low, and the one who suffered most, as usual, was the incumbent.

———

Election day was November 2, the anniversary of the Balfour Declaration—the British announcement in 1917 proclaiming support for "a national home for the Jewish people" in Palestine.

This date was full of meaning in Jewish history. I walked out of my house on November 29 Street to the polling station near my home, and went through the traditional ceremony of cameras, reporters, and microphones. I didn't say a word, just put the envelope into the box slowly enough to let everyone take the picture and get a second shot. Then I went home.

I spent the rest of the day touring the city on foot. I already knew I had won. Two days earlier, representatives of the Haredi parties announced that they were endorsing me. For the first time in Israel's political history, the front page of the Haredi *Hamodia* newspaper ran an ad calling for people to vote for a secular candidate. The ad was signed by the Gerer Rebbe, the Belzer Rebbe, and the other major Hassidic rabbis—and alongside them, the major non-Hassidic rabbis, including Rabbi Shlomo Zalman Auerbach, Rabbi Elyashiv, and a long list of other respected rabbis.

Yet it wasn't the Haredi vote that brought me victory. My lead over Kollek ended up being a lot bigger than what they delivered, but their endorsement made Kollek's defeat overwhelming. I won by more than 25 percent of the vote.

It was a landslide that reverberated across the country.

———

It's hard to believe it now, but when I entered office, Jerusalem was suffering from people leaving the city at a rate higher than those moving there.

The main reasons were the high housing costs and a lack of jobs, especially for young people, as well as a host of additional reasons: outdated infrastructure, insufferable traffic, poor education, and divisions among the different communities—every group to itself, without any sense of being part of a citywide whole.

Jerusalem was a city divided against itself, a place of endless terror attacks, and impoverished. The goal of improving the daily quality of life, the opportunity, the prosperity, the convenience was daunting.

On top of all of that, this was Jerusalem—the most politically delicate city on earth. One uncontrolled event in a sensitive location could spark a fire that would engulf the entire Middle East, the Muslim world, maybe the entire world. How do you navigate through all of that?

———

On my first day in office, I took a tour of the northern parts of the city. I was joined by the director-general of the municipality, the treasurer, the city engineer, and people from the planning division. There were about ten of us. We climbed the mountain that overlooks the turn of the highway coming into the city from Maaleh Adumim, north of French Hill. Today there's an overpass there. I told them that it was crucial to build out municipal Highway 1 (as opposed to the Highway 1 that goes from Jerusalem to Tel Aviv), that runs north to south along the old border between eastern and western Jerusalem. I told the treasurer to allocate half a million shekels to get started on planning. The decision to lay the highway had already been made, but planning hadn't even begun. The new plans were to begin near the Notre Dame center by the Old City, head north past the Central Command, as it was then called, to run past the western slope of French Hill, continue north between Pisgat Ze'ev and Shuafat, and end at Neve Yaakov.

"I want you to get moving on planning and building this road," I told them. "I'll take care of the budget."

Municipal workers weren't used to this kind of talk. They thought it was just opening-day bluster, but I was dead serious. Two years later the road was built. Near French Hill it included a nearly 2,000-foot-long overpass. I came one day to see the enormous machines laying the trestles that would support the bridge. I couldn't help myself.

The roads and highways developed at an enormous speed and scale during my time as mayor.

When I was elected, a huge battle was taking place over the creation of what is today called the Begin Highway, a multilane freeway that slashes across the city from south to north, linking with the Tunnel Road from Gush Etzion near Gilo and ending up near the Ramot neighborhood, where it turns into Highway 443 that heads toward Tel Aviv. The residents of the Beit Hakerem neighborhood put together a pressure group to try to stop the highway, claiming that the noise of the traffic would disrupt their lives. I told them there was zero chance that I would cancel the highway.

When I was elected they had already filed a petition with the High

Court of Justice. A year and a half later, in February 1995, the tractors started moving earth. In June 1998, the highway was dedicated.

Next, we got to work building the highway from Wadi Joz, in the northeastern part of the city, to Maaleh Adumim. This one required digging a nearly mile-long tunnel under Mount Scopus. This, too, was done quickly and opened within two years. It cut the commute from forty-five minutes to about seven. Not only was this a huge boon to commuters, it also fulfilled a strategic goal of making sure Maaleh Adumim, one of the biggest settlements in the West Bank, would never be cut off from Jerusalem in a peace deal with the Palestinians.

———

But the biggest transportation project, not just in Jerusalem but in all of Israel during my time as mayor, wasn't a highway. It was the planning and building of the city's light rail transit system.

Today more than 140,000 people ride the light rail every day. This was the first urban rail transit system in the whole country.

The number of problems in planning and launching the light rail was unfathomable. They included political sensitivities, since the tracks begin near Neve Yaakov, which was in parts of the city that were conquered in 1967. Palestinian pressure caused the Canadian company Bombardier, the biggest company in the world in the field, to pull out of the tender. But there were plenty of other companies willing to bid.

The project itself included countless technical challenges: Widening streets, evacuating and tearing down buildings, upgrading sidewalks along the entire length of Jaffa Street, which was the heart of the train's path, digging a tunnel near the Nablus Gate so that car traffic could be diverted to allow for the trains, laying almost ten miles of track in crowded urban areas, and also a long bridge for the trains that both takes a 90-degree turn and creates an impressive impression at the entrance to the city—since you couldn't stop traffic at the city entrance 200 times a day as the trains went by.

Cost estimates kept changing on an almost daily basis, due to factors that could never have been known in advance. We also needed a maintenance site, garages, and parking for the trains. We needed to reinvent the system of traffic signals to include the introduction of trains in already busy streets. And we had to do it all without anyone in the country having ever done this kind of project before.

The trains have now been running for more than a decade, and the Bridge of Strings is a stunning addition to the city entrance that can compete in its beauty with city entrances around the world.

———

Since I was elected with the support of the ultra-Orthodox, there was an immediate concern that I would upset the delicate balance on religious issues. Since the founding of the country, the question of how to balance between the day-to-day needs of non-Orthodox citizens, who are the large majority of the country, and the symbolic demands of a formally Jewish state has caused furious clashes between ultra-Orthodox Jews and their political parties, on the one hand, and mainstream Israel on the other. As a result, public transportation doesn't run on Saturdays in some cities, while it does in others. In 1999, Prime Minister Ehud Barak's government collapsed in part because of a decision to transport a massive turbine for a power station on a giant flatbed truck on the Sabbath.

Nowhere were these sensitivities more acute than in Jerusalem.

In practice, cinemas in Jerusalem were open on the Sabbath, as were quite a few stores and of course many non-kosher restaurants. Under no circumstance would I allow a change in the status quo of the city. I was pleasantly surprised that Haredi community's representatives didn't go overboard in their demands.

Yet despite this balancing act between the demands of the Haredi and secular communities, during my administration the city's nightlife prospered on weekends. New restaurants opened, while coffee shops and nightclubs were packed. Haoman 17—a club that became famous around the country—drew hundreds and sometimes thousands of guests from the coastal cities, especially on Friday nights, with after-parties lasting into the early morning hours of Saturday.

Of course, something always happens to spoil the party.

A businessman bought a clothing store on Luntz Street, which connects between Ben Yehuda and Hillel Streets in the center of town and is part of the pedestrian mall. He decided to turn the store into a fashion center, and announced his plans to host fashion shows outdoors on Saturday afternoons. What emerged was a totally needless altercation. At the same time, a pharmacy opened up on Ben Yehuda that would be open on the Sabbath. The Haredim were furious.

I told them that I planned on ordering the clothing store to shut down on the Sabbath, and I wouldn't accept fashion shows with scantily clad models in the middle of the street, and certainly not on the holy Sabbath. And yet, I made it clear that I had no intention of closing the pharmacy on Saturdays. Another drugstore was open on King David Street, right opposite the entrance to the King David Hotel. The store was usually busy on Saturdays. The new store on Ben Yehuda was similar.

One Friday, I was at the home of Deputy Mayor Haim Miller, an ultra-Orthodox representative, and we talked about the pharmacy. I told him I was ready to hand the decision over to Rabbi Yosef Shalom Elyashiv, the greatest rabbi of the generation, who had the full respect of the Haredim in Jerusalem. Yet I would insist that the rabbi hear my considerations: I could issue an order to close the store, but then the owner would appeal to the High Court of Justice, and the High Court might reject the appeal. "If that happens," I said, "from your end the problem would be solved. But if the High Court sides with the plaintiffs and cancels the order, the precedent will be significant. Dozens of other stores will open across the city on the Sabbath, and there will be no way to stop it.

"If, despite all this, the rabbi still insists on closing the store," I said, "I will follow his wishes, because I was elected on a promise to preserve the status quo, and I will keep my promise."

The rabbi understood my point, of course, and decided it wasn't worth the risk.

———

Tel Aviv is considered Israel's cultural center. In many ways it's justified. The country's leading theater companies are based there, as is the philharmonic orchestra and the Israeli opera; there are more museums and art galleries there than anywhere else.

As mayor of Jerusalem, however, I refused to accept the idea that Jerusalem was somehow culturally inferior. The Israel Festival, held each spring, was one of the city's major cultural institutions. Some of the world's greatest artists, not just pop stars, have come to Israel in recent years, appearing in special performances in the context of the Israel Festival.

The Jerusalem Film Festival, which grew out of the Cinematheque and its visionary philanthropic founder, Leah Van Leer, is held each year in July. For years the festival grew in size and status, and famous filmmakers came to see it as an honor to be invited. Tens of thousands of visitors from around the world come to Jerusalem, where they meet some of the top figures in the Israeli film industry. The week of the festival leaves its mark on the whole city. The ceremonial part would either begin or end with a speech by the mayor.

It was the only time in my career that I was ever booed.

The film industry brings together the most radical, leftist audience. Without support from the municipality, and without my having gone out of my way to use my personal connections to bring famous artists, the festival would not have been nearly as big a deal. But that didn't matter to the hecklers. Every year I opened the festival with my speech, and every year they booed me as soon as I was announced.

I kept being involved in the festival every year, and ignored the catcalls. Even later, as prime minister, I continued to host the VIPs for dinner, which only added to the festival's prestige.

———

The rising profile of the LGBT community was another major issue I dealt with as mayor.

It's no secret, and I never tried to hide the fact, that my daughter Dana is a lesbian. She came out when she was in college, telling Aliza first and then me. I told her that I loved her with all my heart, regardless of her choices. Her coming out didn't change anything in our relationship or with rest of family. Dana is a source of infinite pride for us. She is brilliant, successful in her academic field, known and respected, and a wonderful mother.

If I were not a public figure, this wouldn't have to be anyone's business. As a person who attracts considerable public attention, however, even this biographical point is part of my public profile.

It became an issue when the gay community wanted to launch a Pride Parade in Jerusalem. I don't know if they had any special expectations of me because of Dana. I also believe that if it were not for this family detail, I would have related to the LGBT community in the same way. I went to the community's center on Ben Yehuda Street and promised I would keep them from being attacked. When they wanted to hold a parade in the streets of the city, I gave my consent. The LGBT community has a right to express its identity as it chooses, and is worthy of backing and support just like any other group of citizens.

The tradition of Pride Parades in Jerusalem began as a relatively modest affair during my administration. Its importance derived from the fact that the Haredim were part of the leadership of the City Council. Despite this, I was not put to the test of their tolerance, and I didn't ask what their reaction would be if the parade took place. I didn't want them to think they were partners in the decision and feel obligated to campaign against it. And so, the first Pride Parade was held along its full course without incident. A precedent was set that couldn't be taken back.

In recent years the parade has triggered acts of murderous violence. That is intolerable. Unfortunately, it's the police that bear the greatest responsibility here. In 2015, just three weeks before the Pride Parade, they released Yishai Schlissel, who had been in prison for attempted murder during the 2005 Pride Parade when he stabbed three people. Now free, he went to the parade, stabbed six people, including sixteen-year-old Shira Banki, who died of her wounds. Letting somebody free who was convicted of a violent attack against participants in the parade, and letting them go back to the scene without supervision—that was an act of negligence.

———

Clean streets in particular was one of the hardest challenges we faced. Jerusalem had a reputation of being a dirty city. From every direction I heard that our city was polluted. That whole streets were filthy. That dumpsters were overflowing and not being emptied. People whose opinions were important to me asked, angrily, what I was even doing all this time, if the city was still so filthy. The criticism hurt, and I couldn't ignore it. The residents paid municipal taxes to receive basic services. Every time I went to Tel Aviv or other cities, the first thing I looked at was the state of the garbage in the streets and dumpsters.

Raanana Meridor, Dan's mother, sent me a letter about how angry she was that our city wasn't clean. I asked her to take me to the places that weren't being serviced properly, and not to tell me in advance which places she thought were filthy. She should take me on a tour, and I would see the blight with my own eyes.

Despite having been through several accidents and being in her late nineties, Raanana Meridor is still sharp as a tack. Back then, she was younger, more energetic, and more foul-mouthed. She started taking me to task before we even began the tour. But I took her criticism with love. A woman like her, who fought in the Irgun and was a university professor, who created a famous family and had the strength to try and do something about the trash in her city—how could I take offense?

We walked through Rechavia, went up Gaza Road, strolled on Ben Maimon Street. Everything was sparklingly clean. Dumpsters had been emptied, the streets were spotless. We couldn't find any of the piles of garbage that had angered her. She was displeased. I was pleased. It was as I had suspected: At certain times of day, between the early-morning cleaning and that of the evening, garbage had accumulated in the dumpsters, and some of the dumpsters were too small. But there was no way to empty them every fifteen minutes, and no city on earth is pristine at all times of day.

Anyone who wants to be a mayor of a city needs to know that he is doomed to an endless stream of complaints. The good things, the things that work and make people satisfied, are taken for granted. There's no need to call the mayor to thank him. But when something goes wrong— and when doesn't something go wrong?—there's an address for complaints and blame. If you're not ready to be that address, look for a different job. In the end, as I said to our municipal employees, it is the public, including those who complain, who pay our salaries. Municipal taxes and fees come out of their pockets, and they have a right to know how the money is being spent. It starts with a broken sidewalk, a busted street lamp, a school bus that runs late, a tree that falls, or a dumpster that isn't emptied. The mosaic of little things that add up to our quality of life and determine how satisfied the residents are.

With time, I felt like the city was transforming. It was a slow process and often painful, but the satisfaction I derived from every small step was great.

———

The struggles surrounding the Machaneh Yehuda market were especially difficult.

The market is not an ancient landmark like so many other places in Jerusalem. But its ambience is unique and special. Its music, too. Not the tunes coming out of amplified speakers, but the voices of the vendors at the stalls, the buyers checking the produce, comparing and haggling, shoppers looking for something special in the alleyways and not finding it but knowing there's nowhere else it can be found.

The market was neglected when I came into office. It is built around two main streets cutting across from Jaffa Road to Agrippas Street, with smaller alleys between and coming off them. One of them is an open-air market, while the other has a corrugated metal covering that, at the time, was dilapidated and collapsing in places. In winter the rain would pour through and the market floor was covered in a pasty mud. Shoppers suffered, and many stopped going there. Stall owners complained that their livelihoods were at stake. I had no doubt that the whole roof needed replacing, as well as adding a new drainage system for the runoff. But how do you renovate a place like that without harming all the businesses? But if we didn't do it, would they be hurt any less?

We entered into a long, exhausting negotiation with the stall owners, and in the end we agreed that the work would be done in stages, without shutting the street all at once. The complaints kept coming, but we got to work, and when we were finished, the covered street was like a palace, and everyone was happy. The stall owners thanked us when it was finished, after making our lives a living hell for the entire time we worked on it.

The same was true for the mostly open-air market on Machaneh Yehuda Street, which runs parallel to the covered market. It's much wider, carries a lot more foot traffic, and required a much more fundamental overhaul. Today it's far more pleasant, more convenient, and a better commercial experience, not just for shoppers but also for the vendors.

You can't understand Jerusalem just by looking at its landmarks. The city is full of them, yes, and they're part of human history and Jewish history, symbolize Israeli democratic sovereign independence, and resonate much more around the world. But the Machaneh Yehuda market is also one of the modern city's biggest symbols. People come from around the world to shop there.

I remember wandering through its alleys, looking for my favorite cheeses, for the warmest, freshest pita breads on earth, and for produce that was fresher and tastier than anything in a supermarket. Today Jerusalem is filled with options for shoppers all across the city, from Malha to Mamilla. But nothing is like Machaneh Yehuda.

———

Jerusalem has more churches, of more different denominations, than any other city on earth.

The tension between Muslims and Christians in the Old City has an impact on decisions made by the municipality, but the divisions among different Christian sects are often much sharper, and the Mayor's Office is the first recourse for bishops, archbishops, and other church leaders.

The most important church is the Church of the Holy Sepulchre, where Christians believe the grave of Jesus is located. Christians from around the world turn their eyes to that church, and it is a mandatory stop for pilgrims from around the world.

The key to the entry gate of the church was given, many generations ago, to a joint guard of the Nusseibeh and the Joudeh families—Muslim families, yes, because the church leaders couldn't agree about which sect would keep the keys. The arrangement has been mostly without incident, but not always. "Saturday of Light," when Jerusalem Christians celebrate the end of the Holy Week leading up to Easter Sunday, draws tens of thousands of Christians each year to the plaza in front of the church. It's one of the most sensitive Saturdays in Jerusalem, and the joy is often overshadowed by the fear of a clash among different Christian sects, and between Christians and Muslims.

One day, an aggressive Muslim man took up a position at one of the parts of the church and began setting up a small mosque there. In an unusual move, all the churches came together and turned to me for help.

They asked the government to intervene, and if necessary to have Israeli security forces remove the man's mosque. It was clear that this could trigger a violent eruption that could have involved thousands of residents.

I received the delegation from the churches. Their leader was Theopolis III, patriarch of the Greek Orthodox Church, the largest and wealthiest church in Jerusalem. Much of the city's land is owned by the church, scattered across the city, including the land that the Knesset sits on, as well as the Prime Minister's Office and the Supreme Court. The Armenian Church is also wealthy, as are the Franciscans. About 15 senior representatives from those and other churches came to me and asked for immediate intervention, or else there would be a riot.

I told my guests that such a decision wasn't mine to make, but rather that of the prime minister. I was prepared, I stressed, to ask for a meeting at Prime Minister Netanyahu's office, as long as all the churches were in agreement. Israel would not take sides in interchurch rivalries.

To top it all off, this was during the week of Passover, when government offices are closed. I managed to get Netanyahu to go to his office. He received the delegation from the churches, and the result of the meeting was the exercise of Israeli sovereign authority, including a mild application of security forces. The Muslims were removed from the church, and quiet was restored.

In light of the waves of violence and terror that the city endured in the years that followed, this may seem like a minor incident. But it's not. The greatest threat to Jerusalem doesn't come from terrorism. Terror definitely requires constant vigilance and fierce measures, but a much bigger threat looms from the holy sites for the different religions. If harm were ever to come to one of them, it could trigger a conflict that could spiral well beyond Israel.

When I started my job as mayor of Jerusalem, just two months after the signing of the Oslo Accords—which recognized the PLO and established under it the Palestinian Authority as the formal government of the Palestinians in the West Bank and Gaza—I was steeped in the populist rhetoric about the Holy City.

"The united, eternal capital of the Jewish people," and many other similar expressions, had become an integral part of my speeches. Like so many others, I, too, thought that one could never speak of dividing the city. As a result, there was no chance of reaching a peace agreement with the Palestinians. They, after all, would never compromise on their demand to make at least part of the city into the capital of a Palestinian state, alongside the capital of Israel.

By the time I left the job a decade later, I knew there was no way to avoid changes to the municipal borders of the city—not because there had been any change in my feelings about Jerusalem as the capital of the Jewish people, but because Jerusalem today isn't the Jerusalem we prayed and longed for over thousands of years.

What does the "capital of the Jewish People" have to do with dozens of Arab villages, refugee camps, outlying neighborhoods, and an airport at Atarot, which were never part of the city and were tacked onto its municipal borders through an arbitrary decision made in the euphoric aftermath of the Six Day War? What does "Jerusalem" have to do with Palestinian neighborhoods in its municipal borders like Jabal Mukkaber, Beit Hanina, or Issawiya?

The necessity of dividing the city is grounded in the simple fact that wide parts of its current territory are not, and never were, part of the Jerusalem that we dreamed about. These areas are filled with hundreds of thousands of Palestinians, and they're the ones who *least* want the city to be divided. They have permanent resident status in the State of Israel, and even though they're not citizens, they can travel freely anywhere in the country.

The Arabs of eastern Jerusalem are, however, a huge security and economic burden to the country. Many terror attacks were carried out by them. The day is not far off when the non-Jewish residents of the city will constitute a majority. We are locked into slogans about a unified Jerusalem. But in reality, the city is not unified. How many Jewish Jerusalemites ever even set foot in Sur Baher or Shuafat, the Palestinian neighborhoods of Jerusalem?

Day-to-day, Jerusalem lives as a divided city. The contact between the two populations is minimal. It exists mainly between Arabs who work in service jobs, usually simple ones, and Jewish consumers of those services—and also in hospitals. The gap in quality of life between the Arab and Jewish sectors of the city is nauseating.

The bottom line is that Jerusalem in its current municipal borders is destined to be divided, no matter how many clichés are tossed into the air by politicians. We can declare as much as we want that Jerusalem is the eternal undivided capital of Israel, but you can't live a normal life in a city where hundreds of thousands of its residents are structurally neglected, discriminated against, live in filth, and to expect them to be law-abiding, respectful of the institutions, and comply with a system that keeps them down.

It hasn't been working for years and it's getting worse. It breaks my heart to admit it: There is no way to keep running the city in its present form. It didn't work, it doesn't work, and it won't work. Before you get to the political issues, the international condemnation, before you raise the issue of whether you can ever have a peace agreement, you have to face up to the disparity between the Jewish and Arab parts of the city. It is a ticking time bomb. It will inevitably cause endless rounds of violence. We can blame the Palestinians for their violence all we want, but we won't unify Jerusalem.

It takes courage to tell this truth to ourselves. I tried to do it, and maybe I sealed my political fate—but there's no other way. In the end we'll get there, and the only question is what price we'll pay until then. How many killed, injured, and traumatized there will be. How many young people will leave the city, because a city at the center of a storm of violence can't prosper and offer affordable housing, good jobs and a hopeful future.

———

The great poet Yehuda Amichai once wrote about the job I held for a decade.

> *It's sad to be the mayor of Jerusalem.*
> *It's awful.*
> *How can a man be the mayor of a city like this one?*
> *What shall he do for it?*
> *He will build, and build, and build.*
> *And at night, the stones of the mountains*
> *Will gather round the houses.*
> *Like wolves, coming to howl at the dogs*
> *That have become the slaves of men.*

I love Amichai's poems for their simplicity, which doesn't come at the expense of emotional depth, and because of his special sensitivity to the land and its vistas, its people, and its daily life. Amichai's words never were especially fancy, but his poems are powerful. He wrote this one during the period before Teddy Kollek and before the Six Day War, when Mordechai Ish-Shalom was mayor, when Jerusalem was a small, quiet, calm, and relatively secure city. It's incredible how he felt the undercurrents that would one day shake the city to its foundations and turn it into a completely different place, depicting the burden of running the city before it was "undivided," before it became a bubbling cauldron that unsettled the lives of its residents, of the citizens of our whole country, and of the international community. Or as he put it in a different poem:

> *What does Jerusalem need?*
> *It doesn't need a mayor.*
> *It needs a ringmaster*
> *With a baton in his hand.*

FIVE

Jerusalem of Blood

The Labor government that took power after the 1992 election was led by two men: Prime Minister Yitzhak Rabin, the old general with a reputation for tough talk and an occasional tendency to bend under pressure, and Foreign Minister Shimon Peres, who as finance minister in the 1980s helped rescue Israel's economy and saw himself as a forward-thinking cosmopolitan, while others saw him as a ruthless behind-the-scenes political player. It was clear to all from the moment Labor took office that the new government would look to make a bold move in the area that had haunted our country since the First Intifada (the violent uprising by Palestinians in the territories) began five years earlier: The question of peace with the Palestinians.

Within months, secret negotiations with the Palestine Liberation Organization came to light. A recognized terror organization that had been attacking Israeli civilians since the 1960s, and which had served as a model for terror organizations around the world, the PLO had been driven out of Lebanon during the First Lebanon War, making their new headquarters in Tunis.

It did not take long before these talks became public and were brought in under the aegis of the administration of U.S. President Bill Clinton.

The Oslo Accords, signed in Washington on September 13, 1993, established the first stage of a process that would ultimately, it was hoped, lead to peace. The PLO, led by the lifelong terrorist Yassir Arafat, would run the affairs of Palestinians in the West Bank and Gaza Strip through an entity called the Palestinian Authority. While Israel would still be in charge of overall security and have the only proper military force, the Palestinians would get control over their domestic affairs, including education, health, transportation, commerce, and their own armed police force.

Although Oslo put the question of Jerusalem—as well as other questions like settlements, the fate of Palestinian refugees, and final borders—off to future talks, the fact that it was mentioned at all represented a major shift in Israeli policy. For the first time since the city had been reunified in 1967, Israel agreed that Jerusalem would be on the table.

We on the right wanted nothing to do with Oslo and refused to countenance any territorial compromise—a position that would evolve over time, not least in my own thinking. But in the early years, the right's rejection of Oslo was so acute that Netanyahu ran a successful prime ministerial campaign three years later, in 1996, on the threat that "Peres will divide Jerusalem."

From the moment the Oslo Accords were signed, however, the sensitivities surrounding the lived reality of Jerusalem changed completely. Anything we tried to build in the city became an urgent matter for the UN Security Council. Any demolition in the Arab sector triggered global condemnation. As mayor, I was the one responsible. I felt we had to build the city, and hadn't expected an endless stream of condemnation. The government may have wanted to create a new reality on the ground, but none of the prime ministers during my decade in City Hall—Rabin, Peres, Netanyahu, Barak, Sharon—wanted to be seen as choking off the development of our capital city.

In one case, we were about to demolish an illegally built Arab-sector building in the Old City, after years of court hearings. I got a call from Prime Minister Netanyahu. "Itzik Molcho is on the phone right now with Arafat," he told me. "Arafat called to say that if the building gets torn down, there will be a violent uprising. You have to put it off." Molcho was Netanyahu's liaison for various diplomatic missions. I told Netanyahu that it was a mistake to capitulate, and I had no intention of playing along. I tore down the building. There was no uprising.

In 1996, one of the big controversies that sparked international criticism was the establishment of the Har Homa neighborhood. Looking back, years after the neighborhood was populated by thousands of families and renamed "Homat Shmuel," I still do not regret building it. The neighborhood, located on the southern edge of the city parallel to Gilo and not far from Bethlehem, established the border between Israel and the future Palestinian state.

Netanyahu, who was then in his first term as prime minister, opposed Har Homa because of the expected international condemnation. I knew that he wouldn't be able to withstand the pressure, so I spoke to Yehuda Harel, who was in Netanyahu's coalition as part of the Third Way Party. Harel was one of the founders of Kibbutz Merom Golan, which was established in the Golan Heights just one month after the Six Day War. Harel explained to Netanyahu that if he blocked Har Homa, he would lose his coalition.

Netanyahu approved it, the neighborhood was built, and his coalition survived.

———

The Oslo Accords allowed, through the establishment of the Palestinian Authority, for the PLO to function in Judea, Samaria, and the Gaza Strip, but not in Jerusalem. Since the fate of Jerusalem would be put off to later talks, Israel insisted that nothing be established within the city limits that would prejudice the outcome of negotiations.

Yet despite this, in early 1994 I learned, through informal channels, that PLO Chairman Arafat was planning on visiting the Temple Mount and praying at the Al-Aqsa Mosque. I was worried. Freedom of worship was not to be questioned, in conditions of calm and an absence of terror, but at that moment I was concerned that his pilgrimage would set off a chain reaction of violent acts from both sides and spiral out of control.

A letter I received, from someone who identified himself as secular, confirmed my fears. He explained that the government had tarnished Jewish honor, and that he and his friends would have no choice but to act.

This mysterious man wrote that the day would come when he and his friends "would know what to do." "All our lives," he wrote, "we have known how to build clever explosives in the security services, and this time we will do it to bring down the Al-Aqsa Mosque from the face of the earth."

I had a feeling that these were not empty threats. I met with Yaakov Peri, the head of Shin Bet, and asked him if it was true that there was a plan to let Arafat visit the Temple Mount. I shared with him my concerns. Peri admitted that he had received a directive from Prime Minister Rabin to prepare a security plan for Arafat's visit. The decision, he said, was not in his hands.

I went to Rabin. He told me that according to the basic principles of freedom of worship, he could not prevent Arafat from visiting the Temple Mount. I told him that if he allowed it, he would be responsible for the horrific results. Rabin was unmoved.

———

I thought about this for a long while and decided to put together a demonstration to protest the visit.

I pulled together Likud, the parties to its right and people from the settler movement, and we held a mass rally on a Saturday night in Zion Square. Thousands of people showed up.

When I came out onto the balcony overlooking the square above the Kravitz stationery store, I saw on the other side of the square a large banner, stretched across a number of buildings, that read: "Death to Arabs, Death to Arafat." This was not my style and not my intention. When I saw the sign, I told the senior people who were with me on the balcony that I wasn't going to speak. That was not something I wanted to be a part of. Benny Begin and Dan Meridor agreed.

In the end I did speak, and I was heckled when I spoke out against that sign. Benjamin Netanyahu spoke as well. The atmosphere and the style didn't bother him, and it didn't bother Ariel Sharon either.

Toward the end of the demonstration, I conferred with the police commander in charge of Jerusalem, Aryeh Amit, and suggested that he not allow the demonstrators to march toward the Old City because it would end with violent clashes with Arabs. Amit, a pompous self-promoter, answered that he had no control over the situation. The march went by the Nablus Gate, and dozens of storefronts were smashed. It caused a lot of damage and ramped up the tension.

The next day I publicly criticized the impotence of the police. Amit responded that he couldn't control how people behaved—ironic coming from the person responsible for public order—and he put the responsibility for the rioting on the organizers of the demonstration. In other words, on me.

I was furious. I summoned him for a one-on-one meeting and told him in no uncertain terms that there was a new sheriff in town, and that it wasn't a district police commander but the elected mayor of the city. I warned him that if he ever again got into a public argument with me, or blamed anything on the civilian leadership of the city, I would make sure that he would be out of Jerusalem. "There is no room here for two commanders," I told him. "There's just one, and it's not you."

I rarely act this way. But I felt like I had to make clear to Amit that as far as what happened in Jerusalem, the buck stopped with me. The warning apparently helped. Amit worked to keep the peace until the end of his service.

I decided not to organize any more demonstrations. The atmosphere frightened me. I didn't participate in them, either, and there were many.

A few days after that rally, I received a visit from Uzi Baram, a government minister and a Jerusalemite. He brought me a message from the prime minister. Rabin, he said, was surprised by the size of the demonstration, and got the message. Arafat would not go to the Temple Mount, and Rabin's expectation in return was that I wouldn't hold any more demonstrations.

Arafat never got to visit the Al-Aqsa Mosque until the day he died.

———

The months after the signing of the Oslo Accords were frustrating and painful. Not only did the terrorism not go away, it grew worse. Nobody expected the Oslo Accords to create an immediate change. It was obviously going to be a long, slow process. But even those, like me, who opposed the accords believed that there would be some positive change, at least temporarily. A pause in the conflict. A moment when people would at least try to see the potential for peace. It didn't happen.

From the very beginning, terror struck around the country. The arch-terrorist Arafat, now chairman of the Palestinian Authority, made no serious effort to fundamentally change course toward peace. Jerusalem was not the main target of the terror, but we also received our share of attacks.

Rabin was frustrated. From the outset he had had doubts about the idea of signing a deal with Arafat. At the end of the day, he chose to give his blessing to the process, and participated in the ceremonial signing with Arafat and President Clinton on the White House lawn. Rabin was a straight shooter, and despite his misgivings, from the moment he decided to go ahead with it, he didn't put any obstacles in its way. Arafat, on the other hand, had other plans. And they didn't include an end to terrorism in the streets of Israel.

The price we paid was heavy. The public expressed its disappointment through often violent demonstrations led by the Likud leader Benjamin Netanyahu and the settlers. I didn't take part in any of them and also distanced myself from the extremism that certain people were whipping up through them. I was worried that it would lead to violence—especially in Jerusalem.

The demonstrations, the extremism, the violence—all these took place in Jerusalem under my watch. I couldn't avoid responsibility for demonstrations taking place in my city, even though it was the Israel Police that approved them all. Where were the chiefs and commanders? Did they not realize that something horrible would happen? That the anger was snowballing? Why didn't they stop the rioters, even with force?

These questions tortured me for a long time after Yitzhak Rabin was assassinated on November 4, 1995, by a far-right extremist named Yigal Amir.

———

Shimon Peres became acting prime minister in the wake of Rabin's murder, and our intelligence agencies started reporting that Arafat was planning a brutal terror assault. The chief of military intelligence was Moshe "Bogie" Yaalon, and we spoke often. Bogie was convinced that Arafat was on the verge of launching a major terror war that would result in many casualties. He even told me that he had turned to Peres, who was also serving as defense minister, and asked him to warn Arafat—but Peres refused, claiming that the intelligence estimates were wrong. Peres often said that intelligence is much better at telling you what happened in the past than what was coming in the future.

On February 25, 1996, bus number 18 exploded near the corner of Jaffa and Sarei Israel Streets in Jerusalem, just before the traffic light. Fifteen people were killed, dozens injured. The shock was awful. We awoke to a new reality.

———

Smoke rose from the remains of the bus when I arrived at the scene. Chunks of metal and personal belongings were strewn in every direction. A few dozen yards away, journalists, photographers and camera crews had gathered. Reporters explained, commentated, asked questions and sometimes answered them. We stood in the cordoned off site of the attack, stunned. With me was the chief of police, Assaf Hefetz. He bent down and picked up an ID card off the road. The name: Yonatan Barnea. The address: 5 Alroi Street, Jerusalem. I couldn't believe it. It was Yoni, the son of the famous journalist Nachum Barnea. He lived just down the street from me.

From a distance I saw Nachum standing among the reporters. He waved. I waved back. He didn't know that his life had changed forever.

I went back to my office. A secretary told me that Nachum's wife, Tammy, had called a few times asking to speak urgently. I asked her to get Tammy on the phone. Tammy asked just one question: Was Yoni there? She had been trying to reach him for hours. "Yes, Tammy," I told her. "Yoni was there."

She said: "I will forever be grateful to you for saving me from the unknown."

I put down the receiver. What can you say to a worried parent who, at that very moment, became an aggrieved mother, whose life would never be the same?

I called Aliza and told her. Later I went home. My son Shaul sat in his room, sunk in grief. He told me, in a broken voice, that every Sunday he and Yoni waited at the same bus stop. They rode that bus together to the central station, and then went their separate ways on different buses. "This morning," he said, "I had a dentist appointment. I wasn't on the bus."

A while later we went to the Barneas' home. Tammy and Nachum had already received the official visit from IDF officials. The house was silent. A small group of friends sat there, not knowing what to say. Tammy and Nachum were bottled up tight. I didn't see them cry, not that morning and not at any other point after. Nachum told me that he waved to me when he saw me at the scene of the attack because he assumed that I would head from there to the center of town and was hoping to catch a ride. I hadn't understood.

———

If Rabin hadn't been assassinated by a Jewish terrorist, he almost certainly would have refused to make any concessions on Jerusalem, ever.

We spoke about this a number of times, but it was during a period when dividing the city was not up for discussion. Rabin was born in Jerusalem and was proud of it. He was also proud of having been the IDF chief of staff who had reunited the city in 1967 and made the Western Wall available to Jewish worshipers.

Leah, his widow, said over and over again after he was murdered that he never would have made concessions on Jerusalem. Leah died in November 2000. When Ariel Sharon was sworn in as prime minister in 2001, in his speech from the Knesset podium, he mentioned a conversation he had had with Leah on her deathbed. Arik said that he knew exactly what Rabin wanted, and would never allow division of the city.

But I'm not convinced Sharon would have kept his promise.

———

In September 1996, riots broke out in Jerusalem in the wake of the opening of the Western Wall Tunnel. The tunnel, excavated by archaeologists over many years since the Six Day War, extended north from the outdoor part of the Western Wall, along the whole length of the wall, all the way to the Via Dolorosa. By breaching the long-sealed northern gate and opening the tunnel to the public, it could become a major tourist attraction.

This was a few months after Netanyahu was elected prime minister for the first time. Later he would claim he had been deceived, that his inexperience had been taken advantage of. This is typical Netanyahu. There's always someone else to blame, someone who led him astray, someone who didn't understand. In the case of the tunnel, it's not entirely false. He wasn't deceived, but the head of Shin Bet, Ami Ayalon, gave him bad advice, and Netanyahu took that advice and charged up the hill with it.

As head of Shin Bet, Ayalon would visit me from time to time at City Hall. We weren't close friends, but we developed a good, open working relationship. Because I was mayor of such a sensitive city, he had good reason to review different issues with me and the potential for violence they entailed.

Ayalon visited me in early September 1996, before the tunnel was opened. Fridays were quiet in City Hall, and the mayor's sixth-floor offices were especially so. A single receptionist was on call, and other than the two of us there was almost nobody around. Ami and I spoke at length. At the end of the conversation I took him out onto a balcony that overlooks much of Jerusalem. When we looked at the Old City, he suddenly asked me, "Why don't they finish digging that tunnel under the Wall?"

I answered that Shin Bet's commander responsible for Jerusalem and the West Bank, Yisrael Hason, was opposed. As Hason had put it, breaking through the final part of the tunnel could trigger a fierce reaction from the Palestinians, who opposed any changes to the status quo in the Old City and were looking for an excuse to riot.

Ayalon wasn't surprised. He said that no time was ever right in Jerusalem. You could always say you were afraid of the reaction. In his view, there was no reason not to open the tunnel up. Some people might protest, but nothing more.

I suggested that he meet with Netanyahu.

I got a call a few days later from the prime minister's personal secretary saying he wanted to see me.

He was in a good mood when I arrived. Ayalon had been there the day before, and the latter had expressed his surprise that Netanyahu hadn't yet given the green light to open the tunnel. I didn't tell him about our conversation when he had said exactly the same thing. I suggested that Netanyahu convene a meeting about it, to work out the details and prepare. He held the meeting a few days later, and included me and representatives of the police, IDF, and Shin Bet.

I have a lot of experience with people who pass the buck. I wasn't surprised that Netanyahu later claimed that because of his inexperience, he was seduced by the head of Shin Bet and by me. He did in fact get advice from Ayalon. But I certainly didn't press Netanyahu to open the tunnel, and he wasn't waiting to be pressed. He really wanted to do it.

And for what it's worth, Ayalon's claim that there wouldn't be rioting wasn't entirely inaccurate. It didn't happen right away. And it was anything but spontaneous. The initial response was quiet, especially in Jerusalem. But Arafat and his people made a supreme effort to provoke the Palestinian street. It took a couple of days, and only then did the riots begin—mainly in Gaza. It was clear that they resulted from organized incitement.

Arafat decided to stir up the territories in light of what he saw as Netanyahu's unwillingness to carry out the Oslo Accords. A few days after the riots, in which 17 Israelis lost their lives as well as dozens of Palestinians, President Clinton summoned Arafat and Netanyahu to Washington. Netanyahu was photographed at the end of the meeting shaking hands at length with Arafat, saying, "I have found a friend."

———

The Oslo Accords were signed on September 13, 1993. Within five years they were supposed to be fully implemented, and then an independent

Palestinian state was to be created. This date was pushed off by two years—because of the many terror attacks, because of the difficulty in getting to more specific agreements, and also because of the intense public controversy among the Israeli public and the weak standing of the governing coalition, which didn't have a decisive majority. The question was: What would happen on September 13, 2000? Would the Palestinians agree to a further delay of independence, and if not, then what?

Ehud Barak, the former IDF chief of staff who had replaced Peres as leader of the Labor party, defeated Netanyahu in a landslide in the May 1999 election and became prime minister. In July 2000, a conference was held at Camp David with the aim of finishing up the negotiations between Israel and the Palestinians. Just before getting on the plane, Barak wanted to meet me. As was typical for him, I was asked to be at his residence at 2:00 a.m.

When I showed up, Barak was busy with phone calls. One call after another. Sometimes he was on two calls at the same time and bounced back and forth between them. I sat there, waited, and kept quiet. In one call he gave instructions to somebody who was in the middle of a negotiation with a Palestinian counterpart, in another he gave instructions to somebody else, and between them he spoke in English with an American official.

The scene appeared surreal. I'm not impressed by people who handle twenty different things at the same time, at two in the morning, while keeping you waiting. It makes for a good show, but at the end of the day (or night, in Barak's case), that kind of performative sorcery doesn't lead anywhere.

He finished his calls and then asked me abruptly if I would agree to join his entourage at Camp David.

I asked him why he needed me.

He said that he thought there was a chance that they would reach a deal on Jerusalem, but it would require concessions. If we had to stand on the White House lawn and announce that an agreement had been reached, Barak said, he wanted me to stand next to him and show my support. This would be crucial in getting the Israeli public on board.

I asked him if he was willing to share with me what exactly he was planning on offering the Palestinians—and the Americans—in Jerusalem. He said the hadn't made up his mind yet, and it was too early to go into details.

I was surprised. He was finishing up a negotiation, and within days he would be sitting with Arafat and Clinton ironing out the final details. How was it possible that he didn't have any general idea of an agreement on such a crucial issue as Jerusalem? Moreover, it hadn't occurred to him that I wouldn't agree to fly to Camp David to be a prop in his play, and especially a play whose contents were unknown to me.

Barak pointed out that if I flew to the conference, I wouldn't be able to leave until it was over. From the moment everyone arrived at Camp David, no one was to come or go.

I suggested that he think through the issue of Jerusalem in advance of the conference. I was interested in negotiations that ended in an agreement, I said, and if there was some way I could help, I wouldn't rule out joining him. But only if I knew in advance what his position was regarding Jerusalem, and if it was something I could live with.

And the end of our conversation I suggested that Barak invite me to another meeting if he thought it necessary. He agreed.

A few days later, Barak summoned me again. And once again, the surreal scene with the phone calls repeated itself, though this time at a more godly hour, around 10:00 p.m. Barak explained again how important it was that I join the conference, especially if understandings would be reached concerning Jerusalem and the mayor of the city stood next to him and lent his weight.

Once again, I explained that I wasn't ruling it out, but I needed to know what his position was on Jerusalem.

Barak just kept on rambling, twisting, raising all sorts of possibilities, but didn't let me know what he was really thinking. Clearly he didn't want to tell me. Maybe he thought that the time wasn't yet right to show his cards. But if so, why drag me there twice to talk about something he didn't want to talk about? I wasn't some parliamentary aide that you could just say "get on the plane" to without explanation.

I didn't go to Camp David.

———

At Camp David, Barak, typically, made every possible mistake.

The famous video of him and Arafat trying to convince each other to go through the door at Camp David first, and he insists, even by force, on pushing Arafat with his two hands, is a meaningful symbol. Whatever Barak himself thinks about it, the image of an Israeli prime minister pushing a Palestinian leader through a door with both hands, against his will, appears in the eyes of every Arab and every Palestinian a symbol of the arrogance that Israel displays toward them.

And that's not all. Barak's refusal to sit with Arafat one-on-one to speak with him, as an equal, was another unforced error. I would never have negotiated with Arafat to begin with. I never trusted him. But to do all the necessary preparations, to go to Camp David with a battalion of advisers and aides, to handle so complicated a negotiation—and then to refuse to sit with the opposing leader? With the man who has to accept what you're willing to offer—and who has to give you what you want to receive?

They sat together for a few meals hosted by President Clinton, and took part in talks that included 15 or 20 other people in the room. But the private, personal conversation where things would be said but not written down, but maybe would enter the heart—only this he refused? To go to Camp David, to spend two long weeks there, to walk down the manicured path with stunning flowers on both sides, to walk by Arafat and turn your head away so that they wouldn't have to greet each other? How insensitive can a man be?

And despite all this, it's still a good thing that Barak went.

I have criticized him and will continue to do so, but I also have to give him credit where it's due. Camp David was a smart move in its timing and content. Some of the participants filled me in about what went on there. I know what was discussed, what was haggled over, and how flexible we were.

I know that Barak went very far. He proposed a framework of a deal that no prime minister had ever dared to offer. There was a rare courage in the offers he made, especially since he knew he didn't have a majority in Knesset to pass it, that most of his coalition partners had already bolted the government, and that he would stand or fall on the results of Camp David.

The failure didn't help him electorally, but there's no doubt that he gave Israel a significant boost in terms of world opinion. Israel had presented a responsible diplomatic face—one that appeared sane, brave, and flexible—which could serve as the basis of an intensive peace negotiation.

The failure of Camp David was first and foremost the result of Arafat's unbending, hypocritical stance. I moved a long way in my own opinions from the days when I believed in the empty slogans of the hard right until the time, a few years later, when I took the flexibility a few steps beyond what Barak offered. I am still convinced that Arafat was incapable and unwilling to make the transition from terrorist to statesman. He believed that he could push Israel into a corner that would handcuff us and emasculate us, forcing us to give in to his demands through the pressure of terrorism and international pressure—without cutting a peace deal in the most fundamental sense of the term.

———

In September 2000, after the collapse of the Camp David talks, there was tension in the air. What would Arafat do? Would the Palestinian Authority stay the diplomatic course, or would it revert to its terrorist origins?

I had planned a trip to the Sydney Olympics, which were to open on September 15, but now I wasn't sure if I should go. I checked in with some Palestinian friends if they anticipated anything major. They said nothing would happen during the Olympics. I decided to take my chances and fly. I was invited by the International Olympic Committee, and that gave me free entry to all of the events.

I had a wonderful time in Sydney.

The day after I got back to Jerusalem, however, I got a call from Ariel Sharon, who had become the leader of Likud after the 1999 elections sent Netanyahu into the political wilderness. Arik now told me he was planning on taking a high-profile tour on the Temple Mount—with all the provocation that this implied—and asked if I would join him.

I told him that he really shouldn't do that, and that as mayor of Jerusalem I certainly would not go with him. I didn't want to have to explain to Jerusalemites why I took part in something that sparked unrest and brought them needless suffering.

I'm convinced that Sharon's tour of the Temple Mount on September 28, 2000, was unnecessary. But it's also absolutely clear that the Palestinians, under Arafat's direction, had already made a decision to launch a terror war and were just looking for a pretext. Amos Gilad, who was then the commander of the Military Intelligence Research Division, was and is one of the most experienced and insightful people about the Middle East. He told me that long before Camp David, he had warned Barak that this was happening. Barak had answered him, more than once, that he had no doubt that Arafat would refuse to make a deal, and that soon after that he would launch a terror war.

Sharon toured the Temple Mount on a Thursday. The next day's Friday Muslim prayers turned into a riot.

At first, the security forces lost control of the situation. Hundreds, maybe thousands, of violent protestors attacked the police and the paramilitary Border Police. They threw rocks down onto the Jews praying at the Western Wall. Some of them hit their targets.

Rosh Hashana, the Jewish New Year, was to begin that same evening. Yair Yitzhaki was now the police commander in charge of Jerusalem. Yitzhaki, a commander revered by his officers, led the charge into the riot, was hit in the head by a large rock, and lost consciousness. He was quickly taken to Hadassah Ein Kerem Hospital. I was on my way to the police station next to the Temple Mount when I heard, and told the driver to head to the hospital. I assumed that police would quell the riot, and I wanted to be by the side of this courageous man. He was already awake by the time I arrived, on a gurney headed into radiology. He fully recovered.

The day he had been hit, before the riots, Internal Security Minister Shlomo Ben-Ami had summoned Yitzhaki to his office, and informed him he was not getting promoted to chief of police. Yitzhaki had answered that he was going to quit the force. An hour later, he was risking his life at the front lines on the Temple Mount. That says everything about the character of those called upon to serve and secure our country and its citizens.

———

Mickey Levy replaced Yitzhaki as police commander in Jerusalem. Levy had been the deputy commander for a few years, and nobody knew the city better than he did. During the entire uprising that followed, he took the lead in fighting terror in Jerusalem. We were on the battlefield together. We saw a lot of blood.

Within a few days, the whole country was a battlefield. The Wadi Ara highway in northern Israel was taken over by stone-throwers and shut down. There were riots in the Galilee, in the Negev, and even in Jaffa. As the Americans like to say, all hell broke loose. The police were charged with quelling the riots among Israeli Arabs. The closing of major roads, especially the highways heading north—this was unprecedented. The police response was also unusual. Hundreds of Arab citizens were injured in the first ten days of October 2000, and twelve Israeli Arabs, as well as one Palestinian, lost their lives.

The Al-Aqsa Intifada, today better known as the Second Intifada, rampaged across the country.

Terror attacks became a daily affair. The heart of Tel Aviv was just as much a target as was Jerusalem. Warnings of imminent attacks caused the shutting down of central arteries for hours on end, disrupting daily life and causing a sense of panic for many citizens. Tourism ground nearly to a halt. And most important: It was clear that the government had no idea what to do about it, and spoke and behaved with complete impotence.

Barak declared that he was giving Arafat forty-eight hours to put a stop to the terror, and that if he didn't, Israel would respond with force. Arafat thumbed his nose at Barak and did nothing. The president of France, Jacques Chirac, invited both of them to Paris. Barak, who had already given the ultimatum, flew there. It was a humiliating farce. Arafat wasn't willing to meet, and didn't agree to Chirac's request to set a timetable and conditions for an end to the violence. They were chasing after Arafat in the Elysée Palace. In short, other than the humiliation and a show of Israeli powerlessness, nothing happened.

———

The situation in Jerusalem went from bad to worse, and I knew the national government wasn't going to help. Shin Bet, military intelligence, and the IDF did everything they could to prevent attacks, but how do you run a city that is under an endless terror assault? When parents are scared to send their kids to school? When people are afraid to take the bus to work? When walking down any street in any corner of the city, or shopping at the market, or sitting in a coffee shop—when any of this is a source of panic?

I asked the director-general of city hall, Raanan Dinur, to put together a checklist for the municipality in the event of a mass-casualty attack. Raanan got the help of Eitan Meir, his deputy. They put together a team that included social workers headed up by Leora Schneider, maintenance workers, first responders headed up by Ziv Ayalon, people from the health department headed by Zion Sheetrit. It was an emergency team that was ready to spring into action at a moment's notice. To help the police cordon off the area to traffic, to keep people away from the scene, to organize detours, to clear and clean up the broken windows, destroyed equipment, posts that were knocked over, objects that had been hurled in all directions.

In every terror attack, the social workers on this emergency team spread out to the hospitals where the injured had been taken. Others went straight to the pathological institute at Abu Kabir, where bodies were taken for identification. A third team of social workers went to deliver the awful message to the families of the victims and then accompanied them. The communications center of the municipality in Givat Shaul was expanded to respond quickly to anyone calling the emergency line to get information or give relevant details, to get help, to express their horror. Another team was sent to the homes of victims of shock. Security personnel made sure that violent groups of Jews didn't start attacking Arabs or vandalizing their property.

I am often asked how average Israelis could tolerate such tragedy, which at the height of the attacks came day after day after day. I try to compare the many horrific events we dealt with during a short period of time in Jerusalem to the trauma suffered by residents of Brussels, Paris, or London—but we had to go through it over and over again—and I am amazed at the relative equanimity with which our residents accepted the attacks. What happened in those cities once or twice became an almost daily affair in Jerusalem. Jaffa Street became a killing field. Buses filled with passengers blew up. Restaurants, coffee shops and stores were targeted.

———

Then they started shooting from Beit Jala, just across the border in the Palestinian territories, into the Jerusalem neighborhood of Gilo.

The distance between them was about half a mile—a fairly effective range for light arms. Since many hundreds of apartments in Gilo were lined up along the street that faced Beit Jala, the shooting caused a lot of distress. Suddenly people weren't even safe in their own homes. Many wanted to bulletproof their windows.

I was aware of the distress, but I refused to bulletproof the homes. We needed to show emotional fortitude. We couldn't play into the hands of the terrorists, who wanted to achieve exactly that: To terrorize, to make us panic. I said then to those who disagreed: What will we do if they start shooting at major Tel Aviv suburbs like Kfar Saba or Petach Tikva? Will we start bulletproofing tens of thousands of homes across the country?

In coordination with security agencies, we decided to build a wall along Ha'anafa Street, six feet high and made of concrete. The idea was to block the view of the entrances to the apartment buildings, and thereby allow people to leave home and come back inside. In parallel, we called on residents to move to interior rooms, away from the street side, whenever they heard gunfire. It was not an optimal solution, and it was a lot easier to say it than to live in a home where the windows might suddenly shatter, but the likelihood of someone actually getting shot was very small.

Even when the attacks on Gilo increased, I adamantly refused to bulletproof the homes. We put up the wall, and Aliza recruited artists from the former Soviet Union to paint the wall with the vistas that were being blocked. The artists were happy to do it. The wall showed a beautiful panorama. Later on, photos of the murals were exhibited at the convention center in Jerusalem.

———

Not long after, Barak announced his intention to resign and announced new elections for prime minister. For a brief period under the Direct Election Law, Israeli prime ministers were elected directly on a separate ticket from the Knesset vote, which was held according to party. (The law was rescinded in 2003.)

Barak's popularity was at an all-time low. His coalition had lost most of its partners, and he was left with 30-odd MKs and no real public support. It was clear that elections were only a matter of time, and Barak had nothing to lose. He tried to change the political reality.

On a Saturday night in early December 2000, I sat with my son Shaul and some friends at Bloomfield Stadium in Tel Aviv for the soccer match between Hapoel Tel Aviv and Beitar Jerusalem. The game was broadcast on television, and the ratings were high. Beitar and Hapoel were the best two teams in the country.

During the game, word spread that Barak had resigned, and would make a special announcement after the game. His resignation would trigger an election just for prime minister, but not for the Knesset. After the final whistle (Beitar won 1-0), I watched his press conference at a nearby coffee shop. The announcement was short and clear. The reasons he offered were not important.

I drove back to Jerusalem. On the way I received a call. A secretary in the office of the prime minister told me that the director-general of the Prime Minister's Office, Yossi Kuchik, wanted to speak with me urgently. Yossi, an old friend who had for some time been the deputy director general of the Health Ministry when I was minister, got on the phone and told me that the prime minister had decided to resign—which I already knew—and that he wanted to urgently bulletproof the homes in Gilo.

"Of course," Yossi added, "there is no connection between these two things."

"Of course," I said. We both laughed and hung up.

We couldn't refuse a decision of the prime minister, so instead we did everything we could to slow-pedal the project. We decided to bulletproof only one window in each apartment facing Beit Jala, after conducting thorough measurements of all the windows. We would also conduct research to see if it was possible to order panels to replace the windows that were all the same size, and so on.

A few years later, when I was prime minister and the shootings in Beit Jala were a memory, I had countless requests from residents of Gilo demanding that we take out the bulletproof panels and put back the windows, since they couldn't be opened. I left that for the new mayor of the city to figure out.

———

At the height of the terror attacks in the wake of the Oslo Accords, back in 1995, I had gotten a call from Rudy Giuliani, at the time mayor of New York City.

The hotels in Jerusalem had emptied almost entirely. The streets were empty. Walking down Jaffa Street was just depressing. Stores were empty. People were afraid to leave their homes.

Giuliani asked me: "What can I do to help?"

I said to him: "Just come here, and together we will ride the number 18 bus, and we'll make sure that all the media cover it." This was just a few days after the second bombing of that bus line. "It's important to me," I told him, "that the world see that Jerusalem is going on with its life."

He was there within forty-eight hours. We walked around the city together, he rode with me on the number 18 bus from Katamonim to the center of town, and paid a visit with me to the injured at Hadassah Hospital. Giuliani was especially moved by the hospital visit. He asked if I could arrange a private room for him for a few minutes.

Minutes went by and he didn't come out. Eventually I knocked on the door and went inside. I found him sitting in a chair, crying.

———

Six years later, as soon as I learned of the September 11 attacks in New York City, I told Giuliani I was coming.

I think I may have been the first foreign guest who came to New York after that horrific day. Giuliani's people waited for me at the airport and drove me to the new command center he had set up in one of the enormous hangars along the Hudson River. He asked me to join a meeting of the emergency command he had set up and also asked me to say a few words to the senior staff.

This was a year into the Second Intifada, and I spoke about the terror attacks we were currently dealing with in Jerusalem. I tried to boost the spirits of his team. Later they arranged an overflight of the site by helicopter. We were joined by Senator John McCain, who was already a major Republican leader and presidential candidate. I asked Giuliani to allow an Israeli television crew to come to Ground Zero, where we were going to land. Giuliani said that no TV crews had been allowed until that moment. "It looks real bad," he said. But he allowed it. Israeli viewers were among the first people on earth who saw from up close the magnitude of the destruction at the World Trade Center.

After another series of terror attacks in Jerusalem, Giuliani called me again, asking to come back to Israel. He added that he would be bringing with him Governor George Pataki of New Jersey and also Mayor-elect Michael Bloomberg of New York.

They arrived in late December 2001, after the triple-bombing on the pedestrian mall of Ben Yehuda Street, in which 11 people were murdered. Giuliani was, at the time, revered around the world, and in Israel as well. It was his fourth trip to Jerusalem while serving as mayor. He told me that over his eight-year tenure, he had left the United States only four times. Each time he visited Jerusalem.

The delegation was a dramatic event. Everywhere Giuliani and his entourage went, they were greeted by hundreds of people cheering them on. Journalists and TV crews were broadcasting live to the world. In the evening I hosted a reception in their honor in the ballroom of the David Citadel Hotel. More than 2,000 guests came.

I introduced the guests of honor. And when I introduced Giuliani, the whole crowd stood and gave him a spontaneous standing ovation. It went on for minutes, and it felt like it would never end. Giuliani was overwhelmed. For one long, symbolic moment, the two cities that had symbolized the pain of terrorism, but also standing strong in the struggle against it, were united. It was an unforgettable moment.

———

The area surrounding the Sbarro restaurant on the corner of Jaffa and King George Streets became a symbol of the crisis our city faced.

Two hours after the horrific bombing there on August 9, 2001, Sharon called me. He told me there had been a warning of a possible attack in Jerusalem. All night long they had been trying to reach Arafat, to warn him that our response to such an attack would be especially harsh. But he was unreachable. They were unable to prevent it.

The next day, I stood at the cemetery and was asked to eulogize the 15 people who had been murdered. Five of them were from a single family. What do you say to such a family, with the bodies of their loved ones lying before them? What prepares a mayor for the moment when he has to stand in front of children whose parents and three siblings have just been murdered? Are there any words that could possibly soften the blow? Is there any way to penetrate the mask of something so awful, the tears, the helplessness, and say something that could actually be meaningful, to help them in any real way?

In my years as mayor, I attended every funeral of every terror victim in the city. I eulogized every single one. Obviously I didn't know the great majority of them personally. They had been unknown to me just a few hours beforehand. But they were sons, brothers, sisters, parents, friends. And you have to say something worthwhile.

These were the worst days of my life. How much suffering can you look at? How much pain can you swallow? Did anyone really believe it was just a passing moment, that you could avoid the abyss? As mayor I didn't have the privilege of being able to show my feelings. I had to make a show of stability, confidence, faith that things would get better, but in my heart there was just a deep, churning, endless pain.

———

The staff from the welfare division were exposed to the most awful scenes and the most painful moments. They accompanied the injured to hospitals, they remained with their families, and they watched as families were destroyed. They accompanied family members to identify bodies at the morgue. They held the mothers and fathers and sisters and brothers and children in their arms, to keep them from collapsing.

It was only a matter of time before they, too, began to crack. It was an almost impossible task, to digest the images, to hear the cries, to carry the look in their eyes that often said a lot more than they could put into words.

One day Leora Schneider, the director of the welfare division for the entire period of the Intifada, who had been with her staff through all the hardest moments, came into my office. She said she had asked a few psychologists to come and meet with her staff in one-on-one meetings, to talk to them and give them an outlet for their own traumas.

"And what about you?" Leora asked me. "Are you also willing to meet with a psychologist?"

I thanked her. It's not easy for a subordinate, no matter how senior, to tell the mayor to get help. I deeply appreciated her sensitivity, but I believed I could handle the hardship, which I suspected was only going to get worse.

Once in a while, after all the funerals and eulogies and *shiva* calls, I would get home and tell Aliza: "It's too much. Nothing is harder than this. I don't know how I can go on." But I had no choice. I had to be the one who constantly projected a sense that things could be better, that there was no way forward other than to deal with the pain and the fear—and that we would prevail in the end.

———

Café Moment was on the corner of Gaza and Ben Maimon Streets, very close to the prime minister's official residence on Balfour Street. In my first years in Jerusalem, in college, it was called Savyon, and was popular among students. Its owners, Yehuda and Moshe, turned it into a popular social spot. One of the waitresses who worked there for a long time had been Aliza Richter, whom I married.

On a Saturday night, forty years later, on March 9, 2002, I was at home on November 29 Street, a few hundred yards from the restaurant, and I heard a deep thud. I immediately understood it was an explosion.

Playing footsie at age two with our family's dog, in Nahalat Jabotinsky, 1947.

With my brothers Ami, Yermi, and Yossi, and our parents, Bella and Nordechai, 1960.

My kindergarten class in Binyamina, 1950.

Documentary evidence of my having graduated kindergarten and been promoted to first grade, 1951.

Reunited with classmates from kindergarten, six decades later, 2007.

As a second-term member of Knesset, I joined cadets much younger than myself in the IDF officers' training course, 1980.

Aliza Olmert

Aliza and I married in July 1970.

As mayor of Jerusalem, welcoming U.S. President Bill Clinton to a Jerusalem school, 1996. Prime Minister Shimon Peres looks on.

With Prime Minister Ariel Sharon and King Abdullah II of Jordan at a meeting in Aqaba, Jordan, 2004.

AVI OHAYON

Leaders of two cities living in the shadow of terrorism. Mayor of Jerusalem and New York City Mayor Rudy Giuliani, 2001.

Speaking before a joint session of Congress, May 24, 2006.

In the Rose Garden with President George W. Bush, 2007.

With Jacques Chirac at the
Élysée Palace, 2006.

Chinese President Hu Jintao, on
state visit to China, 2007.

MILNER MOSHE

Vice President Dick Cheney, at his official residence in Washington, D.C., 2007.

WHITE HOUSE / DAVID BORER

Welcoming two friends—U.S. President George W. Bush and Secretary of State Condoleezza Rice—to the prime minister's residence in Jerusalem, 2008.

U.S. Democratic presidential candidate Senator Barack Obama's visit to Israel, 2008.

U.S. Secretary of State Hillary Clinton and I address the press at the prime minister's residence in Jerusalem, 2009.

Palestinian Authority President Mahmoud Abbas at the prime minister's residence in Jerusalem, 2008.

Aliza and I visit a community center in Shefaram in northern Israel, 2008.

A meeting with President Shimon Peres at the president's residence in Jerusalem, 2008.

U.S. Senator John Kerry at the prime minister's office in Jerusalem, 2009.

A visit to France, 2008.

Hosted by Hirohito, Emperor of Japan, in Tokyo, 2008.

European Commission President
and future Prime Minister of Italy
Romano Prodi in Jerusalem, 2007.

OHAYON AVI

With Turkish Prime Minister Recep Tayyip Erdoğan in Ankara, 2008.

Meeting with Emir Hamad bin Khalifa Al Thani of Qatar and Qatar's Prime Minister Hamad bin Jassim bin Jaber Al Thani (right) on a visit to France, 2008.

Quartet envoy and former British Prime Minister
Tony Blair at my Tel Aviv office, 2009.

Historic summit held at the prime minister's residence in Jerusalem with European leaders the
day after the cease-fire of Operation Cast Lead, 2009.

With French President Nicolas Sarkozy and his wife Carla Bruni, 2008.

Hosting Germany's Chancellor Angela Merkel, 2009.

Russian President Vladimir Putin at the Kremlin in Moscow, 2007.

A return to my roots with a visit from Du Yuxin, the governor of China's Harbin Province, 2008.

Welcoming U.N. Secretary-General Ban Ki-moon at
the prime minister's office in Jerusalem, 2009.

With Egyptian President Hosni Mubarak at Sharm el-Sheikh, Egypt—
in the shadow of terrorism, 2008.

In London with British Prime Minister Gordon Brown at 10 Downing Street, 2008.

U.S. Senator Joe Lieberman, 2009.

New York City Mayor Michael Bloomberg at the prime minister's office in Tel Aviv, 2009.

Within minutes the municipal command center called me with the details. I got in my car. Paris Square was already filled with first responders, while the prime minister's security people were spread across the scene as well as hundreds of police officers. The area was sealed off.

I asked permission to enter. The police commissioner, Mickey Levy, wouldn't let me. "Ehud, I am asking you please, don't go in there," he said. "It will change you forever. I don't want you to go through what I went through."

I insisted. So he asked his people to bring me to the window instead. What I saw inside was horrific. Bodies of people, still sitting upright with friends, as if they were in the middle of a conversation, with glasses of wine next to them, their heads slightly tilted—like a still photo.

But it wasn't a still photo. Life itself had been stilled. It was chilling. I understood why Mickey didn't let me go inside.

The proximity of Café Moment to the prime minister's residence was a matter of chance. Arik wasn't even home. He never spent weekends at the residence. Even on weeknights he almost always went back to his farm. Those were his years of isolation. His wife, Lily, had passed away two years before. To spend the night alone in the official residence, a mansion, was torture for him. He loved his real home, the Shikmim Farm.

I don't think the terrorists were targeting him or even had him in mind. They were looking for a crowded place, and when they found it, they walked in and blew themselves up. With them, they took 11 souls who just wanted to go out for the evening.

This attack resonated unusually powerfully. The suicide bombers had gotten within fifty yards of the security wall around the prime minister's residence, which created the sense that they could reach anywhere. It only added to the Jerusalemites' sense of vulnerability.

———

The attack on the number 32-A bus, at the Pat Junction on its way to Gilo, was particularly awful.

I was at Jacky's barber shop in Talpiot, and just as the barber was finishing up, my guard told me there had been an attack at the intersection next to Teddy Stadium. I told my driver to take me there, as I had always done in every attack. The guard asked me to hold off. They wanted to make sure there wasn't a second bomb. They were completing the security check of the whole area.

I told the driver to go anyway. Within seconds I got a call from the chief of personal security at Shin Bet. "Mister Mayor, sir," he said. "I'm asking you to hold off. We will let you know when the area is clear. As soon as we're done, you can come."

It was a reasonable request, one that happened every time there was an attack. My arrival at the scene of attacks was often covered by the media, and the personal security staff wasn't willing to take the risk. I waited. Then I went.

The scene was horrific. The bus was still smoldering. Police officers and Shin Bet were standing around it. They had finished their check. I asked to go into the charred bus. I know there were people who asked: To what end? Why do that to myself? I have no explanation. I wanted to get on that bus just like I wanted to go into Café Moment.

I wanted to hurt. I wanted to feel the pain inside. Not as a spectator, but as a victim.

The people from Zaka, the volunteer organization that ensured the sanctity of the bodies of victims of accidents and attacks around the country, had removed the bodies and laid them out on stretchers on the sidewalk. Nineteen bodies. One of them drew my attention. The sheet that had covered it was shorter than the rest. It was a twelve-year-old girl. An image I can't get out of my mind.

———

Later on, Ariel Sharon arrived at the scene.

I knew Arik well. I don't remember any time, over decades of knowing him, that I had seen him so angry. He was speechless. Maybe just a word or two came out of his mouth. The look on his face was extreme. Given the opportunity, he would have strangled Arafat with his bare hands.

I have no doubt that at that moment he came to a far-reaching decision. Arik felt that these attacks were a direct and personal assault on himself. I was with him at the Prime Minister's Office when he was told about the murder of a security guard at Kibbutz Magel in the Hefer Valley. Arik went nuts. He was old, a man who fought in all the wars, saw all the horrors, lost the best of friends. It was strange to see him re-acting in extreme anger, pounding on the table as though he were about to charge an enemy who wasn't before him.

Arik felt that these murderers were at war with him—and they were winning. He didn't know how to live with defeat. He had to win, and he decided to win no matter what.

After the attack at the Park Hotel in Netanya, on the evening of the Passover Seder in April 2002, his patience ran out. He decided to go to war. He launched Operation Defensive Shield in the West Bank.

The firepower that the IDF deployed was immense, and the terror-ists were few, but the combat in urban centers, as opposed to massive in-vasions with tanks and artillery and the air force, gave a huge advantage to the terrorists. They ambushed our soldiers, and successfully neutral-ized much of the IDF's natural advantage.

Operation Defensive Shield was a formative event.

The war between the IDF and the terrorists, who were hiding in the refugee camps, was not a normal war. There's no way to avoid showing uncompromising determination to wipe out an enemy that is willing to sacrifice their own family members, their neighbors, and children.

The battle at the Jenin refugee camp was particularly grueling—precisely because the IDF soldiers were careful, responsible, and coura-geous, and did everything in their power not to harm innocents. Rather than go straight in with tanks and armored bulldozers, they sent in infantry and special forces that engaged in house-to-house fighting in a zone laden with booby-traps and noncombatants. Twenty-three IDF soldiers lost their lives, along with fifty-two Palestinians of whom only a handful were civilians. The end was known from the beginning—the IDF defeated the terrorists. But the cost of victory was heavy.

———

The look on Arik's face, when he looked at the nineteen bodies from the number 32-A bus lying on the sidewalk, was burned into my memory and has never left me.

Among the victims was Galila.

Galila was an Ethiopian girl. Not Jewish. Her parents had been members of the Ethiopian Church, which is near City Hall. I knew her father, who worked at the King David Hotel. On the morning of the attack, he had offered to drive Galila to school, because he was worried about bus bombings. She told him that she had learned how to find a safe spot on the bus and wasn't worried. The terrorist had sat down in the empty seat next to her.

When I came to comfort her parents, they were sitting on the floor of the church. The mother, a beautiful woman, was drenched in tears. "Mr. Mayor, sir," she said, "you have influence, you can do anything. Please find out if anything at all was found that belonged to Galila. Even a shoelace. Anything."

I promised to look into it. Nothing had been found. I went back to the mother to tell her, and she couldn't stop crying. I saw a photo of Galila. If she had survived the attack, she might have become a model. She was their only child.

If that wasn't enough, it proved difficult to bury her. We looked for a Coptic cemetery, and there wasn't one available in all of Israel. In Haifa, where there was one, they refused to bury her. In the end we found her a place in a Jewish cemetery. She wasn't murdered for being an Ethiopian Copt. She lived as an Israeli in every way and was murdered as one of us. Her place was with us, forever.

Years later, I spoke about Galila in my address to a joint session of the U.S. Congress, after I became prime minister. It was a speech about turning toward conciliation. I didn't come to Washington to talk about the valor of Israel and our ability to defeat all our enemies. I came to talk about peace and the horrible price of its absence.

As I spoke to a packed chamber about the horrors of the conflict, the members of Congress teared up. At the end of my speech, the Senate majority leader, Harry Reid, told me had had been deeply moved. "I haven't heard a speech like that in many years," he said. I thought it was one of those comments that politicians say to one another. I thanked him, but he insisted it was a deeply moving speech, and that the part about Galila had brought him to tears.

A year later, when I was invited to a briefing of the Senate Foreign Relations Committee, Reid sat next to me. He hugged me and said, "I meant what I said last year. Your speech was wonderful and brought me to tears."

———

In Jerusalem we counted dozens of dead and thousands of wounded, including many who suffered from shock.

Gradually the attacks died down, but the recovery took a long time. The transition from a daily threat—killing, injuries. blood, destruction in the streets, charred busses—to a more normal daily life is much harder than it may seem.

The talk of new elections began to be heard more and more in the public conversation. The 2001 elections had been for prime minister only, according to the Direct Election Law, may it rest in peace. The four-year term of the Knesset would come to an end in January 2003.

With Sharon now in power and a general election on the way, the question of my return to national politics began to occupy my thoughts—and apparently his as well.

SIX

The Road to Balfour Street

My relationship with Ariel Sharon had its ups and downs over the years. I was never part of his inner circle, never invited to his "Shikmim Farm Forum." But Arik knew me as a man of action, someone who could make decisions and help him govern the country. And I knew him as a leader who knew how to make decisions, including unpopular ones, in the interests of the country. He was creative and flexible in assessing the changes that had taken place on the ground, and once he set his mind on a goal, he was an unstoppable force.

In 2002, as talk of elections heated up, Sharon started hosting a series of dinners at the prime minister's residence in Jerusalem, together with his son and political aide-de-camp Omri, myself, as well as a few others.

We talked about the country's future, about domestic and foreign policy, about the sense of national crisis.

By that point, I knew that I neither could nor wanted to remain in City Hall. I wasn't burned out, and the terror attacks hadn't broken me, but I had come to understand that I couldn't keep up the façade of a "unified" Jerusalem, and there would have to be a dramatic shift in our government's position on it. It struck me as unthinkable that a mayor would launch a public campaign to divide his own city. So I'd have to return to the national stage if I wanted to make a difference.

At one of these dinners, Arik asked me if I would quit the municipality and come work for him. He needed me, he said, to fill one of three central roles: finance minister, foreign minister, or defense minister. "I want you to get the kind of experience," he added, "that will prepare you to take over for me as easily as possible in the future."

Those were his exact words.

Did he really mean them? Did he see something on the horizon that would prevent him from carrying out his duties? Or was this just his way of sweet-talking me into leaving the mayor's office and joining his government? Either way, his words dovetailed with my own thinking. I wasn't coming back to national politics as a midlevel minister. My experience, my parliamentary seniority, and my public résumé all gave me a clear advantage over other candidates for the top spots.

Such was the understanding we reached. Nothing was put in writing. That wasn't the way our relationship worked.

The elections were set for January 28, 2003. I announced at City Hall that I would be running on the Likud list for the Knesset and, if elected, would resign as mayor of Jerusalem.

Arik asked me to act as campaign chairman. I worked hard to ensure a Likud victory, and on election day my efforts bore fruit: Likud won 38 seats to Labor's 19. It was an unprecedented landslide, and it was clear that Sharon would be able to put together a government quickly. He brought in Natan Sharansky's Yisrael B'aliyah Party, creating a faction of 40 seats, and then asked me to take the lead in negotiating with Tommy Lapid's Shinui and Effi Eitam's National Religious Party. I brought them in, as well as the National Union Party. Together, we had 68 seats.

We had our government. Now came the task of dividing up the ministries.

———

The weather in February 2003 was unusually harsh for Jerusalem. Heavy snow fell.

The time was drawing near when I'd need to announce my resignation as mayor. A new law, passed at the urging of my rivals in Likud who had looked on with concern as my status in the party grew, prohibited any sitting mayor from also serving in the Knesset. There was no real principle behind it. It didn't apply, for example, to the secretary-general of the Histadrut labor union or other prominent public officeholders. But if I didn't quit as mayor, my seat in the Knesset would automatically vacate.

I called up Sharon. I told him that I'd need to make an announcement the following day, but it depended on exactly one thing: Would he keep his promise to appoint me to one of the three top ministries? If not, I would stay on as mayor and quit the Knesset, and it wouldn't be a big deal.

Arik said it had never occurred to him that I wouldn't be in the government. Promises would be kept. He told me to go ahead and make the announcement.

The next day, I did exactly that. From that moment on, my fate was entirely in his hands. If he didn't keep his promise, I would look like a fool.

A few days later, he called me into his office. The work of crafting the government was drawing to an end. He told me that he had been deliberating about which senior position to offer me. Naturally, he said, in light of the broad international network I'd built during my decade as mayor, he was inclined to offer me the Foreign Ministry.

Back in November, Labor had decided to bolt the coalition, with the aim of running as a clear alternative to Likud and Sharon. At the time, Binyamin Ben-Eliezer resigned as defense minister, as did Shimon Peres as foreign minister. A few weeks before the election, they were replaced by Shaul Mofaz at defense and Benjamin Netanyahu as foreign minister. Sharon had described both of these as temporary appointments, only good until the election. But since Mofaz had concluded his role as IDF chief of staff just four months earlier, I assumed there was no chance he would be replaced after the elections. As for the Foreign Ministry, Sharon had called to reassure me that Netanyahu's appointment was temporary.

Now it was after the election, and we sat in his office. Arik told me that upon reflection, he had decided to leave Netanyahu in the Foreign

Ministry. All dealings with the United States specifically would be handled by Sharon himself. The Foreign Minister would deal with areas like Africa, Asia, and South America. "Anyway, they can't stand Bibi in America," he added.

So, he offered me the position of finance minister. "If you accept," he said, "I'll make an announcement, and it'll be official."

I told him that I preferred the Foreign Ministry, but finance was one of the three he had promised, so I would be fine with that.

We shook hands.

Arik asked me to join him for lunch in his office. He brought in Dubi Weisglass, his chief of staff, and told him that he had picked me for finance. After lunch, he said, Dubi would fill me in on the negotiations with Washington regarding loan guarantees. He added that it might be good for me to fly to D.C. the week after the government was sworn in to close the deal.

We hugged. Just before I left, Sharon asked me if I had any thoughts about who should chair the Knesset Finance Committee. I told him I wanted Avraham Hirschson, the former deputy speaker of the Knesset and deputy chair of the Finance Committee. Sharon picked up the phone, called Hirschson, and told him that I would be the new finance minister, and that I wanted him to chair the committee. Hirschson readily accepted.

———

"Sharon to Olmert: You're Finance Minister." That was the front-page headline the following morning in *Yediot Aharonot*. The body of the article mentioned details from our meeting that were so accurate it was obvious Sharon had leaked them.

I went to the Knesset first thing in the morning. People came up to me and shook my hand. Some offered to serve as aides or advisers. But then, a few hours later, the news reported that Sharon had met with Netanyahu and offered to name *him* finance minister. They were, apparently, in talks. And then another report: Sharon had met with Silvan Shalom, one of Netanyahu's biggest rivals in Likud, and offered him the Foreign Ministry instead of Netanyahu.

I was stunned.

He had never really cared about what job Silvan Shalom would have, but suddenly Arik had given him one of the most important roles. Arik had, apparently, been listening to people who claimed Silvan had enormous influence inside the party, and that any insult to him could undermine Sharon's hold on power. I decided to duck out of the Knesset and bide my time.

The entire day was filled with reports about Sharon's negotiations with Netanyahu. At the end of the day, it was said that they'd reached a deal. Bibi would be finance minister instead of me.

Sharon had left me out in the cold.

That evening, I got a call from the Prime Minister's Office. Arik's secretary said he wanted to see me. We set to meet at his office at 9 p.m., one hour before the Likud faction was convening to hear from Sharon about the allocation of ministries.

I went to meet Arik. Dubi was in the office as well. Arik squirmed in his chair. He said that the circumstances had changed, and he would not be able to fulfill his promise. He offered instead that I become minister of industry and trade, with additional responsibility over the Broadcasting Authority, as well as assistant prime minister.

I thanked him for the offer, but told him I couldn't accept. I had no intention of serving in the government under the new circumstances. After leaving the meeting, I would announce my intention to resign from the Knesset, and from political life in general. But I would have no personal beef with Sharon, I said, and in the next elections I would be happy to serve again as campaign chairman.

Arik tried to persuade me. I refused to even discuss it. He asked if I was willing at least to explain why I wanted to leave politics. I said I would, but only if Dubi left the room. "I don't want anyone else to hear what I have to say to you," I added.

Dubi walked out. It was just the two of us. "Why don't you want to join the government?" he asked.

I told him I had no intention of serving in a government being led by a liar.

"For an entire day, you negotiated behind my back," I said. "If you had called me before your meeting with Bibi and said you couldn't honor our agreement and wanted to make me a new offer—I might have been okay with that. That's politics. But to close a deal with me, to shake my hand, to ask me to fly within the week to Washington, to appoint a Finance Committee chair on my recommendation—and all the while, you're negotiating behind my back? All this, after I gave you the opportunity to walk back your promise before I resigned as mayor, and after I led the campaign to an amazing victory, and also put together your coalition. After all this, how can I take an oath as a minister in your government?"

Sharon asked me not to say anything publicly. "Let's leave it till the morning, okay?"

I told him what I had told other prime ministers: When the prime minister asks me for something, I don't say no right away. I agreed to let it wait until morning. The next day there was going to be a formal announcement, which the Knesset would need to approve.

I went home. Sharon told the faction who the ministers would be, with the exception of industry and trade. In the media they said there was a crisis, and that it looked like I was quitting politics. I was flooded with calls. Not, of course, from members of the Likud Central Committee, or from incoming ministers who were now potential competitors. Just from friends, important people in the business world, and even ordinary folks who begged me to serve in the government despite everything.

———

At 7:00 a.m. I received a call from Ruvi Rivlin. He had been named speaker of the Knesset. He called to say that Sharon wanted to come to my house for breakfast.

I thought that under the circumstances, Aliza did not deserve the punishment of having to make breakfast for Ariel Sharon. And I wasn't in the mood for games. He was the prime minister. If he wanted to have breakfast with me, he should invite me to the residence.

Ruvi got back to me and asked me to be there at 9:00 a.m.

Arik waited for me on the third floor, in the prime minister's living quarters, in the kitchen. The table was full of food. He said he had given it all another thought, and he wouldn't present the government to the Knesset at all unless I agreed to be a member of it. He asked me to consider accepting his offer, and said that in addition to an expanded

Ministry of Industry and Trade, he would also give me responsibility for both the Broadcasting Authority and Channel 2.

"What about the Israel Land Authority?" I asked. I knew that Sharon, every time he had been a minister, had always insisted on controlling the Israel Land Authority. In a country where the majority of the land is government-owned, the Land Authority is a major center of power.

He immediately answered: "You can have the Land Authority."

"One more thing," I said. "If you want me to serve in your government, I will need to have the role of deputy prime minister." As opposed to assistant prime minister, which is merely a title, the deputy is defined by law as first in line of succession. If the prime minister were incapacitated, only the deputy prime minister would automatically replace him as acting prime minister.

Sharon agreed without hesitation. I added that I would also need to be a member of the security cabinet and receive the same top-secret intelligence material as the prime minister. Arik accepted this as well. I said that I would have to be part of any diplomatic negotiations that were launched, and of any security or diplomatic forum, with the exception of his private meetings with foreign leaders or chiefs of the Mossad and Shin Bet.

Arik agreed to everything.

"Good," I said. "Now, I will put it in writing. If by four o'clock this afternoon, when the Knesset session begins, I get something on official letterhead of the prime minister with the text I prepare, I will agree to be in your government."

Arik asked: "Why do you need a letter?"

I answered him bluntly: "Because I don't trust you."

Sharon looked at me and smiled. "You're tougher than I thought."

I got the letter from Arik by courier before four o'clock that afternoon.

———

The experience of being a government minister was not new to me, of course. The biggest difference between national and municipal leadership, which bothered me deeply, was in the relationship between decisions and execution. The powers of a mayor are much more immediate than those of a minister. I'm a doer. Most ministers give recommendations to career professionals. They make a lot of speeches and declarations, but few real decisions. They don't execute.

My approach was different. I believed in taking responsibility. As a minister, I tried to impose a managerial culture that was unknown in national government at the time and is still unusual today. In my new role, that would include the development of new industries and fulfilling the nation's potential as a high-tech superpower. This occupied my thoughts from my first day in office.

Soon after I took office as minister of industry and trade, I received a call from Elisha Yanai, the CEO of Motorola in Israel and vice president of the global Motorola Corporation at the time. He wanted to meet urgently.

I asked him if he could come to my office that evening. He was surprised. "You mean tonight, as in *tonight*?"

"You said it was urgent. Urgent means today."

Yanai arrived. I asked him to start from the end. He showed me a PowerPoint, the bottom line of which was that Israel's technological power depended on two factors: The number of students completing degrees each year and joining the workforce as engineers, and the government's investment in research and development.

I agreed completely, even without all his impressive statistics. Israel's high-tech sector had started to blossom in the early 1990s, when the government had created the Yozma Fund, launched by Minister of Industry and Trade Moshe Nissim and Yigal Erlich, the ministry's chief scientist. Since then, Israel had developed its venture capital industry, and a huge amount of capital had been invested in high-tech startups to help them get to the stage of product development and prepare them for manufacturing and marketing. As the number of engineers grew, so did the opportunities to start new companies and develop new products.

At 4.9 percent of gross domestic product (GDP), Israel's investment in research and development is the highest in the world. Very few countries even come close.

The chief scientist of the Ministry of Industry and Trade is responsible for budgetary allocations for high-tech companies. He thoroughly investigates every start-up and its potential to turn a brilliant idea into a commercially viable product. The bigger the investment, the greater the risk the state takes on. But when a start-up successfully develops and sells its product, the chief scientist's office takes a percentage, and the company becomes a viable concern on its own.

From the beginning, I made a decision to increase the government's investment in research and development far beyond what it had been before. To achieve this, we launched joint funds together with international conglomerates and foreign governments. The first of these had been the Bird Fund, created together with the United States government more than thirty years ago. We signed similar agreements with state governments in Maryland, California, New York, and Florida, as well as the province of Ontario in Canada and the Australian state of Victoria. We signed with European countries as well as South Korea and Japan. Additional deals were made with IBM, Microsoft, Oracle, Motorola, Cisco, Huawei, and dozens of others.

Making new connections and strengthening the old ones, all around the world, required me to travel often. These were not ordinary business trips. I would take with me as many business leaders, and as few aides from my end, as possible. Hundreds of meetings took place on each trip. On some trips we brought as many as one hundred entrepreneurs, with each of them having up to ten meetings. I played the role of both host and visiting dignitary, showing my face at many of the meetings, making introductions and offering a few words of endorsement, which gave each meeting a sense of state-level importance. To my meetings with heads of state and top cabinet officials, I usually brought along five or six prominent Israeli CEOs to make it clear that we hadn't come just to chat. We flew to Romania, Turkey, South Africa, China, India, South Korea, attended major conferences of the Organization for Economic Cooperation and Development and the World Trade Organization, and much more.

And all of this was just for *one* of my jobs, as minister of industry and trade—in addition to my work on the Broadcasting Authority, the Land Authority, and the security cabinet.

The diplomatic atmosphere was relatively calm during the years I served as deputy prime minister. Sharon himself met with Palestinian President Mahmoud Abbas a number of times, and invited me to come along. I attended, along with other senior ministers, a summit in Aqaba with Abbas, King Abdullah of Jordan, and President George W. Bush. The meeting's importance was underscored by Sharon's closing statement reiterating his commitment to the two-state solution.

This was during Bush's first term. Colin Powell was his secretary of state, and Condoleezza Rice was national security adviser. Bush asked Sharon and Abbas at a certain point to meet him privately. They sat outside on stone benches overlooking the Red Sea. We couldn't hear what they were saying, but it was a stirring image: three leaders sitting comfortably, full of smiles and hand gestures, engaged in a lively conversation. Almost like a family photo.

Nothing about it recalled the hate and hostility of the intifada, but it was clear to everyone that if something didn't change, the calm would not hold for long.

A number of NGOs started putting together peace initiatives in 2003. Most of them tried to set parameters that would enable Israel and the Palestinians to go back to the negotiating table. It was a popular topic: You could go around Europe and North America and, on an almost weekly basis, attend a conference or roundtable about the conflict. It became a cottage industry. Every conference produced a document, revolutionary in the eyes of its authors, and disseminated it to political leaders, public figures and, of course, journalists.

Ami Ayalon, former chief of Shin Bet, launched the The People's Voice together with Sari Nusseibeh. I had met Nusseibeh a few times. He was a kind of Palestinian "prince," the son of Anwar Nusseibeh, a former minister in the Jordanian government and mayor of East Jerusalem prior to the Six Day War. Sari was an impressive intellectual who graduated with honors from Oxford and had a PhD. His English was as good as his Arabic.

Now he was president of Al-Quds University, with campuses in eastern Jerusalem and Ramallah. He was a great conversationalist. I had no doubt that he genuinely wanted peace—but his political influence among the Palestinians was marginal. He wasn't part of any of the groups that made the major decisions. His cooperation with Ayalon was interesting but pointless. Two men, lacking influence, well intentioned, smart people, eager to contribute to the cause of peace—but powerless. Their "People's Voice" didn't bring any practical results but contributed to a growing sentiment in the Middle East in the early 2000s that something good was happening and should happen quickly.

Around the same time, we saw the beginning of what became the Geneva Initiative to bring a solution to the Palestinians issue. This was a much more serious effort, based as it was on experienced political actors, and I have no doubt that it was fueled by a large amount of European money. But like the People's Voice, the Geneva initiative couldn't offer a serious basis for an agreement. Again, its main effect was to get people talking—and in Israel, there was a lot of talk.

Arik was aware of the talk and didn't take it too seriously. But he knew pressure was coming. It concerned him.

He had been through it all—the field of battle, years of political struggles, taking heavy fire, disappointments, rejection and being blackballed—and he defied all expectations and became prime minister. More than anything, he loved the pose that Reuven Adler, his communications adviser, famously crafted for him: Father of the nation. A quiet, level-headed man. The adult in the room, whose mere presence assured us all that everything would be okay. At the age of 75, Arik was not looking for adventures, neither military nor political. The Geneva Initiative was, for him, a sign of trouble.

———

I was restless. I felt like we couldn't keep going this way without taking action of our own. But what steps could we take that would build trust with the Palestinians without bringing down the coalition?

I realized we had to start thinking about getting out of the Gaza Strip, and I began to think of ways to begin expressing this idea in public. For decades, Gaza had been an insufferable burden on Israel: For the sake of a small number of Israeli settlements, we had occupied a densely populated, hostile stretch of land with little strategic or historical importance to us. Unlike the West Bank, it seemed that withdrawing from Gaza unilaterally would be a relatively easy sell to the majority of the Israeli public.

On November 30, 2003, I attended the wedding of a colleague's son in the northern city of Afula. On my way back to Jerusalem, around midnight, my cell phone rang. Dubi Weisglass from Sharon's staff was on the line. The next day there was going to be a national memorial ceremony for David Ben-Gurion at Sdeh Boker, in the northern Negev desert. Arik was supposed to speak, but he had taken ill. He had asked if I could take his place.

I agreed. I asked him how exactly I was supposed to make it to Sdeh Boker by 11:00 a.m. when I was on my way back from Afula after midnight. Weisglass promised to arrange a seat for me in the helicopter taking President Moshe Katzav to the ceremony from Jerusalem. I asked him to fax me, at home, the speech that Arik had prepared. I thought it would be a good idea to stick to his official line.

The draft was waiting for me when I got home at around 2:00 a.m.

It was a surprising speech, with quotes from Ben-Gurion backing up one central message: Israel had to be prepared for wide-ranging concessions. We had neither the need nor the desire to give up on our dreams, which were the basis of our national rebirth, but we would have to find a point of compromise between these dreams and the realities on the ground.

Knowing Arik, I wasn't surprised so much by the direction he was taking as by the sharpness of his words. I decided not to plan my own speech yet, and instead got to bed in order to be as fresh as possible in the morning. This memorial service, I sensed, was an opportunity.

What I usually do before every speech is to mentally spell out a few things I want to say, turn them into sentences, and try to put together a chain of ideas whose internal flow expresses my exact feelings. When I finally sit down to write, the words pour out. I knew exactly what I wanted to say. The memorial ceremony at Sdeh Boker was a significant national event, as appropriate for our nation's founding father. Foreign dignitaries would be there, along with the IDF top brass including the chief of staff, as well as top police officials and the political leadership, with the president at center.

I was called up to the podium. I don't think anyone expected much from my speech. I was standing in for the prime minister. They expected the usual platitudes. I chose a direction and style that were unexpected, however. I quoted Ben-Gurion's words in the Knesset in 1949, in the wake of the cease-fire agreements. "When the question arose of having all the Land of Israel without a Jewish state, or a Jewish state without all the land of Israel—we chose a Jewish state without all the land."

After a pause, I continued. "Two decades later, David Ben-Gurion declared, after he was already a retired statesman, that in exchange for a real peace, Israel would need to give away the great majority of the territory it had conquered in the Six Day War. Since then," I added, "much water has flowed. Facts were set on the ground. Agreements have been signed. The international order has changed beyond recognition. But the bloody conflict with the Palestinians has never ended. It's time to end it."

When I finished speaking, there were rumblings in the audience.

"A disaster!" said Ruvi Rivlin as he rushed over to where I was sitting. "You will cause an earthquake in the Likud. This speech is the beginning of the end." Ruvi and I, again, were never very close. But to his credit, he always told me exactly what he thought.

I understood there would be a reaction. I just had no idea how big it would be.

Shimon Peres, at the time a private citizen, came up to me as well. "An excellent speech," he said. Ehud Barak, also out of office, hugged me and called it "a historic speech."

Back in Jerusalem I started hearing the echoes. News broadcasts summarized my speech. Commentators were thrilled at the new direction, while enraged colleagues in Likud didn't mince words in attacking me. I understood that I'd just put myself in the line of fire.

From one direction, however, there was silence. The line between the Shikmim Farm and Jerusalem went dead. No phone call, no reaction, not from Arik, not from his inner circle, not from his official spokesman. I had no idea what it meant. Did it suggest assent? Or was it the silence of repressed fury? Arik knew how to repress, and nobody had fury like his. But I stayed calm, confident that I had said the right things in the right place and time.

I went back to my office at the Knesset. Bill Burns, the U.S. assistant secretary of state for Near Eastern Affairs, waited for me there, along with U.S. Ambassador Dan Kurtzer. We talked, among other things, about the speech I had just given. I was curious about Kurtzer's reaction, but he was tight-lipped. That was good. For reasons I never understood, Kurtzer wasn't well liked in Israel. He was, of course, an Orthodox Jew who loved the country, but he had come up through the State Department as one of James Baker's people, so he was presumed hostile. Before being posted in Tel Aviv, he had been the U.S. ambassador to Egypt. I liked him. He had no problems criticizing Israel in private. He had a lot to say about Israeli policy on settlements, especially before Sharon became prime minister. But I liked him anyway. The Americans had long hoped something like this would happen, something that would change the dynamics in the region as a whole.

I imagine a lot of diplomatic cables went back and forth between Tel Aviv and Washington that day, mainly asking whether my speech reflected just my own views or a wider policy shift.

With time I came to understand that, without my knowledge and independently of anything I had done, Arik had been exploring the possibility of a similar unilateral move on his own.

Two weeks before that, I later learned, he had met in Rome with Elliott Abrams, the senior director for Near East and North African affairs in Bush's National Security Council, who would later serve as deputy national security adviser in Bush's second term. On the Israeli spectrum, Abrams would be considered far-right. He and I were good friends, but he took issue with my diplomatic approach when I became prime minister. His way of telling me this was to send me regards from his wife, Rachel, who had passed away from cancer. Rachel was just as right-wing as he was, but he was an administration official and she wasn't. So she would "send me regards," and then add that I shouldn't give away the store.

When Sharon met Abrams in Rome, he mentioned the possibility of unilateral action. I only heard about it later from Arik himself, after I'd given the speech. Sharon had already reached the same conclusion I had, and was willing to share it with Washington.

————

It was close to midnight when I finally got home.

Aliza was asleep. She left me a note saying Nachum Barnea had asked me to call him at any hour. Nachum was the most senior journalist in the country. We'd attended Hebrew University together, and as the editor of the student paper, I had known him as curious, sharp, and smart. He blazed his trail to the top of Israeli journalism the hard way, by reporting from the field. He wasn't one of those dilettantes who sits in their room and shares their musings with the public. Barnea wrote about things he saw with his own eyes.

He came to my office the next day, in the late afternoon. I said to him, "Start writing."

I spoke for an hour and a half. I got everything off my chest. I was on fire. I didn't let him get a question in. After I was done, there was nothing left for him to ask. Nachum edited it, artificially inserting his own questions into the text, but there had been no need to ask them.

The interview appeared on Friday, December 5, 2003. The boldface, front-page headline in *Yedioth Aharonot*, at the time Israel's largest-circulation daily, said: "Ehud Olmert: Withdraw from All the Territories." Quotes from the interview were all over the news section, as were responses from across the political map. The full interview appeared in the paper's weekend supplement. Barnea told me they had software that showed references to the article appearing in media across the world in real time. Within an hour, my words were echoing across the globe, in a thousand radio and television broadcasts, newspapers, and websites. In Israel the reactions ranged from total dismissal, as though I were some marginal political figure, to those who assumed I was acting as a surrogate for the prime minister himself.

And still—total silence from Shikmim Farm.

At around two in the afternoon, I finally got a call from Dubi Weisglass. "Amazing," he said. "This is the right path. Keep on going." Then he added: "Arik will call you soon. Don't worry, it'll be a good call."

Half an hour later I was on the phone with Arik's secretary. She said she was connecting me to the prime minister.

———

Ariel Sharon had a special sense of humor. A combination of sarcasm and warmth. He knew how to be cold and cruel, but also warm and human at the same time.

"Peace be unto you, Mr. Deputy Prime Minister!" he began. "First, I have big news for you: I have recovered from my illness! I am completely healthy, and you may now unburden from yourself the heavy mantle of filling in for me. You may now enjoy your weekend."

I laughed and thanked him and waited for the blow to land.

"By the way," he added, "where am I catching you?"

I said I was at home, in Jerusalem.

"Yes, yes, that was exactly my question," he said. "What part of Jerusalem? The part that you've already given to the Palestinians, or the part that's still ours?"

I said I was in the part that's still ours.

Something in his tone told me that I was going to come out of this just fine. "Okay," he said. "Well, that's a relief." He added that the interview with Nachum was very interesting, just as my speech was at Ben-Gurion's grave. I told him that we should get together to talk, and he said of course. We agreed to meet Monday at the Knesset.

Sharon's call came at the perfect time, from his perspective. If he had waited, the delay would have felt more portentous than necessary. On the other hand, if he had called me first thing in the morning, it would have suggested he had been especially agitated. A call in the middle of the day sent the message he wanted to send. The hours that had passed since the article came out and the commentators on the radio gave both Sharon and me time to assess the initial impact my words were having. I felt like he was telling me: True, we didn't coordinate, and you gave me room to distance myself if I wanted to, but overall it was the right direction.

———

"Gilad thinks there's no alternative to unilateral action," Sharon said when we met the following Monday. "It's the only way to get away from this Geneva Initiative." Along with his other son Omri, Gilad Sharon was one of Sharon's closest advisers and confidants. Arik told me about his meeting with Abrams in Rome and how he'd made it clear to the Americans that he was planning a unilateral move. He hadn't fully worked out the scope of it, but that was the direction. He told me that my interview, which spoke of withdrawal from not just the Gaza Strip but almost all the West Bank including parts of Jerusalem, was understood in the White House and the State Department as reflecting his own opinions and was therefore taken very seriously.

From that day forward, things were on a new track, which became a policy that changed forever the Israeli political map, Sharon's life, and my own.

Sharon decided to give Yoel Marcus, the chief political writer for *Haaretz*, the next scoop.

On February 2, just over a month after my interview with Barnea, Sharon invited Marcus to Shikmim Farm. On his way back from the farm, Marcus dictated to the people at *Haaretz* that Arik had told him he was planning a unilateral withdrawal from the entire Gaza Strip, including the dismantling of 21 settlements there, as well as a few in the West Bank. By the time the Likud members of Knesset held their weekly meeting that day, the news was out.

It landed like a cluster bomb on the political landscape. I hadn't known about it ahead of time, but again I wasn't surprised. It was clear to me that sooner or later he would take that step. The exchanges we'd had were unambiguous. Now we had gone past the published opinions of a deputy prime minister to explicit words coming from the prime minister himself. There was no turning back.

———

In the last two years of his life, Sharon was a different man.

He tired easily. He lost a lot of his vitality, and sometimes had a hard time staying awake and sharp in meetings. It was impossible to miss. He may have understood that his end was near. Maybe his solitude in the wake of his wife Lily's passing in 2000, before he had had a chance to fulfill his lifelong dream of serving the country as prime minister, weighed on him.

Years later, President Bush asked me what kind of man Sharon was. I was surprised by the question. It was widely believed that he and Sharon were close.

Bush said that in truth, he never knew what Sharon really wanted, what his vision was, what he expected to happen—except of course for the disengagement from Gaza, which Bush supported and saw as a courageous move.

I told him that I didn't know what Sharon's complete vision was either, and I doubted Sharon himself knew. He had to put all his remaining energy into getting through the tumult of that period, and perhaps he didn't want to or couldn't look beyond that horizon.

Sharon's biggest contribution to the withdrawal from Gaza was the actual decision, the uncompromising stubbornness with which he defended the plan and refused to back down, with the exception of one specific, incredible moment, which to this day I do not fully understand.

———

The decision to dismantle settlements had a financial side to it. We needed a formal vote of the government in order to allocate the budget for the withdrawal. Sharon had already given his plan the name that would go down in history: Disengagement.

He called me on a Thursday. I was up north, on my way back from a tour of a few factories. He sounded troubled, and said he had decided to change the proposal he was bringing to the government for approval. There wouldn't be a full withdrawal from all the settlements in Gaza. He said he was thinking of just dismantling four of them.

I was taken aback. I asked if he thought he would have a majority for the decision. He said he thought that he would.

I told him I wasn't so sure. I, for one, would vote against it.

He asked me why. I said that I was against playing games. Dismantling just four settlements would mean paying the price without reaping the diplomatic benefits. What good would it do us?

I asked him not to make any decision until we had a chance to meet. We agreed that I'd come to the farm the next morning.

I rarely ever went to the farm. I arrived at 11:00 a.m. sharp. Arik came down to welcome me, and we sat in the reception room. His sons Gilad and Omri joined us.

Arik said he'd had enough. He had no patience for the "pathetic extortionists" who were trying to pressure him. He was especially annoyed by a harsh exchange he had just had with Danny Naveh, the minister of health and an acolyte of Netanyahu.

Naveh opposed the entire plan. He battled with Arik and said explicitly—according to Sharon—that he would formally oppose it if it came to a vote in government on Sunday. After a long argument, Danny had added: "Tell Dubi to call me, together with my lawyer, and we'll work out the details of a new proposal."

"This *nobody*," Sharon concluded, "this total *zero*, sends *me* to talk to his lawyer? I've had it. I can't do this anymore."

I was surprised. Not by Naveh's behavior—he was always arrogant. I was surprised at how fragile Sharon seemed. It seemed that the endless battles against him inside the Likud, which had gotten worse since he had begun promoting disengagement, the insults, the constant needling from Netanyahu, his unstable health, the signs of which we couldn't fully see but which had weighed heavily on him, the various criminal investigations and the publication of suspicions against him, the interrogations of his sons—all of these had brought him close to the breaking point.

I said it would be a tragic mistake to capitulate on disengagement, and with his own two hands he would bring down the government and ruin his reputation. "If Danny Naveh can make you buckle," I said, "tomorrow you'll show up to a Likud Knesset faction meeting and somebody will say out loud, 'Who's the fat guy?'"

Arik was miffed by my words, but I was undeterred. "You can fold, sure," I went on, "but then why bother dismantling four settlements? Give up on the whole plan and explain that you came to the conclusion that you didn't have the necessary support. But if you're going to stick with it, go all the way. You're Arik Sharon. There's nobody like you. You have never caved—and now, of all times, when you're prime minister—now you cave?"

"Ehud's right, dad." Gilad weighed in.

Arik picked up the phone and asked that he be connected with the government secretary, Israel Maimon. "Cancel the offer I made yesterday," he said. "We're going back to the original plan. Whoever's with me is with me, whoever's against me is against me."

Later he asked me to join him at the hay barn. On Fridays, he would gather his friends and family there for barbecue. I ate a delicious steak, fresh off the grill, and took my leave.

I was worried about Sharon's health. He was recovering from one illness and now had shown himself to be weak. I didn't know whether he had in him what was necessary to regroup, fully engage his fighting spirit, and take this fight to the end.

―――――

Before the final vote in the government on disengagement, in August 2005, Netanyahu announced his resignation. The eventual split between Likud and what would become the Kadima Party was now just a matter of time.

A few months earlier, in February 2005, when the Knesset was about to vote on the budgetary aspects of disengagement, a few other ministers, including Danny Naveh, Israel Katz, Limor Livnat, Silvan Shalom, and Netanyahu, all threatened to oppose it. The rest of us sat with Sharon at his Knesset office, and someone came in and said that Bibi and a few other ministers wanted to meet with the prime minister. Sharon understood it was a trap, and said that he had to get back to the plenum. He got up, walked to the main chamber of the Knesset, and took his seat at the government's table.

The TV cameras caught the other ministers, supporters and opponents alike, running around the hallway outside, trying to figure out what to do. Sharon sat in his seat, upright and motionless. It was a brilliant pose. This image, which was shown on every news broadcast, became a symbol of his determination in the face of all opponents. They were running around the halls, and Sharon sat alone, unmoved and un-moving.

Then the vote started. It was a roll-call vote. The ministers who had threatened to vote against it entered, one by one, with their tails be-tween their legs, and voted in favor. When the Knesset recorder called out the name of Benjamin Netanyahu, even he said "Aye." Arik whis-pered to me, "I told you he would sweat. I know him."

That was back in February. Now, in advance of the final government approval of the plan, Netanyahu quit as finance minister. Just him, alone. His rebellious friends kept their cushy chairs.

That evening, at one minute to 9:00 p.m., I got a call from Asi Shariv, Arik's spokesman. "Turn on your television," he said.

The *Mabat* news hour opened with a report that the prime minister had appointed me as finance minister instead of Bibi, in addition to my other duties. Sharon hadn't said anything to me. The only hint had been a call I'd gotten from Reuven Adler, Sharon's communications person, right after the cabinet meeting. He told me that I should be finance minister and that he'd speak to Arik about it.

I called Sharon. He said that, for once, the media were telling the truth.

————

I took office as finance minister on August 8, 2005, just before the disen-gagement plan was carried out.

The country was in turmoil, with the public divided between a loud, "orange" minority that opposed Disengagement and a "blue" major-ity that understood the necessity of getting out of Gaza. (The color of the anti-disengagement movement was borrowed from the Ukrainian Orange Revolution that had taken place just a few months before.) And the government was busy planning the withdrawal from the settle-ments and relocation of thousands of settlers who lived there, pulling the IDF out of the strip and preparing for whatever happened next.

We were not worried about soldiers or police disobeying orders or undermining government or military authority. But we expected resis-tance, possibly even violence, from many of the residents, along with thousands of supporters who had gone to Gaza to help them, including not a few troublemakers and provocateurs.

On the ground, at the moment of truth, the army and police operated "with determination and sensitivity," as IDF Chief of Staff Dan Halutz put it. There was violent resistance, but nobody lost their lives. All the settlements of Gush Katif were evacuated, as well as four others in northern Samaria. The houses were demolished. The synagogues, which we left standing due to pressure from the Orthodox, were ransacked and destroyed by Palestinians immediately after we pulled out.

———

During that summer, Condoleezza Rice reached out to me and asked to speak in person in Washington. She wanted to know what the next step would be.

When I told Arik I was going, he suggested we meet beforehand. I arrived at his office in the Knesset around midday, after Sharon had just finished a meeting of the Knesset Foreign and Defense Committee. He looked pale and exhausted.

"What happened?" I asked. "You look awful."

Dubi Weisglass said that Arik had been the target of nasty attacks from the extreme right, which would never forgive him for disengagement. The most hurtful was Effi Eitam—the former IDF brigadier general and leader of the pro-settlement National Religious Party—who had shouted at him, "You're a gangster! A criminal! A thief!"

Sharon had expected to get some backing from the chairman of the committee, Yuval Steinitz, but he didn't. He was too exhausted and distracted himself to answer back. But the experience was apparently upsetting to Arik. It's incredible to think of all the things this man had gone through in life—wars, political clashes, the personal tragedy of losing a son, both his wives, and brothers-in-arms on the battlefield—and then, at the age of 77, to sit as prime minister in a Knesset committee and be attacked in this way.

I said a few things to try and calm him. I'm not sure it helped.

Sharon asked what I planned on saying to Rice.

I told him I wanted to tell her that disengagement was, in my mind, just a first step, and that I wanted to push for a much wider withdrawal in the West Bank. It should start with negotiations, but if the Palestinians wouldn't be willing to work toward a final-status agreement, we would pull out unilaterally again. I wouldn't offer her specifics on the scope of the withdrawal, but it should be clear that this would create a more convenient security reality for us and bring an end to unfair accusations of occupying land that wasn't ours. We would be freed from having to rule over another people.

Sharon didn't like the idea. He asked me to dial it down.

I answered that I would be speaking entirely on my own behalf, and I would also emphasize this fact in Washington.

Arik didn't have the energy to fight with me on it.

I met Rice in late August. Washington felt like it was on fire. Like other American cities, Washington knew how to freeze over in winter, but in summer it became a hot swamp. I prefer Israeli winters, and also Israeli summers. But there's a calm to Washington that lifts my spirits.

Rice was open to my ideas. She agreed with the overall direction, but we didn't go into details. I assumed there would be time in the future. I never imagined that less than five months later, I would be prime minister, and that the things I had said privately to Condi Rice would be understood by the Bush administration as official Israeli policy.

———

The withdrawal from Gaza, the issues of resettlement and compensation for the evacuated settlers, the split within Likud over disengagement, and the resulting formation of the Kadima Party—these took up most of my time until the end of 2005.

In November, Amir Peretz narrowly defeated Shimon Peres for leadership of the Labor Party. Peretz pulled Labor out of the unity government Sharon and Peres had created in order to get disengagement passed, and new elections were now called for March 28, 2006. With elections on the way, the split over disengagement between Sharon's faction in Likud and Netanyahu's camp would now lead to a formal rupture of Likud. On November 21, Arik formally announced he was leaving Likud and launching Kadima ("Onward"). Naturally, I was with him. Within days, Peres would leave Labor and join Kadima as well.

Peres's decision to leave Labor, along with a few others, to join Kadima was shocking to many. Kadima was made up mainly of former

Likud members, so leaving Likud did not feel any different to me from previous political adjustments within the national camp, such as when, decades earlier, Herut had joined with other parties to form Likud. The national camp had its parties that came and went and evolved, as it still does. Peres, on the other hand, was in a different situation. Even though he denied it, the departure of Peres from Labor felt like the end of an era. Few realized at the time that this was the beginning of the end for the movement that had led the founding of the country. Labor would never again compete for rule of Israel as a leading party. (In the 2021 election, it received just seven seats.)

In the middle of December, Arik was rushed to Hadassah Hospital with what turned out to be a minor stroke. I had been on my way north to the Kiryat Eliezer Stadium in Haifa to attend a soccer match between Beitar Jerusalem and Maccabi Haifa when I received the call. I told the driver to turn the car around and head back to Jerusalem. On the way I asked Arik's people whether there was any point in my going to the hospital. They told me, correctly, that such a visit might be seen as inappropriate. I went home instead.

Sharon was released two days later and looked good.

A few days after that, it was reported that the doctors felt he should undergo a thorough examination of the arteries leading to the brain to make sure there wasn't any clotting that might trigger a fatal stroke later on.

Speculation about his health swirled. Articles suddenly started appearing about who would replace him if he were incapacitated. Other articles reported a conflict brewing between me and Justice Minister Tzipi Livni about which of us would get the number-two spot in Kadima—but in light of Sharon's health, it felt more like a discussion of succession.

Sharon's team did not like these reports. For my part, I didn't speak with anyone about them. It would have been foolish to do so.

A few days later, Sharon summoned Tzipi and me to the prime minister's residence. Our meeting was delayed, and we took a few minutes together in a side room. There was a computer there, and I took a look at the YNet news site, where the lead headline claimed that Arik had reprimanded the two of us for our bickering. Apparently Sharon had decided to get ahead of the story by leaking a reprimand that hadn't actually happened.

When we walked into Sharon's office, I laughed. "Okay," I said. "I see that you've already reprimanded us. Let's move on." Sharon said whatever he said, and then added that he was planning on heading back to the farm.

"Why not stay in Jerusalem?" I asked. "You're not feeling well. Stay here a few days, close to the doctors and the hospital."

"I don't like sleeping in this house," he said.

I told him he was being irresponsible. He was adamant about going to the farm.

What I learned from the nonreprimand story was that Sharon wasn't actually worried about me and Livni. I knew he saw me as number two and had no intention of promoting her at my expense. He had his doubts about whether she was ready. She, of course, was certain that the opposite was true. If there were to be a race for the job of prime minister, she wouldn't hesitate to run against me or anyone else.

This can wait, I thought. I had no idea how little time there really was.

———

Ariel Sharon was scheduled for another round of tests at Hadassah Hospital on January 5, 2006. Two days before that, on January 3, Channel 2's evening news had opened with a dramatic announcement. An Austrian citizen visiting Israel had been arrested on suspicion of bribing the prime minister to the tune of $1.5 million. It was like a bomb had gone off, at the most inconvenient possible time for Sharon.

The next day, January 4, a ceremony was held at the Prime Minister's Office marking the sale of the state-owned shares of Bank Leumi to Cerebrus Capital in New York. As finance minister this was my event. It was agreed in advance that a representative of the buyers would speak, as would someone from Bank Leumi, the chairman of the Bank of Israel, and the finance minister. We all said the usual things for such an event. Sharon spoke last. But he didn't read from prepared remarks as he usually did. Instead, he spoke as if he were talking to himself. Among other things, he said that he had never imagined the job of prime minister to be so appealing or important, but when he now saw how many people were standing in line for it, he realized he must have been mistaken.

Was he talking about me? No other candidate for the job was in the room. When the ceremony was done, I had planned on rushing to my office, where the Japanese ambassador was waiting to meet me. Instead I was flagged own by Marit Danon, the prime minister's secretary. "Arik wants you to step into his office," she said.

In the room sat Sharon together with his personal assistant, Lior. He was working on putting together the Kadima list for the next election. He wanted to hear my thoughts about a number of people he was considering. He said that the following day, he would be handing over the powers of the prime minister to me for a few hours, since he would be under full anesthesia for a medical procedure.

Although he was being jovial, I could see a sadness as well. Maybe it was connected to the headline about the alleged bribe. I told him I intended to take advantage of the few hours of prime ministerial power and replace all of his advisers. He said that was fine with him, as long as I didn't replace Marit. I promised. She was still standing in the room, and she blushed.

———

I never saw Arik again.

That evening, I attended a ceremony at the president's residence, and from there I rushed to the Israel Museum, where I took part in the hundredth anniversary celebration of the Bezalel Art Academy. I then went home, picked up Aliza and headed over to dinner at Darna, to meet our good friends, the philanthropists Charles and Andrea Bronfman, along with Michael and Judy Steinhardt and a few of the other founders of Birthright Israel, which has brought hundreds of thousands of young diaspora Jews on free ten-day trips to Israel. The next day I was to be the guest of honor at the Birthright "Mega Event" at the convention center, instead of Sharon. At dinner we were supposed to go over the achievements of this incredible Zionist project in advance of my speech.

At around 9:30 p.m., a security guard standing in the corner signaled me. I walked over to him, and he whispered that I had an urgent call, and that I should take it outside. I stepped out. On the line was Israel Maimon, the government secretary. He said that Arik had had another stroke, apparently more serious this time. He was on his way to Hadassah Hospital.

Maimon suggested that I go home and wait for developments. I walked back inside and told my friends that they were about to hear reports that Arik was on his way to the intensive care unit with a stroke. "I think," I said, "I'd better go home." I apologized and expressed hope that I'd still attend the Mega Event. My driver rushed me home. I turned on the television and followed, like the rest of the country, the nonstop coverage.

At 11:10 p.m., the phone rang. On the line was Maimon, along with Attorney General Meni Mazuz. Maimon gave us a quick update on Arik's condition—he was at Hadassah and being put under—and then got to the point.

"What's clear," he said, "is that right now we need to undertake an act of transfer of power, and this is backed up by the medical opinion of the service's doctor, his personal doctor, and also the doctors at the hospital. What I suggest is that we hand over powers without a time limit, until the treatment is completed. After we get off the phone, we'll update the ministers of the government." An announcement from the Prime Minister's Office would follow our call.

Mazuz and I agreed, and that was that. A three-minute phone call. I told them I'd be reachable at home.

From that moment, my life changed forever. The powers of the prime minister had been transferred to me, "without a time limit."

At around midnight, there was a loud banging on the front door.

I went downstairs to answer. The first to enter was L., and after him another six Shin Bet officers. "Sir, we are the prime minister's security detail," L. said. "From this moment on, we are your detail. We have closed off the street to vehicular traffic. The press is gathering, and we've backed them off a few dozen yards. Do you need anything?"

I smiled. L. had detailed me many times in the past, and I had known and worked with both him and his staff for years. I told them everything was fine. I had no intention of going anywhere that night. They said they'd be outside.

Later that night, I heard hammering outside. I didn't know what it was, but assumed Shin Bet was on top of it. I didn't let the noise bother me. I watched the news.

I called a staff meeting for 6:30 a.m. and told everyone to prepare for a packed day. I asked Arik's staff to attend as well. At around 4:00 a.m., I went to bed. I remember hearing Aliza say, "Udi, what have we gotten ourselves into?" but I don't remember answering. I passed out.

At 6:00 a.m., I got up, shaved quickly, and managed to down a cup of coffee.

Aliza kissed me and said, "I don't know what you're going to do, but I wish you success."

Outside, I saw that the hammering during the night had given birth to a new roof covering the driveway outside my home. The prime minister's motorcade was there with engines running. I got into one of the cars. The motorcade charged ahead, and this was a strange thing: No traffic lights. No red lights or green lights, just flashing blue lights on the roof of the car, sirens cutting through the silence of the sleepy neighborhood of Rechavia, and within five minutes I was in my office at the Ministry of Industry and Trade, where I planned on working that day.

Thus began my first day as prime minister of Israel. It was Thursday, January 5, 2006.

SEVEN

Prime Minister of the State of Israel

In all of Israel's history, the powers of the prime minister have never been transferred so suddenly. When Levi Eshkol died in 1969, his powers briefly went to Yigal Allon, but Eshkol had been ailing and his death was expected, and Allon was soon replaced by Golda Meir. When Yitzhak Rabin was assassinated in 1995, Shimon Peres was named acting prime minister, but it wasn't automatic and required a government vote the night of the murder. When Menachem Begin resigned in 1983, he had already tapped Yitzhak Shamir to succeed him. In all these cases, there was a natural successor, backed by a political party that was prepared to accept his leadership.

In my case, the party was in the process of being created, my role as successor to Sharon was not a political given, and a date for elections had already been set. But in the meantime there was a country to run, and I hadn't received a proper handoff.

This was all running through my mind the evening I was thrust into the nation's highest office. I spent the night doing what every other Israeli was doing: Watching the news. In the hours that passed, I spoke frequently with Shlomo Mor-Yosef, the medical director at Hadassah, who updated me on Arik's condition.

I couldn't ignore the possibility of a state funeral. I recalled that Arik had asked to be buried next to Lily, on a floral hill overlooking Shikmim Farm. Later that night, I discussed this with Maimon and quietly gave my first directive as prime minister: To prepare for that possibility. In the months that followed, it became clear that Arik was, in fact, made of special material. Mor-Yosef said he had never seen a man stronger than Sharon. He spent eight years in a coma before he finally succumbed.

———

Dawn broke as the motorcade rushed me to the Prime Minister's Office, where the staff would be waiting. It was almost 6:30 a.m.

Israel Maimon and I had agreed to set a meeting of the full cabinet for 9:00 a.m. It would be brief. The ministers would be updated on Arik's condition and there would be a formal announcement of the transfer of his powers to me.

There was no time to waste. Alongside a constant flow of diplomatic and security issues that needed to be addressed on a minute-to-minute basis, and alongside the personal shock of Sharon's sudden collapse, there was also an election set for March 28, a date picked when the Knesset dissolved the previous November. If Arik wasn't coming back, I would need to take a series of steps in the coming hours and days to build a consensus around my leadership of Kadima.

Despite the early hour, Sharon's staff showed up in full force, with Dubi Weisglass being the most senior among them. The team, he said, would help with anything I needed. I told everyone that this was an extremely difficult moment for all of us—first of all for Sharon's family, but also for everyone present and for myself. We would all have to show restraint and patience—especially with regard to public statements.

As we were about to get up to leave, Asi Shariv, Arik's media adviser, raised his hand. "I would like to ask you a personal question, and I hope you take it the right way," he said.

"Please go ahead," I said.

"Do you plan on sitting in Arik's chair during the cabinet meeting?"

I was neither surprised nor insulted. This transition would be extremely sensitive. The idea that I would sit in Arik's chair, just hours after his collapse, never occurred to me. I understood the question, and the heart-wrenching pain that was behind it. I wanted to send everyone on Arik's team a message, and the moment seemed right.

"As you all know," I said, "it is accepted practice that in all ministerial committee meetings, the chair of the committee sits in the prime minister's chair. I am the only one who has never done it. The first time I chaired a committee, the committee secretary motioned me over to the empty chair. I told him: 'That chair belongs only to Arik. I'm comfortable where I am.' If that's what I have done up till now, there's no reason for me to do anything different, especially today."

I could see the relief on their faces.

———

After the meeting, Major General Gadi Shamni asked to see me one-on-one.

The role of military secretary to the prime minister is unique. He is privy to the most classified state secrets and reviews intelligence materials of a breadth and variety that no one other than the prime minister gets to see. Not even the defense minister. I quickly grew to respect Shamni and put my full faith in him.

"There is an urgent operation," he said, "that we absolutely have to approve today." I told him I would free up later in the day. He warned me that I would need to dedicate a lot more time to security matters than I might be aware.

At that moment, I was also finance minister and minister of industry and trade. But as acting prime minister I would also, within a few days, take over the portfolios of the Foreign, Health, Agriculture, and Education Ministries—which were all about to be vacated with the resignations of Silvan Shalom, Danny Naveh, Israel Katz, and Limor Livnat, who all followed in Netanyahu's wake.

I had to be careful. The entire country would be watching the cabinet meeting. Any incorrect gesture, unnecessary word, or improper smile would leave an impression that could never be erased.

I called my own staff into my office at Industry and Trade. I asked them to continue with their day as usual, and that none of them would join me for the cabinet meeting. "I will be walking on eggshells," I said, "and I don't want even the tiniest hint that could be interpreted as creating new facts on the ground. I don't plan on setting foot in the prime minister's own office. I'll go straight up to the conference room, and at the end of the meeting, about five minutes later, I'll come straight back here. Wait for me and watch the broadcast. We'll continue working from here for the foreseeable future."

It was almost 9:00.

I put on my jacket, folded the piece of paper on which I'd scribbled a few sentences I planned on saying in the meeting, and got up to leave. The motorcade took only a few minutes to get me to the Prime Minister's Office.

The building was silent. Nobody wanted to stand out. I entered the office of the government secretary and asked to get Mor-Yosef on the line. I wanted to be as up-to-date as possible about Arik's condition before the meeting started.

Arik, he said, had just come out of surgery and was unconscious. "We do not expect him to regain consciousness in the coming hours or days," he said. "Perhaps not at all. The medical picture is quite grave."

I wouldn't be the bearer of good tidings. I asked Marit, Arik's personal assistant, to join me. She was crestfallen. I recalled our joking around with Arik just the day before. We embraced. She broke down in tears. I tried to console her, and told her I would not set foot in Arik's office.

Later, somebody told me that Marit had been livid, back in 1995, when, the day after Rabin's assassination, she came into the Prime Minister's Office and found Shimon Peres sitting at Rabin's desk. "Rabin isn't even buried," she said at the time, "and this guy has already taken his seat."

———

The conference room was crowded yet hushed. I walked in and took my regular seat. Even the journalists, normally a noisy bunch, approached the table in silence.

I began the meeting. I told the assembled ministers that the night before, just after 11:00 p.m., the prime minister's doctors determined that he was unable to fulfill his duties, and accordingly, the government secretary and the attorney general informed me that the powers of the prime minister had been transferred to me.

I paused for a few seconds. Then I mentioned that I had just spoken with the medical chief at Hadassah, who told me that the operation on the prime minister's brain had been completed, the prime minister was still under anesthesia, and there was no way of assessing his condition at this stage. I shared my hope that he would recover, thanked the medical staff who treated him through the night, and added that our hearts and minds were with Omri and Gilad and the entire family.

The government was divided. Netanyahu had left, and four more ministers were about to join him. But suddenly their resignations had to be put on hold. A couple of them raised their hands and said they would do everything to help in the coming days. It was a respectful, and helpful, gesture.

I adjourned the meeting, thanked everyone present, and left. A group of journalists followed me. It was clear I wouldn't say another word. The motorcade bolted back to the Ministry of Industry and Trade. When I got to my office there, about half an hour after I'd left it, a metal detector had already been set up at the entrance. The lobby was filled with people. My office was noisy as well. I told everyone to calm things down and to clear out anyone who didn't need to be there.

———

I couldn't get my final days with Arik out of my mind.

We had almost never embraced. Arik knew how to be warm, but generally refrained from physical contact. I'm not like that. The last time we met, I spontaneously hugged him before we parted ways. Now, sitting alone in my office, holding back the deluge for just a few more minutes, I reflected on the man who lay unconscious at Hadassah. Could he know what was happening to him?

I felt horrible for him. His final days had been sad ones. What a shame for these to be the final chords in a magnificent symphony of a life.

But the drama that swirled around me didn't allow for too much reflection. In addition to the immediate questions of government, I also held the keys to Kadima's parliamentary list for the coming election, and I was flooded with meeting requests.

Meir Sheetrit, the minister of transportation, was the first to show up on my first day in office. He told me he had no intention of running against me for the top spot in Kadima, and that he wanted to be finance minister. I told him it was too early to hand out ministries. He later claimed, falsely, that I had promised it to him.

Tzipi Livni was next. This meeting was tense—it was just two weeks after the much-reported fight between us that never happened, triggering a reprimand from Arik that also never happened. Unlike Sheetrit, she really did want my job, though she knew it was, for the time being, out of reach. She said she wanted the Foreign Ministry, which Silvan Shalom was about to vacate, as well as the number-two spot on the list. I didn't promise her anything either, but didn't rule it out, and promised not to fill the post without speaking to her first.

Avi Dichter, the former chief of Shin Bet, kept calling the office, demanding a meeting. I finally returned his call, and he told me a phone call wasn't good enough, he had to meet in person, so that he could advise me on strategy and put himself by my side from that moment on. I had no idea what he could teach me at this stage, but eventually I agreed to a brief meeting. I quickly discovered that Avi, who had only recently joined Kadima, just wanted to make sure his position in the party was secure. I reassured him. Later on, I would ask myself more than once whether it had been such a good idea to appoint him internal security minister. He had been an excellent Shin Bet chief, but as a minister and member of Knesset he revealed himself to be surprisingly unstable, shallow, and impatient. He once told me that he divided his life into ten-year segments. Now he was starting his ten in politics, which would end with his becoming prime minister. He was surprised to discover that nobody else felt that way.

The final meeting of my first day in office was with Defense Minister Shaul Mofaz. He opened with a recollection of promises he claimed Arik had made to him, that he would continue as defense minister after the elections as well. I decided to be polite, but reminded him that in the current circumstance, I had no way of independently verifying what Arik may have promised him.

This was not entirely true. Arik and I had in fact discussed Mofaz. Arik was angry about how Mofaz had announced he was leaving Likud for Kadima and then changed his mind—"because you don't leave your home." A few weeks later, when he realized how poor his prospects were in the Likud primaries, he suddenly discovered that sometimes you do leave your home, and switched back to Kadima. Arik told me explicitly that he hadn't promised Mofaz a damned thing after the elections.

After my one-on-one with Mofaz, Shamni joined us for a security briefing. They said a few words about an operation that would require my approval. Then a few other senior security officials came in to talk it through. The operation was complicated and sensitive, including significant risks, and the decision was on me. I had heard about such operations in the past, and in some cases even knew how they turned out, but I had never been asked to approve one.

I listened carefully to each of them, asked for clarifications, made a few brief comments and then summarized the meeting. With time, they would learn that I really did not like long meetings. They would get used to my opening each discussion with, "Start from the end."

I told them to prepare the next meeting for the purpose of getting my final green light.

My first day in office was exhausting. Aliza waited for me at home. As we had for many years, we sat together in the kitchen. She made coffee and we talked. "Do you really understand what is about to happen to us?" she asked. "Do you really want this so badly?"

The question was rhetorical. We hadn't had time to prepare for the change. It just happened. She knew I had no intention of turning it down. She was just sharing her feelings. I knew they came from a place of love, of concern for my health, and also for herself and our children. Before I turned off the bedroom light, she said, "This is the first time I've ever gone to bed with a prime minister."

I fell asleep before I could even laugh.

———

Shimon Peres came to see me the next day. It was bizarre. Peres was of a different generation. He, who had held almost every possible office and who had decided to come on board after Sharon announced the creation of Kadima, came to offer his experience but also to make sure his understandings with Sharon would be honored. I wondered whether it crossed his mind that the roles should have been reversed: That he, the veteran, the elder, should be the candidate for prime minister, and I should be the one looking for a job.

Meanwhile I started to get calls from diplomats and world leaders. The first was from Secretary of State Condoleezza Rice. Then came calls from the Egyptian President Hosni Mubarak and King Abdullah II of Jordan. I knew all three personally and we could skip the formalities. We all agreed on regular conversations and that we would meet in person soon. Then Vladimir Putin, the Russian leader, called, as did his foreign minister and a string of leaders from Europe, Australia, Canada, and others.

The most important call was from President George W. Bush. "Isn't it strange, the paths that our lives can take?" he said. "When you and I first met, I was the governor of just one of fifty states, and you were a mayor. Now I'm president and you're prime minister."

He asked me about Arik's condition, and wondered out loud if he would survive. "If God forbid he passes away," he promised, "I'll come for the funeral."

In almost every meeting I had with him subsequently—and there were probably a dozen of them—Bush asked after Arik's condition. Once he even wondered whether it was appropriate to leave him in his current state, without any significant signs of life. I answered that Arik's sons were convinced he would one day return to us.

"If that's what they believe," he said, "I fully understand them."

It never happened, but that was what his children wanted.

I went back home for another round of phone calls. Dinner was just Aliza and me.

———

One of the names that came up often in context of the Kadima list was Ehud Barak.

He called me and asked to meet. I had no reason to refuse. We set to meet at my house on January 23, close to the date I'd have to finalize the Kadima list. It was really quite late in the game. Uncharacteristically, I was the one who showed up late. Barak was waiting in my dining room. He started talking and didn't stop until the meeting ended. I managed to get a sentence in at the very end. I'm not sure he heard it.

The essence of his pitch was that I needed to understand just how complicated the role of prime minister was, and how many risks were involved. "You will be in many situations where you'll want people with you like me and Dan Meridor," he said. Barak's proposal was to include him on the Kadima list. To ease any concerns I might have had that he wanted to challenge my leadership, he offered to sign a letter and leave it with his attorney, Eli Zohar, saying that he committed not to run against me or compete with me, and to be unwavering in his loyalty.

I said I'd think about it, and we would surely speak again in the coming days. After he left, I kept thinking about the conversation we had just had—more of a monologue, really. I had once had great respect for Barak. He impressed me with his eloquence, the breadth of his knowledge, and the vast experience he brought with him into politics. When Netanyahu claimed, during the 1999 election campaign, that "Barak will divide Jerusalem," I defended him. I was caught on tape singing his praises at a reception in his honor at City Hall. But he proved to be a terrible prime minister, possibly the worst in our nation's history.

After he left my house, I wondered when Barak had become an obsessive talker. It had never occurred to me that he might compete with me for the party's leadership. If anything, I was more worried that having him on the list would be an electoral liability. All the campaign's internal polling showed that he was the least popular politician in the country.

But he was relentless. A week later he showed up at my home again, and the whole thing repeated itself—another monologue that threatened to last into the night. And the more he spoke, the more my doubts dissipated. I ended up informing him, by phone, that there was no way to move forward. He refused to accept it. "It doesn't matter where I am on the list," he said, "it can be the twentieth spot."

I lost whatever was left of my patience. "Sorry," I said. "It's just not happening."

Then he sent Eli Zohar to speak with me. I told him the same thing. I couldn't put Barak on the list, and I wasn't sorry about it. After the election in March, and after the Second Lebanon War in July and August, he kept calling me and taking every opportunity, every chance encounter, to get me to put him on the list.

Barak, of course, later denied the whole thing.

———

I didn't just want former Likud people on the Kadima list. So I included two esteemed academic figures, Uriel Reichman, the founder and president of the Interdisciplinary Center in Herzliya, and Menachem Ben-Sasson, who would later be president of the Hebrew University in Jerusalem, as well as several other cultural and intellectual figures.

The Kadima list in 2006 was an all-star team of the most talented, experienced, and serious people who ever ran for office. And it was obvious that a list like this could come together only when just one person was putting it together, or at most two or three, who didn't have to worry about primary elections. A list like this can't be the outcome of backroom deals and vote-bundling. I knew it was a winning list.

On January 5, my first day in office as prime minister, a poll was conducted by the veteran pollster Mina Tzemach. With me as head of the Kadima list, we would get 38 seats. In the previous poll, with Sharon leading the list, Kadima had 40. Not much difference. This was encouraging, but I knew it was foolish to rely too much on polls, especially in the tumult surrounding Sharon's incapacitation.

During the campaign, Sharon's media advisers told me I should do a major TV interview—and that I should keep my answers short, and stay strong and silent like Sharon. These were the same people who had gotten him elected, campaign veterans. I was inclined to follow their advice.

Nissim Mishal is a legend of Israeli television. He was the obvious choice to do the interview. Channel 2, prime time, my first interview as prime minister and as a prime ministerial candidate. We prepped the interview, and I delivered quiet, short answers. The broadcast was widely viewed.

The first reaction I got was from Aliza. "Did something happened to you?" she asked.

"No," I said. "Why?"

"You acted like you were trying to be someone else," she said.

I watched the recording over and over, and then I understood. Reuven Adler had pushed me to act like Arik Sharon. But Sharon and I were very different people. For Sharon the pose made a lot of sense: Father, maybe even grandfather, of our country. His massive physical presence left a strong impression. He could allow himself to say little, to be reticent. I was a new candidate. Unknown. I understood this had been a mistake, and that I would have to be myself from then on—so that the public would get to know me as the present candidate and not feel nostalgic about the one who couldn't run. I would have to be assertive. Confident. Ready for battle. I decided to change course.

There was no need to try and sell me as a skinny Ariel Sharon. The campaign would have to figure out how to sell Ehud Olmert.

In the end, I think I did okay. I had certainly expected more than the 29 seats we got, but the reasons we didn't had nothing to do with my personality or the way Adler ran the campaign. Three days before the election, Kadima shed 4 or 5 seats after a poll showed the Pensioners Party led by Rafi Eitan getting past the threshold. They ended up with 7 seats. They threw a wrench into everyone's predictions and significantly cut away from our total.

There was another reason we won only 29 seats. During the campaign I took a few major steps that flew in the face of everything the advisers were telling me. Adler, Eyal Arad, Lior Horev, and the pollster Kalman Gayer—they all were furious. Despite this, I told them that I intended to grant a series of interviews and say exactly what I planned on doing on the Palestinian issue if elected. These veteran politicos were in shock: "Who on earth says what they plan on doing before the election? You only say the things the customers will buy. What's the rush?"

Before the 2003 elections, Sharon had come out against withdrawal from Gaza, and many of his voters felt swindled when he later announced disengagement. I didn't want to fall into the same trap. I would rather lose votes than be accused of stealing them.

My first major action in this area, even before the election, involved the evacuation of Amona.

Amona was a West Bank settler outpost, established in violation of Israeli law. It was built on privately owned Palestinian land north of Ramallah. Numerous court orders were issued obligating the settlers to leave. But they didn't. Even the Supreme Court ruled repeatedly that the evacuation of Amona could not be further delayed. The land had to be returned to its owner.

In late January 2006, I pulled together the relevant team, including the defense minister, IDF chief of staff, the chief of police, the attorney general, and representatives of the state attorney's office, Shin Bet, and the West Bank civil administration. The attorney general told us we could get another delay in the evacuation if we told the court that a month and a half before elections was the wrong time for such a move.

But I don't believe in putting off decisions. What looks difficult, impossible, harmful today can easily become much worse a few months down the road.

I wanted it done.

My advisers thought I had gone off the rails. They patiently explained that evacuating a settlement outpost just before elections would only sharpen divisions with Netanyahu and Likud, and might blur the line between Kadima and Labor. But that was exactly what I was trying to do. To go off the "rails" that the experts had laid for me, to blaze my own trail instead.

Under my watch, judicial rulings would be honored. Settlers would not act like they owned the country.

The night before the evacuation I held a conference call with all the relevant officials. There was no disagreement, because my reasoning was simple: The High Court had ruled, and we would obey, without any games whatsoever. My approach to the rule of law would not change in the future. This didn't help me later on, of course, when the State Attorney's office turned me into a target. But we'll get to that.

"Gentlemen, evacuate Amona," I said. "Demolish it. Uphold the law. Show restraint, do not use excessive force, but carry out the mission." The next morning, on February 1, it was done. There was violence. Thousands of extremists barricaded themselves in the outpost, throwing rocks, eggs, and paint at the officers. In the end, 86 police officers and 140 civilians were injured. But the evacuation took place.

————

The other message I delivered on the eve of elections was that if elected, I would take unilateral steps to complete our divorce from the Palestinians. I granted interviews to all the media, laying bare my diplomatic vision. I called it "Convergence" (*hitkansut*).

The plan was to open negotiations with the Palestinians with the aim of reaching a final and full peace agreement. If we succeeded, great. If not, we would unilaterally withdraw from the great majority of the West Bank, including parts of municipal Jerusalem. We would establish a permanent border for our country.

These were unprecedented statements I was making—not just for a prime ministerial candidate, but for pretty much any Israeli politician. I knew I was taking a risk. I could lose a lot of votes from people who wanted a more moderate government but didn't like the vision I was offering. I understood this, but had made up my mind to lay the foundations for a brave new diplomatic course. I didn't want anyone to claim after the elections that they didn't know where I had planned on taking the country.

I granted an interview for *Haaretz* with Aluf Benn. He was the paper's senior diplomatic correspondent and later became its editor-in-chief. He ended the interview by asking me, "What do you want the country to look like when you finish your term in office?" I answered without hesitating: "One that's fun to live in."

I still feel that way.

————

If I was going to launch a peace initiative, I felt I needed the Labor Party in my government. Amir Peretz had led his party to 19 seats. Rafi Eitan, leader of the Pensioners Party, told me he would be happy to join my coalition. Kadima together with Labor and the Pensioners made 55 seats. We needed just one more party to get to 61.

Netanyahu knew where I would lead the country and had no intention of bringing the Likud in. He probably didn't have the power to do it even if he wanted to. The National Religious Party (NRP) and the National Union, which joined forces to garner 17 seats together, were locked into the camp of the right together with the Avigdor Liberman's Yisrael Beiteinu. Shas had 11 seats and was a natural partner, but I would first have to talk to Labor, the second-largest party.

The final vote tally was certified on Friday, March 31. I intended to launch coalition talks the following Sunday and complete them as quickly as possible. At the same time, there were discussions among and within parties about whom to recommend to the president to give the mandate to form a government. I was hopeful that as leader of the party with the most seats, I would be given the mandate automatically.

In the afternoon Haim Ramon called. Together with Shimon Peres and Dalia Itzik, Haim had decided to leave the Labor Party and join Kadima. He told me, with some urgency, that Amir Peretz had checked in with a few other parties, including Shas and NRP, and that Peretz was looking to put together a government without Kadima. Ramon added that even as we were speaking, Peretz was on his way to close a deal with Yaakov Litzman of United Torah Judaism that would ensure the support of six MKs from the ultra-Orthodox party. He urged me to reach out to Litzman and bring him in. "Give him one or two ministries, whatever he wants, just cut him off from Amir," Haim said. "Otherwise we're lost."

I told him he was being delusional. "Amir Peretz has no chance in hell of forming a coalition," I said. Ramon cut me off and said that Liberman had also closed with Peretz. I laughed.

I really do like Haim Ramon. I told him that I had already made plans for the evening, a dinner at the home of a good friend celebrating his fiftieth birthday. "There will be a lot of rumors going around," I said. "If I lose my cool now, what kind of image will that project? There may come a day when I have to make crucial decisions on Iran. Who will feel they can rely on me then, if a single rumor caused me to prostrate myself before another party?"

On my way home after dinner, almost at midnight, the phone in my car rang. Uri Shani was on the line. "Amir Peretz," he said, "called me up and said you need to meet him urgently, tonight." I wondered what could possibly be that urgent. Shani said Peretz wanted me to close a deal with him before I spoke to other parties. Peretz was worried I was going to set up a government without Labor.

I met with Peretz late that night. He said that I was obviously the one setting up a government, and he wanted to be a partner. We talked about different possibilities and agreed to continue the conversation the following day. I ended up naming Peretz defense minister.

The political positions I had expressed before the elections, the evacuation of Amona, the Convergence plan that stood at the center of Kadima's platform, and the coalition agreement—none of these could have been the basis for any coalition with the parties of the right.

I needed one more party, and would have to choose between two ultra-Orthodox parties—United Torah Judaism and Shas. I knew that Shas would be a more comfortable partner. To them it was urgent to get back into government, and their leader, Eli Yishai, had his eyes on the Ministry of Industry and Trade. His demands were in line with what was normal for negotiations with an ultra-Orthodox party. And I had worked together well with their representatives in the Jerusalem City Council, which made things easier.

This partnership ended up proving itself. During the negotiations with the Palestinians, Yishai warned that Shas would have to pull out of the coalition if the subject of Jerusalem were even discussed. But he didn't follow through on his threat. I personally told him about the talks, and that I was talking to Abbas about Jerusalem, but he didn't know what kind of generous offers I was making, and the understanding was that they really would pull out if we reached a deal that included concessions on Jerusalem. But he didn't get in the way of the negotiations themselves.

And so, on Thursday, May 4, 2006, five weeks after the election, the 31st government of Israel was presented to the Knesset for approval. Sixty-seven voted to approve. That day I announced the appointment of Dalia Itzik as speaker of the Knesset, the first woman ever to fill that role.

———

Immediately after the election, as is customary, I was invited to Washington to meet with the president of the United States. The trip was scheduled for the third week in May 2006. Only this time, I was also invited to speak before a joint session of Congress.

This is an honor that few world leaders enjoy, but I was not the first Israeli prime minister to do so. Netanyahu had given such an address in 1996, and would again later in 2015.

Nothing emphasizes our special status in the United States, or the bipartisan support we enjoy, like a speech of an Israeli prime minister before Congress. Presidents come and go, but Congress is forever, and our relations with both Democrats and Republicans on Capitol Hill are the key to the stability of the alliance. Such a speech is broadcast live across America, in Israel, and around the world. It's also accompanied by meetings with key members of both the Senate and the House. I asked the veteran D.C. pollster and political consultant Frank Luntz to help me prepare the speech. In my life I never prepared as intensively for any speech as for that one.

Such trips include countless receptions and private meetings that become part of the folklore of the Prime Minister's Office. There are always disagreements over who gets to stay at Blair House and who at a hotel. And above all, over who gets to attend the first meeting with the president. The Americans said that they'd have six people there, including Bush. We couldn't flood the office with our whole entourage.

The most important thing, I felt, was to build relationships that were warm and founded on trust.

I wanted Bush to understand what I wanted to achieve in my term, and that above all that he could put his trust in me as a reliable ally. But there was also a diplomatic goal to this trip. From the moment I announced the Convergence plan, on the eve of the election, it had been subject to endless interpretation. The Americans had supported disengagement from Gaza and helped Sharon carry it out, but they would have been happier if there had been a negotiation with the Palestinian Authority and we had pulled out from Gaza in a coordinated fashion.

When I started talking about Convergence, I emphasized that I intended to first negotiate with the Palestinian Authority. If no agreement could be reached, we would withdraw to a new border, which would be our final border with the Palestinians in any future peace deal. The idea of unilaterally setting a permanent border without a negotiated settlement was unsettling for many. The fear was that another end run around Abbas would signal to the Palestinians that the PA was irrelevant. The Americans wanted to better understand my practical intentions, both in the short and long terms. We agreed that we'd spend time on this issue during the trip.

Now, in the White House, Bush and I shook hands. Then he gave me a hug.

"Where's Mrs. Olmert?"

I told him that this was a working meeting, and Aliza thought it more appropriate to stay at Blair House. Bush said he'd decided to change up the schedule, and that he wanted to talk to both of us. "Can you bring her over?"

She was there ten minutes later. Bush invited us up to the living quarters. He took us out onto the Truman Balcony, which overlooks the South Lawn and has a direct view of the Washington Monument. We sat and smoked cigars and chatted.

As is often the case, the conversation began a little hesitantly but quickly warmed up. We talked about everything under the sun. We sat there for three hours, far beyond what was planned. During the third hour, his aides came out every few minutes to remind him of the journalists waiting outside. "Let them wait," he said. "I'm enjoying the conversation."

There was one unusual moment. We talked about Iran, and I told him the Iranian nuclear threat was the most vexing issue for Israelis. "Who knows," I added, "if for exactly this purpose God has appointed you to be president." When I said that, he jumped.

"I'm amazed," he said. "A few hours ago, Elie Wiesel sat exactly where you are sitting and said the exact same thing. Elie is a prophet. There's nobody like him. He said that the obligation to stop Iran before they get a nuclear weapon is a 'divine mission.' Do you understand what it means when Elie Wiesel says words like that?"

I told him that Elie was a friend and that I shared Bush's reverence for him. He promised that he would do whatever was necessary to work with us to stop Iran, but immediately added that he didn't think it would require direct military confrontation. "There are many ways to handle Iran," he said. "Together with a few friends, we'll do what we have to."

———

A speech before a joint session of Congress follows certain protocols. The speaker waits in a side room. A group of senators and representatives from both parties comes over to welcome him and then escorts him into the House chamber. The first to greet me was Senator Hillary Clinton, followed by others including Senator John McCain, who would run for president two years later against Barack Obama.

Hillary and I knew each other from when Bill Clinton was president, and she greeted me warmly. When we entered the chamber, they seated Aliza in the VIP gallery together with Elie Wiesel and his wife, Marion. They had come to Washington from New York just for this. Elie, who passed away in 2016, was in my eyes the most important Jew in the world. Presidents and kings opened their hearts and doors to him.

My speech presented a call for peace between Israelis and Palestinians, and it was received warmly. But speeches of this kind need to be especially awful in order to not get a warm reception. The invitation itself is an expression of appreciation for the speaker and his country. So I wasn't surprised that I received multiple standing ovations, the most of any foreign leader at the time except British Prime Minister Tony Blair. But what surprised me was the reactions beyond the expected protocol, especially from Israelis who had seen it on television.

More than anything else, it was important to emphasize our policy of peace and my intention to lead the way. From the first moment, I wanted to create momentum for peace, and to get the Palestinian Authority and the Arab world to wake up. The speech got the message across. The rest would be up to me.

I did what I had come to do. I also laid the foundations for a good working relationship with Bush and key members of his team, especially Vice President Dick Cheney, Secretary of State Rice, and White House Chief of Staff Joshua Bolten.

———

I came home to a difficult reality.

The situation in the south was fluid. Hamas was incessantly provoking us with rocket fire and infiltration attempts. To the north there was ongoing tension as well. Every week or two, Hezbollah also tested us with rocket fire in one sector or another along the border.

During the six months that passed between January 5 and July 12, 2006, I held six lengthy security briefings on the subject of Lebanon. No subject troubled me more, or took up more of my time. We weighed options and risks. We tried to assess Hezbollah's military capability. We talked about the destructive potential of the Katyusha rockets and other missiles in Hezbollah leader Hassan Nasrallah's possession. I was shown different war plans that the IDF had prepared as a potential response to a range of possible threats. They all had grandiose names: "Shield of the Country," "Waters from on High," "Ice Breaker." All of them proposed, in different variations, landing a heavy blow as the first step, with different possibilities for a ground assault.

The discussions included the leaders of all the military divisions: The IDF chief of staff, the chief of Military Intelligence, the commander of the Air Force, the chief of operations, the chief of human resources, the northern commander, and all the rest of the senior officers who took part in preparing a campaign on the northern front—as well as the chiefs of the Mossad and Shin Bet. The briefings were all led, for the first two months, by Defense Minister Mofaz. The assumption was that before long, Hezbollah might try a repeat of the attempted kidnapping of soldiers at Har Dov in 2000, in which three of our soldiers were killed. In order to retrieve their bodies, along with a living civilian, Elhanan Tannenbaum, the government decided to release 400 prisoners as well as the bodies of dead Hezbollah fighters, including that of the son of Nasrallah.

Since then, the government had been replaced, and I was a freshman prime minister, certainly new to the subject of clashes in Lebanon, and it was clear to everyone that Nasrallah would want to test me. Immediately upon my taking office, they started launching minor provocations, mainly in the western sector of the Lebanon border, and they had a regular pattern: Hezbollah would open fire with light arms and position heavier weapons close to the border. We would respond with artillery fire. They would shoot back, and within an hour or two things would quiet down.

The question was how to respond if Hezbollah upped the ante by setting an ambush and killing or capturing soldiers. All the participants in the discussions, without exception, agreed that a nonresponse would be a recipe for strategic catastrophe. The question, therefore, was how broad a response should be.

But before we were forced to answer that question with the events of July 12, we were confronted with another serious crisis to the south.

———

Early in the morning, on June 25, 2006, an Israeli Merkava tank was idling in place while securing the Gaza border near the kibbutz of Kerem Shalom. Suddenly, Hamas terrorists emerged from a tunnel just past the border, launched a rocket-propelled grenade (RPG), and hit the Merkava tank in a vulnerable spot. Two members of the tank crew— Lieutenant Hanan Barak and Staff Sergeant Pavel Slotzker—jumped out and charged the attackers. They were both killed. The terrorists threw a grenade into the tank and started to head back to the tunnel in Gaza. A third soldier, Corporal Roi Amitai, sustained a head injury in the driver's seat of the tank and was knocked unconscious. (He has since recovered.) A fourth, Corporal Gilad Shalit, was sitting in the gunner's position and was lightly injured. His loaded rifle was by his side. He also had access to the tank's machine gun. He had the opportunity to look through the window and open fire on the terrorists. Instead, he jumped out of the tank, unarmed, and surrendered. They hadn't planned on taking prisoners. But they were more than happy to receive the gift. They crossed the fence with Gilad and ran into the Gaza Strip. Thus began a saga that lasted five years and four months, and came to a humiliating end from Israel's perspective.

From the day he was taken prisoner until the publication of this book, I have kept silent about the affair. What I have to say is not pleasant, but it's the truth.

The abduction of a soldier was one of the worst scenarios we had planned for. As opposed to other countries, Israel's experience had taught us that we were willing to pay an extremely high price to free an abducted soldier. Not just high, but one that kept going up every time it happened. These prisoner exchange deals strike a dagger in the heart of Israeli society.

It was absolutely clear that Gilad Shalit had not acted according to what was expected from an IDF combat soldier.

The circumstances are no longer classified. Everything he said when he was debriefed upon his return has been revealed. Every combat soldier goes through extensive training to prepare him for contact with the enemy. The IDF does not train soldiers to surrender, but rather to fight—and to give up their lives if necessary. That's what Hanan Barak and Pavel Slotzker did. They died as heroes.

I do not mean even to hint that Gilad should have suffered the same fate. But to fight, to pick up his weapon, and open fire at the retreating terrorists—this he should have done.

What was going through his mind in those crucial minutes, I cannot fathom.

———

I knew I would have to pay a completely unreasonable price for the release of Gilad Shalit.

Many in the security establishment believed, as I did, that Hamas saw him as a high-value asset and would keep him alive and healthy. We had good reason to believe that they would guard him carefully in order to extract as high a price as possible. This proved accurate. Shalit, by his own testimony, was not tortured. He spent more than five years in the same exact place. They were careful with him.

I did, however, want to get him home. I told Yuval Diskin, chief of Shin Bet, that if we could rescue him through a military operation, that would be a seminal moment in the war on terror, and would send our enemies a powerful signal that there's no place we can't reach.

Yuval understood this without my help. But he failed to locate Gilad, and he would come to see this as his only major failure during his tenure. We could guess, based on a complex and intensive intelligence operation, that he was being held in the southern part of the Gaza Strip, but nothing precise or reliable enough to base an operation on.

Gilad's family, meanwhile, launched a public campaign to pressure the government to make extreme concessions. I completely understood their desire to bring their son home at any price. Who wouldn't do the same for their son? But that's exactly why family members should not influence government decisions. A government has other factors to consider. Foreign leaders kept asking me why on earth we were strengthening Hamas's hand by pressuring foreign governments to mediate Gilad's release. They reminded me how Israel was the one who always lectured the world about never negotiating with terrorists.

I had some very difficult conversations with the Shalit family. Aviva, his mother, kept mostly quiet, her face sullen, her eyes damp. Noam, the father, did most of the talking. I could never tell if he understood he was speaking with the prime minister, who bore the responsibility for the lives of all our soldiers, or if he was sunk so deep in his personal horror that he couldn't hear anything I was saying.

I never raised my voice or told him off, but there were moments I really wanted to. Something about the metallic coldness of his words put a distance between us. I knew what responsibilities I carried, what I could say to him, and what I had to keep to myself.

Captivity, no matter the conditions, is a horrible experience not just for the soldier but no less for the family. I wish they could have been spared it. In the end he came home, in exchange for an intolerable price. Gilad Shalit is neither a hero nor an example—not as a fighter, not in his courage or self-sacrifice, not even in basic soldiering.

I'm glad he's home, but I'm not glad that the Netanyahu government that succeeded mine gave in to extortion. The great champion of never negotiating with terrorists ended up freeing more than a thousand prisoners, including the most horrible of murderers, and sacrificed the national interest in order to win votes.

———

We were in the thick of a campaign of punishment against Hamas in early June 2006, but my mind was on the north.

I was worried Hezbollah would try to replicate Hamas's success. I kept asking Defense Minister Amir Peretz to make sure we were still on high alert along the Lebanon border. I called the IDF chief of staff myself. His answer was reassuring. The IDF, he said, was locked and loaded for a war in the north.

I kept telling myself that if things heated up with Hezbollah, under no circumstances would I be dragged into a major ground invasion in

Lebanon. What was possible in 1982—and even then it cost us nearly 700 fatalities—was impossible in 2006. We were stuck in the Lebanese quagmire for eighteen years, until Ehud Barak correctly pulled our troops out in 2000. True, I had my doubts at the time about the way we had pulled out, like a thief in the night—but the decision itself was the right one.

———

I met with the Shalit family on the morning of July 12, 2006. Just two and a half weeks after Gilad's abduction, and this was, I think, my first meeting with them. Immediately after the visit I was scheduled to go directly to the Prime Minister's Office for a reception for the prime minister of Japan, Junichiro Koizumi. When Gadi Shamni, the military secretary, suddenly showed up as I was getting ready to leave, I assumed he had come to prepare me for the reception. Instead, he walked up, apologized, and handed me a note.

It read: "An IDF half-track was ambushed by Hezbollah next to Zarit. Two soldiers killed or possibly taken captive."

I looked at the note. The room was quiet. I handed it to Noam Shalit. He read it and didn't react.

It was clear that my entire schedule, and that of the government as a whole, had just been upended.

———

"Just say the word, and we will send Lebanon back to the Stone Age," IDF Chief of Staff Dan Halutz said to me the next morning.

I figured it was just military tough talk. That he really meant to say that our response would be such that the enemy would not quickly recover. But I didn't like the way he said it, and was concerned it would be misinterpreted. I told him that for now I wouldn't allow any widening of the range of artillery fire. That evening we would have another briefing and decide what to do, where, and with how much force.

It was clear that we were moving to a war footing, and it needed to be handled carefully. I directed my staff to ready the office at the IDF headquarters in Tel Aviv, and I'd start working from there, to be closer to the General Staff, the Defense Ministry, and other security forces. I told Aliza not to wait up.

Calls started coming in from around the world. The first one was from Condoleezza Rice. She wanted to know how we would respond. I told her, simply, that I wasn't planning on launching a war against Lebanon as a whole, but that I did hold the Lebanese government, led by Fouad Siniora, responsible. At the same time, I understood that this war was being launched by Hezbollah, not the Lebanese army, and they would be our primary target of operations.

Rice was satisfied. I knew the Americans liked Siniora, a Christian. When he was first elected, he toured Europe and the United States and left the impression of a moderate, someone they could work with. For all I know, he was exactly that—but he was also easily pressured, and it was clear that the one pulling the strings now was Hezbollah's leader, Hassan Nasrallah.

I had meant what I said to Rice: I had no desire to launch a war on Lebanon as a whole. About half the country's five million citizens were Christians. They were caught between the Syrians and Hezbollah, they weren't involved in terrorism, and they had no desire for war with Israel. Punishing the entire country would be, I felt, a mistake. We would hit Hezbollah with everything we had. We would place responsibility on the shoulders of Siniora and the Lebanese government, because they were in fact responsible, but we would keep open the possibility of dialogue.

My staff relocated to the Tel Aviv office. The military secretary was being updated on an ongoing basis. My diplomatic adviser, Shalom Turjeman, and chief of staff, Yoram Turbowicz, were in constant contact with their counterparts in the United States, the United Kingdom, France, and Germany. I sat in my office getting ready for the military briefing that I'd called for later in the day, and for the cabinet meeting that would follow it at 8:00 p.m.

In the meantime, I consulted with the chiefs of the Mossad and Shin Bet. Together we updated the situational assessment and sharpened the key points that would be raised in the briefing. The overall direction was agreed upon in advance.

Israel's biggest military operation in more than two decades, which would come to be known as the Second Lebanon War, was now under way.

EIGHT

The Truth about
the Second Lebanon War

It has been widely claimed that our decision to go to war on the night of July 12, 2006, was an angry overreaction to the second abduction of IDF soldiers in three weeks.

Nothing could be further from the truth. We spent months discussing our security situation along the Lebanese border, the endless threat of light arms and rocket fire, the interminable pressure on residents of border towns. We discussed a range of scenarios. The one that most concerned us, for which we planned most intensively, was the one that in fact happened: A Hezbollah ambush that would lead to the death or abduction of soldiers. Such an attack, we all agreed, would require a massive response.

Time is both dear and fluid at moments like these. All the brainstorming and critiquing and raising of alternatives—the "known knowns" and "known unknowns," as U.S. Secretary of Defense Donald Rumsfeld once put it—all of this discussion needs to happen, and many decisions made, in advance. If you don't respond immediately to so flagrant an attack, you lose the upper hand and encourage even more aggression. There are things you can do today that you can't do a week from now. A quick response takes advantage of international outrage and sympathy.

And indeed, the sympathy on July 12 was wall-to-wall. Even Arab states condemned Hezbollah's Nasrallah. But such a consensus can be fragile and short-lived.

I called a meeting in my office in Tel Aviv that afternoon to decide on our immediate response. Joining the meeting were Defense Minister Amir Peretz, IDF Chief of Staff Dan Halutz, Chief of the IDF Planning Directorate Ido Nehushtan, Chief of Operations Gadi Eizenkot, Chief of Military Intelligence Amos Yadlin, the chiefs of the Mossad and Shin Bet Meir Dagan and Yuval Diskin, and a number of aides and advisers. The head of the National Security Council, Ilan Mizrahi, took part in every discussion along the way. And of course my own top aides, Yoram Turbowicz and Shalom Turjeman, as well as the military secretary Gadi Shamni, were there.

Halutz recommended, in the name of the IDF, a plan to destroy the civilian infrastructure of Lebanon. I don't know whether the other generals supported it. It was a slightly less brutal reformulation of his earlier offer to blast Lebanon "back to the Stone Age." Lebanon was the responsible sovereign government, the argument went, and we shouldn't let it off the hook for what happened from within its borders.

I made it clear that I would not allow the destruction of Lebanese civilian infrastructure, and that no such proposal would even come to a vote. Even if we destroyed it all, we wouldn't get rid of Hezbollah. At the same time, it's fair to assume the international community's sympathy would evaporate, followed by an imposed cease-fire, a UN condemnation, and an international investigation into the killing of noncombatants. Nasrallah would continue to command the border, a few dozen yards from our towns. Thousands of Israeli citizens would continue to live within range of light arms fire, and the impossible reality that prevailed before the war would continue indefinitely.

Yadlin, the chief of military intelligence, offered instead a list of targets in southern Lebanon. It included hundreds of rocket launchers and missiles that were hidden in identified private homes. The list had been assembled through painstaking intelligence work over many years.

The main difficulty was the crowded airspace: we would need to plan every warplane's approach and escape route, and precisely orchestrate each second of the attack, to hit the most targets in the shortest possible time.

What I approved during this first meeting was the bombing of dozens of rocket launchers, the Al-Manar TV station in Beirut, and the command centers of Hezbollah, as well as the runways at the international airport in Beirut. We also imposed a naval blockade of Lebanon. The army asked for permission to hit a power station. I said no.

We also talked about the expected retaliation from Hezbollah and the exposure of our civilian population to potentially massive rocket fire. It was agreed that after the briefing, the full cabinet would meet. My plan was to inform the government of the creation of a smaller "Forum of Seven" for making decisions—including myself, Defense Minister Amir Peretz, Foreign Minister Tzipi Livni, Deputy Prime Minister Shimon Peres, Minister of Transportation Shaul Mofaz, who had previously been both defense minister and IDF chief of staff, as well as the former Shin Bet chief Avi Dichter and Eli Yishai, the head of the Shas Party.

The full cabinet met at 8:00 p.m. The atmosphere was tense. I asked Yadlin to give a full report on the ambush and abductions. After him the IDF chief of staff spoke, and then the heads of the Mossad and Shin Bet. I wanted every member of the government to get a detailed briefing on what happened, on what the status was in the theater of operations, on the balance of forces among the different factions in Lebanon, on the capabilities of Hezbollah and the extent of its dependence on the support of Syria and Iran, and on what was likely to happen as a result of our response.

It was clear to me that this meeting would enter into the annals of history, that every word of every minister would one day be picked apart and analyzed by future researchers—what they knew, what they didn't know, what was kept from them, if anything, what exactly the prime minister wanted, which ministers opposed action, and what their reasons were. I didn't want the ministers to have missed a single detail that they should have known about, or to claim later that they didn't have the full picture.

———

The cabinet was in a belligerent mood. Without exception, every minister supported a military assault against Hezbollah. I told them to prepare for a campaign that could last weeks. I emphasized that Hezbollah's missiles could reach Haifa and even further south, and hundreds of thousands of Israelis would head to bomb shelters.

This would require urgently preparing the home front, starting with a thorough inspection of shelters, including the installation of televisions, air conditioners, and chemical toilets in every public shelter in the north. Hospitals across the north, too, would have to go on full alert.

At a certain point Haim Ramon passed me a note. "You're scaring the ministers," he wrote. Ramon was especially aggressive, saying we should respond with full force. Peres spoke as well, saying that whatever our attack plans were, we needed to be thinking about the second phase of the campaign as well. Tzipi Livni, who was fully supportive of a massive assault, said there was no chance on earth of rescuing the abducted soldiers through military means. Everyone agreed.

I was asked more than once why we demanded the return of the soldiers and why we later dropped that demand during negotiations for the cease-fire. There were even those who went as far as saying that the entire campaign, which was eventually called the Second Lebanon War, had failed because we hadn't brought them home. That's nonsense. We knew we wouldn't be able to take back the POWs through a military operation, but it was right to demand it anyway. There are things that have to be said even if there's no chance of achieving them. We also wanted the issue to be high on the international agenda. If we had issued an official government statement that didn't include demanding their return, it would be tantamount to giving up on them. (Two years later, we would close a deal for the return of their remains. Both soldiers had, it turned out, been killed during the initial ambush.)

During the meeting, Livni asked how we should define victory. If she hadn't, I would have raised it myself. It was important to set realistic expectations. I didn't want anyone to come out of the meeting thinking that by dropping a few bombs we'd bring Hezbollah to its knees.

Halutz said this explicitly. "There will be no knock-out," he said.

The best we could expect was a long battle that would eventually lead the UN Security Council to intervene, hopefully on terms that would change the equation in southern Lebanon.

At the end of the meeting, the government issued a unanimous decision that emphasized Israel's right to retaliate against the attack on its soldiers and citizens and repeated the demand to release the abducted soldiers. The precise military response would be decided by the Forum of Seven.

———

"What is the likely outcome of targeting rocket launchers hidden in residential homes?" asked Meni Mazuz, the attorney general, whom we invited to the next meeting, which combined the Forum of Seven with the heads of the military and intelligence branches. We were worried about civilian casualties. Nobody wanted them, but these weren't ordinary civilians: They had agreed to put launchers and missiles in their homes. Were they legitimate military targets under international law? This was obviously not just a legal question, but I wanted the attorney general to know we were asking it, and to put his opinion into the record.

A discussion ensued. How many casualties were we talking about? Hundreds, thousands, fewer? Did the answer depend on whether the missiles were about to be fired at Israeli cities and towns? It was crucial to us not only to limit civilian casualties in reality, but also to limit our exposure to claims of violations of international law—and to do so while achieving our objectives, restoring safety to our own civilians in the north, and while fighting an enemy that had no qualms about using its own civilians as human shields.

We approved the assault, as well as the attack on runways at the international airport in Beirut.

———

The Air Force executed astonishingly well.

Within thirty-four minutes, our warplanes, operating in an extremely crowded airspace, destroyed dozens of surface-to-surface missiles and launchers, enforced a no-fly zone and a naval blockade, and devastated the Al-Manar TV station (which quickly resumed broadcasting from a different location).

Hezbollah was, naturally, infuriated. On Thursday, rockets fell across the north. Hundreds of thousands of residents were in shelters. We continued the aerial bombardment. Together with IDF Chief of Staff Halutz, the Forum of Seven decided we needed to start driving the population of southern Lebanon northward. Our aim was clear: To completely confound the lives of hundreds of thousands of south Lebanese, getting them to start moving toward the middle of the country, in order both to put pressure on Hezbollah and also to make it easier to attack what was known as the "nature reserves"—the underground network of military posts and tunnels operated by Hezbollah throughout southern Lebanon. They were well fortified and used for hiding rocket launchers as well as the Russian-made Kornet anti-tank missiles that were especially effective against our armored personnel carriers and Merkava tanks.

———

I wasn't thoroughly familiar with the IDF when the war launched, about six months after I had originally taken office as acting prime minister.

A day before the war began, I met with the IDF General Staff in Tel Aviv together with the defense minister. The chief of staff ran the meeting, and I asked the generals to speak freely. I couldn't stand the thought of having meetings where participants only said what they thought I wanted to hear. I always wanted to hear the truth, and you can only get that if everyone can speak their mind.

Some of the generals complained of a lack of resources, insufficient exercises, and a lack of battle-readiness among the fighting units. Others said the opposite. Everyone of course wanted more budgets. What general doesn't? When did an IDF chief of staff ever say that the IDF has too many warplanes or tanks? So the complaints about resources sounded all too familiar, and I confess I wasn't especially impressed by them. I was very impressed, however, by the words of Major General Yishai Beer, who at the time was president of the Military Court of Appeals, the IDF's highest court. He said the IDF was a "hollow shell" of an army due to its lack of supplies and preparedness.

The deputy chief of staff, Moshe Kaplinsky, took the opposite tone.

He said the army was ready for any mission, even though there was an urgent need for exercises and to replenish supplies.

The bottom line was that there was clearly a need to do a thorough review of the IDF, and to do it urgently. People who came later and claimed that they had sounded the alarm about problems affecting IDF readiness—these were not people who actually made decisions. What exactly was I supposed to do on July 12, just after hearing all this? Tell Nasrallah that he had attacked us at the wrong time? That we'd circle back in a few months when we were ready? We needed to retaliate immediately with the tools at our disposal at that moment, in a calculated and determined fashion.

———

On Friday, July 14, two days after the abductions, the Forum of Seven convened to talk about further escalating the military response.

The IDF chief of staff, Halutz, requested an assault on a complicated target in Beirut, in the security quarter run by Hezbollah, known as Dahiya, where the homes and offices of senior members of Hezbollah were located. Halutz assessed that destroying specific buildings would bring about the collapse of their communications system and severely hamper Hezbollah's command-and-control across the country. "We should assume," he added, "that we will take out actual senior Hezbollah commanders."

A discussion followed. The Air Force commander, Major General Eliezer Shkedi, was the first to speak, explaining the details of the operation and expressing complete confidence in the ability of the Israeli Air Force (IAF) to execute. Meir Dagan, chief of the Mossad, concurred that Dahiya was the nerve center of Hezbollah and should be targeted. The neighborhood had already been emptied of most of its residents and no one was allowed in other than Hezbollah members. Hitting it would deal a major psychological blow to the terror group, he said.

The IDF's chief of operations, Gadi Eisenkot, emphasized that Hezbollah would respond with fury, including launching missiles deep into Israel. Halutz said Hezbollah had no strategic asset more valuable than Dahiya. In his view, such an operation would make the whole war a lot shorter.

Tzipi Livni and Avi Dichter were worried about civilian casualties. Tzipi added that the Americans and Europeans were asking us to avoid escalation, and an attack on Dahiya might be seen as disproportionate. The chief of Military Intelligence, Yadlin, responded that if Al Qaeda leader Osama bin Laden were hiding there in a bunker, the Americans would be dropping ten-ton rather than one-ton bombs. Mofaz said that Hezbollah was for us what Al Qaeda was for the United States, and Nasrallah was bin Laden. So there should be no problem carrying out an operation aimed at taking out its top leadership. Eli Yishai agreed with Mofaz. Only a "disproportionate" response, he said, would change the equation.

In the end, four of us—Mofaz, Peretz, Yishai, and myself—voted in favor of the operation. Two—Livni and Dichter—opposed. Peres wasn't there, and I updated him by phone, and he submitted his vote in favor.

———

Later that same day I sat next to Shkedi, the Air Force commander, in the IDF high command's underground war room in Tel Aviv, known as "the Pit." On a TV screen that ran the length of the entire long wall of a very large room, we could see the operation unfold in real time. At a certain point Shkedi said to me, "Soon I'm going to say to the pilots, 'Go,' and 52 seconds after that, you will see missiles entering each building, to the left and right, via the third-floor windows. The missiles will dive into the buildings and hit the lower floors, where the Hezbollah command centers are located."

Shkedi then said, "Go." I watched the screens. The buildings were right in front of me. A timer ticked away on screen. At exactly 0:52, the missiles entered the buildings through the third-floor windows and detonated.

The buildings collapsed. No civilians were hurt—but the Hezbollah leaders had all managed to escape from Dahiya.

We kept bombing them for days. We flattened buildings and dropped bunker-busters. We didn't get to Nasrallah, who remained hidden elsewhere. But little was left of Dahiya when we were done.

———

To get a better sense of the battlefield, I needed to move closer. I decided to pay a visit to the Northern Command on Saturday, July 15, to understand the military options and capabilities from up close, and to convey my intentions directly to the commanders.

"I want to create," I announced after the generals had finished their survey of the war, "a strip about two or three kilometers [one to two miles] deep along the entire length of the border, that is completely free of Hezbollah positions."

Hezbollah's comparative advantage was its ability to ambush us along the border, to lay improvised explosive devices (IEDs), and to run diversionary moves against our forces. Ours was in the power of our fire and the precision of our weapons. "We need to create a new reality on the ground," I told them. "We're not going back to the First Lebanon War, we're not launching an all-out invasion, but rather something very careful, built on our superior firepower and ability to neutralize the main Hezbollah bases along the border."

Major General Udi Adam, the impressive Northern Commander who hosted my visit, said that his forces were prepared for this kind of operation, and to an extent had already started. I directed him to keep going.

Why did we fail to decisively achieve this aim? Why couldn't we, despite our massive advantages, break their forward line?

The central story of the failures of the Second Lebanon War concerns the functioning of the commanders who sent in the troops. The question isn't what the government wanted or what strategy was approved by the cabinet. The political level's decisions were unambiguous: To stay near the border and push back the threat by one or two miles. Everything else was executed well through a long string of successful bombing campaigns, both from air and land. The failures were in specific battles in limited locations, very close to the border. Dozens of soldiers were killed in these battles, and that altered the image of the war as a whole.

———

On Sunday, July 16, I met with Tzipi Livni. Turbowicz and Turjeman were in the room. It was right after the weekly cabinet meeting. Livni came alone. We talked about the emerging picture of the war.

At the end of the meeting, Livni asked to speak one-on-one. I asked Turbowicz and Turjeman to step outside. They later recalled that the meeting lasted two or three minutes, that we were standing the whole time, and that I immediately told them what had been said. Livni told me she was wrong to have voted against the Friday attack on Dahiya. She said she had no intention of running opposition to my proposals, and if I had updated her in advance of the meeting, she would have voted in favor.

I told her that I don't hold grudges and I accepted her explanation.

The problem with one-on-one meetings is that without a witness, either participant can later claim things that were never said. It's your word against theirs. That meeting would come back to haunt me.

———

In the days that followed, our Air Force started targeting long-range missile launchers. The intelligence behind this operation had been painstakingly assembled. Israeli warplanes identified the targets, fired precision ordnance, and destroyed dozens of medium- and long-range missile launchers—often together with their operators. In some cases, when Hezbollah successfully fired missiles in the direction of cities to the south of Haifa, the launcher was destroyed just seconds after missiles were fired. We had the ability to detect the launch and instantly take out the launcher.

Such achievements don't usually appear in statistics about the Second Lebanon War, but they left a major impression on the leadership of Hezbollah. Nasrallah was the one who said, at the end of the war, that if he had known how Israel would respond to the abductions, he would have avoided the adventure entirely. "If I had known on July 11," he said in a televised interview, "that the operation would lead to such a war, would I do it? I say no, absolutely not."

Hezbollah's capabilities were deteriorating by the day. But a weeks-long war would take its toll on us as well. Every casualty, whether soldier or civilian, added to the pain. I knew I had to be patient. I knew that I would pay a price for the number of casualties, the failure of any given assault, and the public image of the war as a whole. Anyone who wants to avoid paying a price should avoid public service to begin with. I decided that I would never lose sight of our mission, a Lebanese border without Hezbollah, among the agonies of the moment.

————

More than two weeks into the fighting, a clear image of the battlefield emerged. Incoming rocket fire continued, and intelligence was saying Hezbollah could keep up the fire indefinitely. The mission of destroying their bases was nearing its end, but it came at a high price. At Bint J'bail, Maroun A-Ras, and other Hezbollah bases, we achieved most of the military objectives, but the casualties on our side were much higher than expected, with more than a hundred soldiers killed.

In a briefing held July 26, the fifteenth day of fighting, things appeared stable. A huge number of launchers, rockets and missiles had been destroyed. The incoming rocket fire inside Israel had almost completely ended. Alongside the weakness we discovered in our ground attack, intelligence was signaling a significant weakening of Hezbollah. Now the question was whether to significantly expand our ground operation.

Halutz, the IDF chief of staff, supported preparing for a major operation and even calling up reserves. But then he took a contradictory tone. "Now I'll give you two or three reasons why a major ground invasion, beyond the experience of 1982, will reduce our international legitimacy. First: Because we'll again look like invaders. With the aerial assault we aren't conquering territory. Second, in my assessment it could, in some scenarios, increase the potential of drawing Syria into the war. Third is the cost in casualties. We have to take that into account. Even now there are casualties, and the question at the end will be whether we are paying twice. Doing one thing now, and then doing something different and paying again. I think that at the end of the day the correct mix is a gradual one, one that could eventually lead to a wide ground assault, which we should prepare for but which I am not recommending."

Defense Minister Peretz responded. "If we give up on the aerial assault and want a ground invasion, it's a much more complicated story. We need the next ten days, because we have to complete the work of destroying all those fortifications they built along the border. That itself is an important thing. That in itself justifies continuing the war for a few more days to finish the job. And it's a complicated job. Not simple. We need to build a defensive strip there. Very important."

I summarized the meeting with the understanding that a wider ground offensive would remain on the table, but that we would need to make sure it was thought through and planned carefully, with the aim of further degrading Hezbollah's capabilities rather than conquering territory, and above all to do everything to make sure Syria stayed out of the war. Our discussions continued.

––––––

The Forum of Seven met daily, sometimes two or three times a day. It prepared position papers on every aspect of the war: Diplomatic, military, communications, coordination with allies, and communication with Arab states, many of which condemned our enemies for the first time in history.

The civilian casualties on our side were limited. I'm not a big fan of building massive civilian bomb shelters—and I was especially troubled when, the following May, the Supreme Court ruled the that the government had to build them for residents in the south.

It only took a few years after that for us to develop the correct approach to missile defense: The Iron Dome system.

Before that, there had been two competing missile-defense technologies on offer. Each had serious people supporting them. The Nautilus system was based on lasers. Its advantage was a low cost of use, but the development looked to be both lengthy and expensive. This was a joint venture with Lockheed Martin and had the support of a former Air Force commander, as well as Rafi Eitan, a former senior Mossad official.

But I decided to go with the product being developed by Rafael, the Israeli military development firm: Iron Dome, which could detect a missile's trajectory, determine whether it was heading for populated areas, and intercept it with a rocket. I passed the question on to the chief of arms development in the Defense Ministry, Shmuel Keren, and his team came back to me with an unambiguous recommendation for Iron Dome.

From its first battle test during Operation Protective Edge in 2014, Iron Dome proved itself as an efficient defense against short-range rocket attacks. And it continues to improve, saving countless Israeli lives and giving us a great deal of operational flexibility to choose the specific scope and targets of retaliation as we see fit.

———

On Saturday night, July 29, Condoleezza Rice landed in Israel. While she was in flight, the media reported rumors that our conversation would be a tough one—mainly, for some reason, concerning the Shaba Farms, a fleck on the map along the Golan Heights, which we had conquered from Syria in 1967. The Shaba Farms were now part of Israel along the Lebanon border, and Syria, which still saw the Golan as its own, had "donated" the land to Lebanon in order to create a pretext for continued conflict.

Discussing it now with Rice struck me as absurd. What did Shaba Farms have to do with ending the war? Our main demands concerned stopping Hezbollah's terror operations, stopping the import of weapons via Syria, having the Lebanese army and an international force take over the border with Israel, and other aspects of security.

We came to understand that the rumors had been leaked by a senior member of Rice's entourage. I had seen this before, when the Americans leak the contents of a conversation in advance so that the other side has time to prepare.

I received Rice in the evening. The conversation was pleasant. We went through the various issues discussed in talks between our staffs. Everything was also cleared with the British, French, and Germans, and Rice was in constant touch with their foreign ministers.

Near the end of the conversation, she raised the subject of Shaba Farms. Without our giving up on that small piece of land along the slope of the Golan Heights, she said, there was a chance that there could be no deal to end the war. I had a feeling she had had bought into the rumors spreading about how our achievements in the war were disappointing and that we were in a hurry to end it—even if it meant a loss of prestige.

I quickly made things very clear. "I expect another ten days of fighting," I said, and proposed she begin counting them from the following day. As for Shaba Farms, I reminded her that before the war, I had told her I'd be willing to discuss it if the UN came to the conclusion that it was in fact Lebanese territory, and if Hezbollah actually complied with UN Resolution 1559, which required it to evacuate southern Lebanon. "However," I added, "I said those things at a different time. I can't imagine doing this now, after what Hezbollah has done. The Shaba Farms are not part of any deal."

Her face turned grim. "Your position," she said, "is not acceptable to the United States."

"With all due respect," I said, "that's something only the president can say to me. We can call him right now if you'd like."

She caught herself. "I apologize. I was out of line. Let's go on to the rest of the issues." We came to agreement on everything else. Rice said she was heading out the next day to Lebanon to meet with Prime Minister Fouad Siniora. In her view, Siniora was ready to support the core provisions of a proposal along the lines we were discussing. "If he does," she added, "I'll fly on Monday to New York, and we'll see that on Tuesday the Security Council passes a resolution calling for an end to the war."

Tuesday would be August 1, which seemed reasonable. The provisions we agreed on offered an excellent formula, from our end, for ending the war.

With this spirit of agreement we said farewell.

———

In the morning, we started getting reports of a disaster in the village of Qana, east of Tyre in southern Lebanon. The initial reports spoke of an apartment building destroyed in a bombing by the Air Force, with more than one hundred civilians, including many children, dead.

A firestorm erupted that engulfed the Middle East. Rice, who was still in Israel, was in shock, mainly because she was afraid of losing momentum for a Security Council resolution. Siniora immediately announced that there was no point in her coming to Beirut.

It was not our policy to bomb residential homes, certainly not multistory ones. I ordered an immediate inquiry into the event. (It would later turn out that we had in fact bombed it, on the basis of flawed intelligence that told us it was empty.) Rice cancelled her flight. She asked to meet me immediately after the cabinet meeting. *Haaretz* continued insisting we were having a major dispute about Shaba Farms.

I had no doubt Rice was furious. If we met immediately, her anger would get the best of her and likely undermine our relationship. I decided to push our meeting off until later in the day, with the hope that she would show up more restrained. I sent Turbowicz and Turjeman to see Elliott Abrams and David Welch, her two closest advisers, to explain that my schedule of meetings with foreign leaders and foreign ministers in Israel at that moment was jammed and I couldn't cancel them. The meeting would take place, just later in the day.

In the afternoon I received an update from our sources in Washington: The president was not angry. In wars, things happen, including disasters like this, and one shouldn't overdo the anger or the pressure on Israel.

When I saw Rice, she was still upset, her plans for ending the war scuttled. I told her we would get to the bottom of what happened at Qana. There wasn't much either of us could do. The war's end would be delayed until things calmed down.

———

Talks about a Security Council resolution to end the war continued. So did the fighting. Losses continued to mount. Hezbollah's leaders and commanders were stunned: They hadn't counted on Israel's tenacity, or on the deterioration of their own forces due to the endless hammering they were taking. They saw what the Israeli media did not see—and they started moving toward an agreement. Nasrallah's representatives pressured Siniora to improve the terms, but failed. They had no leverage.

The Forum of Seven held a series of meetings about ending the war, beginning on Saturday, August 5. One of the subjects that concerned us was the possibility of a Syrian attack. Our intelligence assessments suggested this was possible, and we directed the IDF to prepare for it. I doubted that Syrian President Bashar Assad would take the risk, which could lead to catastrophe for him. Syrian air defenses would not be able to stop our air force. The Syrian missiles looked impressive, and were much more fearsome than Hezbollah's, but their use would mean all-out war, and such a war would end, from his perspective, in certain disaster.

After the fact it was clear I was right. I sent Damascus a number of messages over the course of the war, especially when we were operating close to the Syrian border, that under no circumstances should they attack us. They got the message.

Eisenkot talked about preparing ourselves mentally for a longer stay in Lebanon. The defense minister proposed we get ready for a bigger operation, but emphasized we would need to take into account the diplomatic timetable. At the end of the meeting at which this was discussed, I directed the IDF to continue grinding down the sources of fire in southern Lebanon. I emphasized that the continuing bombing of residential areas be coordinated with the attorney general whenever necessary. I wanted to make sure we didn't end the war exposed to claims of excessive force against civilians, and I took Mazuz's advice seriously.

In a meeting two days later, on Monday, August 7, Halutz took an aggressive stance. "The only way to completely stop the rocket fire," he said, "is to conduct a ground invasion to control all of southern Lebanon."

In the opinion of Halutz and Eisenkot, the IDF could launch a major ground operation using three divisions as soon as August 9. It would take ninety-six hours to conquer the entire area, if not fully cleanse it of Hezbollah positions. I directed the IDF to prepare for such an operation, but not to focus on conquering territory or staying there. Instead, the goal should be to take out the sources of fire, an approach that better fit the diplomatic efforts. As the Qana disaster faded, we believed the Security Council would be voting on a resolution within days.

On Wednesday, August 9, the cabinet met to approve the operation. During the meeting, Condoleezza Rice kept trying to get me on the phone.

I had never avoided a call from her before, but there were advantages to holding her off just a bit. I understood that reports of a broader ground operation, which had been percolating in Israeli and international media outlets since the morning, would help make a Security Council resolution happen. Her call was a sign that I was right. I told my secretary to tell her I was in the middle of a cabinet meeting and couldn't take her call.

After a few more tries by Condi, each more urgent than the last, I suspended the cabinet meeting and called her back. She was agitated. She hoped, she said, that we had not yet made a decision on sending ground forces into Lebanon.

I told her I had suspended the meeting to call her back, but my intention was to approve the proposal.

She said that the United States and its allies had accepted all of Israel's demands for a Security Council resolution—including the disarmament of Hezbollah—and had secured a commitment of 15,000 Lebanese troops taking up positions in southern Lebanon immediately to put the brakes on Hezbollah.

I said that the Lebanese army had no credibility, and no capability, to put any brakes on Hezbollah.

Rice added that there was also an agreement to bring to southern Lebanon 12,000 NATO soldiers under the UN framework known as UNIFIL (the UN Interim Force in Lebanon, which was established in 1978). Until they were fully deployed, the IDF could remain in southern Lebanon, with the backing of the Security Council. The passage of weapons from Syria into Lebanon would be forbidden.

She went into more and more details, and it became clear to me that we were going to end this war under highly favorable terms.

I told Rice that everything depended on when the Security Council resolution passed. She answered that the decision would take no more than two days, by Friday, August 11. I told her I would delay the operation, but not past Friday. If the Security Council failed to act by then, I would direct the IDF to move in.

The cabinet approved the ground operation, delegating the timing of the final green light to myself and the defense minister. I clarified, before the vote, that if there were any possibility of the Security Council passing the resolution as Rice had reported—including the multinational force—within the next two days, then the invasion would no longer make sense.

The IDF was chomping at the bit. Commanders and fighters couldn't understand the delay. This is what the defense minister and chief of staff told me that same night. I reiterated that we would not take an action, on the day the UN Security Council was to vote on a fantastic resolution for us, that I hadn't been prepared to do for the first twenty-nine days of the war.

On Thursday, August 10, the Security Council didn't pass the resolution. Turbowicz and Turjeman sat with Assistant Secretary of State David Welch, revising it. Because of the time difference, late Thursday night in New York was early Friday in Israel.

Slowly the picture became clearer, and it started to emerge that disputes among the members of the Security Council would prevent a decision Thursday night. Peretz and Halutz came back to me and pressed me to give the green light. I said, again, that there would be no immediate action. I had set Friday as the deadline, and I would stick to it. I told Halutz that if he wanted, I would speak directly with the division commanders and explain it to them. He accepted the offer, and reminded me that a decision to start their engines would be needed by around 5:00 p.m., to take advantage of nightfall.

I was soon on a call with Gal Hirsch, Eyal Eisenberg, and Guy Tzur, the three division commanders. They, too, reported that the soldiers were eager and ready for battle. "Give the order, and we will charge."

I explained that the picture I saw was different from theirs. I was thrilled that the soldiers were ready, but it would not be right to launch the attack if a few hours later the Security Council passed a resolution that we ourselves wrote and pushed for. They needed to stay ready, but to give me another day.

It was an important conversation. Halutz and Peretz calmed a bit. At 10:00 p.m. Thursday, Turbowicz and Turjeman reported that they were finishing up talks with Rice's people in Israel. And then the phone rang.

Tzipi Livni was on the line. "I've decided to fly to New York," she said, "to continue the negotiation."

"When are you flying?" I asked.

"In an hour," she said.

I told her there was no reason to fly. It would be a mistake to run to the UN, to stand before 15 members of the Security Council and make our case. That's not how you negotiate.

"You're forbidding me to fly," she half-asked, half-said.

"If that's how you want to put it, the answer is yes," I said.

The next day, I read in *Maariv* about how I had banned our foreign minister from flying to New York. Whatever. The whole thing was childish and irresponsible.

I went to sleep Thursday night having been told that I would be presented with a final version of the resolution in the morning, which would be approved by the Security Council the following evening.

Late at night, however, Danny Gillerman, our UN ambassador, tried to reach me. The secretary passed him to Turbowicz. He told Turbo that he had received a call from the U.S. ambassador to the United Nations, John Bolton. "We have agreed that France will be submitting the resolution," Bolton reported, "but it doesn't look anything like what was agreed to with Israel."

Turbo decided to let me sleep.

———

The next morning I woke up to find that nothing of what Rice and I had agreed to appeared in the French draft. I summoned my staff to the prime minister's residence. At 10:00 a.m. Israel time, I couldn't get Bush on the phone. It was 2:00 a.m. at his ranch in Crawford, Texas.

We tried to track down Steve Hadley, the national security adviser. They said he was on his way to see the president. Condoleezza Rice? En route to New York for the meeting of the Security Council.

I needed to make a sharp, bold move. I had chosen Friday as the latest date for a UN resolution, but that was assuming a completely different text. We needed to create leverage at that moment to change the decision.

I knew that by the time I was able to bring the Americans and French back on track, the window for military action would close. And I knew that what had caused Rice to panic on Wednesday would make her panic even more on Friday.

I directed Israel Maimon, my chief of staff, to give the IDF the order to launch the offensive. Amir Peretz was thrilled. I saw it as way of forcing the Security Council's hand. I hoped it could happen very quickly.

I spoke to Halutz. I asked him how many hours' warning he needed to stop the operation from the moment I gave the order. Halutz said it was like an aircraft carrier—it required a few hours to bring it to a halt.

"How many hours?" I asked.

"Eight hours," he said.

I told him he had to be prepared for an immediate stop at any moment. He accepted that.

On Friday at 5:00 p.m. Israel time, the operation began.

Turbowicz had managed to get Hadley on the phone. Hadley wanted to know why we had decided to move forces. Turbo told him it was a direct result of the change in the text. Hadley said he knew nothing about it. Turbo emailed him the new version submitted by the French.

Hadley was in shock. He said it was completely different from the version he had, and he sent that one to us.

While they spoke, I was able to get Rice on the phone on her way to the UN. She asked for time to verify the details and promised to get back to me. Calls and emails shot around the world. By 7:00 p.m., we had reached an understanding with the Americans about a new version of the resolution. It needed a few final changes. It was agreed that Turbo and Hadley would go over it and work out a final text.

That took about two hours. Then I spoke with Rice again and we went over it together, line by line, to make sure we agreed on every detail. Now we needed to get the rest of the members of the Security Council on board. This, too, took an additional two hours.

And so, at around 11:00 p.m. Israel time, we began to see the fruits of our labor. In New York it was 4:00 p.m. Rice called to tell me that the president wanted to speak with me later on. She expected the Security Council to vote that evening at 8:00 p.m., or 3:00 a.m. Israel time Saturday.

UN Secretary General Kofi Annan called me to ask how long it would take for the IDF to stand down completely from the moment the Security Council approved the resolution. I promised to get back to him. Halutz then told me he wanted ninety-six hours. I told him that was too much time.

We agreed with the secretary general on a timeframe of forty-eight hours from the passage of the resolution. Since we expected it to happen at 3:00 a.m. Saturday, I told him that at 8:00 a.m. Monday morning, the IDF would completely cease fire. It was agreed that Israeli forces could remain in Lebanon until the Lebanese army and the multinational force deployed into Hezbollah-controlled areas.

At around 1:00 a.m., President Bush called me.

It was our first conversation since the beginning of the war. As usual, he was warm, and apologized for not having called me during the war. As he put it, his advisers had told him to call me a few times, but he had refused. "They wanted me to tell you to stop the war, but I didn't want to do that. So I thought it was better just not to call you." As long as I believed the campaign was effective, he said, and that I could really weaken Hezbollah, why should he pressure me?

At 3:00 a.m. Israel time, the Security Council passed Resolution 1701 unanimously. Fifty-three hours later, on August 14, at 8:00 a.m., the exchange of fire stopped in southern Lebanon and northern Israel. It was the first time an Israeli military operation had been brought to an end by a Security Council resolution whose terms had been dictated by Israel, and the text of which had been approved by us in advance.

———

Immediately with the end of the war, Netanyahu and his allies began working overtime to undermine public perceptions of the conflict. He, along with his then aide Naftali Bennett and others on the right, with the benefit of ample funding from abroad, turned the war into a tool to bring down my government. Three sets of parents of fallen soldiers—all of them members of the Likud Central Committee—started protesting against me, backed by Netanyahu.

Indeed, there were reservists who were justifiably angry at the end of the war. Fighters from the Alexandroni Brigade were in shock when they discovered their emergency storage sheds half empty. Even during the war, they and other units lacked equipment to a degree that hampered their ability to carry out their missions.

Was this a strategic failing? Did it justify bringing down the government? Certainly not. First of all, it was a failure of the IDF. A failure of mismanagement of the sheds, and of the commanders who didn't solve those problems by borrowing equipment from the storage facilities of other reserve units that hadn't been called up.

You can definitely look at this as a national failing. You can get caught up in the failures of one battle or another, in which the IDF got ambushed or failed to achieve its objectives. Every failure demands that lessons be learned. But the basic question about the war should be: What were its goals, and were they achieved?

The goal of this war was victory. Not a total victory, which was impossible, but a victory that would change Hezbollah's thinking with respect to what was worth doing and what wasn't. In order to change the calculus of this bloodthirsty terrorist group, there was no choice but to hit them harder than any Israeli government had dared to.

It was the policies of previous Israeli governments, spanning decades, that gave birth to Nasrallah's infamous speech about how Israel could be cleared away like a "spider web." We talked tough, but at crucial moments we capitulated and compromised and then sold these compromises to ourselves as achievements. Nasrallah and his people knew exactly which side had caved each time. Israel's weakness whetted their appetite and incentivized them to provoke us on our northern border over and over again.

The Second Lebanon War brought a new calculus—and, as of this writing, a decade and a half of relative quiet.

———

The opposition fostered a sense of frustration and disappointment among the public. That hurt our government and especially hurt me. It distorted people's ability to correctly assess the results of the war, and helped my rivals create a sense that my days were numbered.

There were immediate calls to establish a National Commission of Inquiry. I was against it. I didn't believe in 2006, and I don't believe today, that a country can be run by commissions of inquiry. The media bought into the manipulations of the opposition, but I didn't take the bait. Amir Peretz did, however, and took action on his own. His mistake almost brought our government down.

As defense minister, Peretz was troubled by the criticism. He decided to establish a commission of inquiry inside the Defense Ministry that would examine the IDF's performance in the war, headed up by former IDF Chief of Staff Amnon Lipkin-Shahak. Amnon was a wonderful, honest man. But appointing him to investigate the IDF, without any similar body examining the performance of the government, was a big mistake.

Nobody gets immunity for testifying before such a commission. Any soldier who talks takes the risk that his words will be used against him if any subsequent inquiry has access to his testimony. As a result, the IDF chief of staff announced that he would order any soldier called before Lipkin-Shahak's commission to say nothing in order to avoid self-incrimination.

In public the announcement met with harsh criticism—it looked like an attempt by politicians to avoid responsibility. I couldn't abide this. I had no choice now but to set up a formal commission of inquiry in accordance with the law. It was my only way out of the corner Amir Peretz had backed me into.

The government tasked the commission with investigating every aspect of the war, including both the political and military decisions. It was headed up by Judge Eliyahu Winograd, a retired president of the Tel Aviv District Court, and also included Ruth Gavison, one of Israel's most respected legal scholars, as well as two retired IDF generals and the renowned historian Yehezkel Dror. It was decided to grant full immunity to anyone who testified, and that testimonies would be sealed. This last part would later be overturned in part by the Supreme Court, and many uncomfortable statements, not all of them true, saw the light of day.

I prepared my testimony. I didn't try to find out what people were telling the commission, neither politicians nor military leaders. I knew the details of what actually happened, had access to the documents and the recordings, the careful records kept by my office. Most important, I had nothing to hide.

I was asked to testify last. I assumed that any important issues would come up in their questions to me. My testimony was relatively short, lasting only a few hours. When I finished, I noticed that I wasn't asked any questions, nor was I asked to expand on any of the issues that should have been of interest to the commission. It was strange.

This commission was supposed to be investigating a wide range of issues involved in waging a military conflict, to draw conclusions about the quality of the performance of the political level and to go into depth about the way the war ended. Instead, it focused on trivial things, mainly on complaints raised by the public. And indeed, one of the generals on the commission, Menachem Einan, even said as much later on to the journalist Amnon Dankner. "We capitulated to the atmosphere of the street," he said.

———

The commission published the first part of its report on April 30, 2007. In accordance with the process set out when it was established, the commission submitted the report to the prime minister and the defense minister. After the official presentation at the Prime Minister's Office, the members of the commission presented key findings at a major press conference, broadcast live to the world.

My staff and I went through the report, and the more we read, the more we understood how shallow and simplistic it was. The commission, it seemed, had chosen to play to the public instead of conducting a serious investigation.

In brief, the commission blamed me, the defense minister, and the IDF chief of staff for deciding to go to war through a rushed decision, which we hadn't; for not taking into account the alternatives to war, which we did; for not being militarily prepared, which was only true in part and not in a way that undermined the achievements of the war; for insufficiently including the foreign minister in our decisionmaking, even though she was part of the Forum of Seven and present in every crucial meeting. The commission finally accused me personally of "a serious failure in exercising judgment, responsibility and prudence," which is, with the perspective of many years, transparently untrue.

One of the most shocking things in the report was Tzipi Livni's testimony that she had offered a proposal to end the war early through diplomatic means. She claimed it had happened during that two-minute meeting when we were alone, standing up the whole time, when the only thing she had actually said to me was that she had been wrong to vote against the operation in Dahiya. I've gone through the most top-secret transcripts and records, and at no point throughout the war did she ever even hint at ending it early through diplomacy.

But aside from what it says about Tzipi Livni, more shocking is that the commission never asked me about it before including it in the report. Again, I was the final witness. Did they not think it significant that a senior minister had suggested ending the war early and that I had turned it down? Didn't they want to know, for example, why I hadn't accepted the offer? If they had asked, they would have learned that it had never happened. But they didn't bother.

———

Predictably, there were calls for my resignation coming from the opposition and especially Netanyahu. I called a meeting of all of Kadima's cabinet ministers that evening. I started by pounding on the table. "I want to be perfectly clear," I said. "I have no intention of resigning. I'm not going anywhere. There is no room for debate."

As I was saying this, Justice Minister Daniel Friedmann walked in. Before sitting down, he lay the report on the table and said, "What a pile of rubbish. We don't need to take it seriously."

Shimon Peres asked to speak. No one in the room was as experienced as he was. He had sat in that same room with Ben-Gurion. "As with any such report," he said, "you have to read it and study it. But you can't get worked up by it—and it would be wrong to draw any conclusions from it."

The meeting didn't go long. Nobody raised the possibility that I should resign.

Later on we called a meeting of the entire Kadima faction in the Knesset. We also invited mayors of northern towns. Some of them asked to say a few words at the beginning of the meeting. Among them was Shlomo Buhbut, mayor of Maalot-Tarshiha. "We need to bless the prime minister," he said. "This war saved the north. We can live our lives in peace now. All of us support Olmert. Anyone who comes out against him, we will attack them with everything we've got."

The veiled threats were aimed at Tzipi Livni, who had publicly hinted I should resign. While nobody else in the party felt this way, in the media her position was widely publicized. A deputy prime minister saying that the prime minister should quit—that's great fodder for journalists.

The next day I summoned Tzipi into my office. She was tense, the way she always gets in situations like these. I didn't want to argue with her. I told her she needed to release a statement, and I handed her the text. It included support for the prime minister and accepting his authority. I didn't want anything else in it. I felt that any more than that would come across as insincere. I told her that the alternative was relieving her of her posts as foreign minister and deputy prime minister. She was free to express her opinions about me, but not in the roles she currently held.

Livni released the statement exactly as I'd written it. I didn't need more than that. The most important goal was to nip her political maneuvers in the bud. I wasn't worried, and I knew she had no backing within the party. All I wanted was to stop the circus. Having achieved this, I left her alone.

———

All this was happening soon after we had learned that Syria had been, under our noses, building a reactor for the production of nuclear weapons. The irony was not lost on me or the close staff around me. On the one hand, you can't ignore the campaign of incitement being launched by politicians both outside and inside your party. On the other hand, you have to focus all your energies on the tightrope walk of sensitive steps to remove an existential threat facing your nation. All this, without anyone sensing that you are feeling the slightest sense of crisis. I had to draw up every ounce of mental strength I had.

And in the thick of it all, I was also running negotiations with the Palestinians. It was crucial to me that Palestinian President Mahmoud Abbas not come to the conclusion that I was a lame duck. A prime minister with a target on his back. I appreciated the fact that he kept coming to see me every few weeks, and we'd spend hours in deep, personal conversations. I interpreted this, and still do, in a simple way: He sincerely wanted to reach a deal that both of us could get approved by our respective sides.

The final months of 2007 were a blur of competing priorities that would decide the country's fate. At a certain point I learned that the final part of the Winograd report would be released in late January 2008. The entire country was on edge. The atmosphere was tense. All kinds of stories were floating around about arguments within the commission: Should they include personal recommendations regarding political and military leaders? Could you even do that without sending warning letters to relevant parties? (The Supreme Court would rule that no, you couldn't.) The rumors had it that at least two of the members threatened to resign if such warning letters were sent out, which would make such recommendations possible, and which would move the commission to a new phase involving lawyers and investigations. It was clear to me that the resignation of two of the five members would inevitably lead to dismantling the commission and burying the final report.

The IDF operation that sent three armored divisions into southern Lebanon in the final forty-eight hours of the war became the main focus of both the final report of the commission as well as the public debate around it.

Again, the purpose of that operation was clear: It was meant to force the hand of the UN Security Council to adopt a favorable resolution to end the war, one that would bring stability and calm in our north. And it achieved exactly that.

I felt that whatever the public sentiment was at that moment, if the commission itself came to the conclusion, as was loudly claimed by people like former IDF Chief of Staff and future Defense Minister Moshe Ya'alon, that the final forty-eight hours of the war were nothing but a PR move—if that were the case, it would be difficult to deal with the consequences. But if the commission acted more responsibly, then all the criticism would eventually die down, and my political rivals' latest effort to use the families' tragedies to bring me down would fail.

The day arrived. On January 30, 2008, I invited Judge Winograd to submit the report to me and to Ehud Barak, who had defeated Amir Peretz in the Labor Party's primaries and had now taken his place as defense minister, in the Prime Minister's Office in Jerusalem. Winograd handed us two copies of the report, said a few polite words, and I offered a few of my own in response. I thanked him and the members of the commission, and he took his leave.

Only Barak and I were in the room. I knew that if this report were as bad as the first one, there was a good chance he would quit. We started to leaf through the report. My staff started going through additional copies the judge had left behind in a separate room. Within minutes, we started to understand—Barak and I both—that this time, the truth would be told.

My small staff came back into the room, a massive sense of relief was on their faces. The final forty-eight hours of the war were a necessary action that yielded a significant portion of the war's achievements.

Somebody turned on the TV. Judge Winograd was explaining that the final operation of the war was an "almost completely necessary" move that had yielded major results. The threat of the Winograd Commission had, finally, passed.

———

Today it is possible to look back on the war and draw real conclusions. The fundamental question behind the Second Lebanon War is as relevant today as it was on July 12, 2006: What should Israel do if an enemy abducts or kills soldiers or heavily bombards our civilians along the border? Should we absorb every assault, in the hope that the enemy's missiles will just stop on their own?

Some people felt that way. There were people who said so during the summer of 2006. That was, in fact, the prevailing policy prior to the war. But I could never understand it. It never occurred to me that the Israeli government should even consider such a posture. It's not just a question of being cowardly—it's also suicidal. A country surrounded by terror organizations can't allow itself that degree of restraint.

Ehud Barak said, after the cease-fire had been announced, that we should have taken a time-out thirty-three days earlier and considered our response.

But we had thought everything through in advance. For months. And we had reached the conclusion, together with the leaders of the IDF, Mossad, Shin Bet, Military Intelligence, the General Staff, and the defense minister, that absorbing this kind of attack, restraining ourselves after such an escalation, would be so harmful as to constitute a strategic catastrophe. We had also explored the nature of the appropriate retaliation in depth and from every angle, in advance. The conclusion had been clear: Israel had to use its power in a measured way, always using its inherent advantages, its air superiority, its use of precision ordnance, and its use of special forces, to clean out a strip along the border one or two miles deep.

We executed exactly what we had concluded would be the appropriate response. For years afterward, my political rivals, especially Netanyahu, would endlessly attack the conduct of the war and especially me. A lot of people fell for it. But the results speak for themselves. We have enjoyed a decade and a half of quiet on our northern border.

Yes, it's true that since the end of the war, Hezbollah has built up a large arsenal of missiles and rockets. People speak of tens of thousands, maybe even more. It is described as a strategic threat to Israel as a whole, not just the north.

I don't want to downplay the threat of these missiles, even if, as I suspect, the numbers are exaggerated. Israel is capable of destroying missile storehouses and neutralizing the ability of most of them to launch. To the best of my knowledge, the threat is much smaller than a lot of people—including those who know better—make it out to be.

Because it's not enough to have a weapon. You need to be willing to use it. For fifteen years, Hezbollah has avoided conflict with Israel. Nasrallah does not have any desire to use his weapons. That is a direct result of his crushing defeat he suffered in the Second Lebanon War.

It's called deterrence.

NINE

Why Syria Doesn't Have
a Nuclear Bomb

They say that the job of prime minister of Israel is almost as hard as that of the president of the United States.

The daily threats that the prime minister has to deal with are innumerable. He must assess all the risks and weigh up all the possible short-term implications and long-term consequences—all while dealing with political machinations, and keeping steady control of the government by maintaining his inner balance and a cool head. He must also remember that he is never alone. Millions of eyes, both within the country and around the region and the world, are watching his every move. His behavior will determine how other nations respond, and whether his people can bear the burden.

In 2007, Syria was still one of Israel's most serious strategic threats. This was a few years before our neighbor to the northeast collapsed into a horrific and multifront civil war that has, to date, cost half a million lives and created many millions of refugees both within the country and across the region. The authoritarian regime of Bashar Assad was, at the time, one of only five nations designated as state sponsors of terror by the U.S. State Department. It worked with Iran to send arms and funds to the Hezbollah terror group in Lebanon. It was Syria, together with Egypt, that had launched major wars against Israel in 1967 and 1973, and had taken us on head-to-head during the First Lebanon War that began in 1982. For decades under the regime of Assad's father, Hafez al-Assad, Syria had been trained, supplied, and funded by the Soviet Union, and it remained close with Russia even after the fall of the Soviet Union. Syria has maintained a state of permanent war against Israel from day one.

So when we discovered, in March 2007, that the Syrians had been secretly building a plant designed specifically for creating nuclear weapons and were just months away from activating it, the issue quickly rose to the top of our agenda.

We destroyed the reactor in September 2007, and prevented a radical shift in the strategic reality, not just for Israel but for the whole world.

Successfully destroying the Syrian nuclear reactor was, without question, the most important achievement of my career. And it happened against the unbelievable pressures of internal politics, endless legal threats and accusations against me, and the surprising opposition of the president of the United States.

———

At least once a week, the prime minister holds a meeting with the chief of the Mossad. Sometimes the meetings are one-on-one, but usually the Mossad chief brings along aides, division chiefs, and mission commanders. The IDF secretary, who is privy to all state secrets, was always by my side at these meetings.

On March 1, 2007, I had a regularly scheduled meeting with the chief of the Mossad, Meir Dagan. At the end of it, a few other senior officials entered the room, and a debate ensued about how to interpret some newly obtained intelligence about suspected nuclear activity in Syria. The information, which came from a variety of sources, was disturbing, but not yet sufficiently clear or comprehensive to become our highest priority. Although both the Mossad's and Military Intelligence's greatest focus would continue to be on Iran, I ordered intelligence-gathering operations that would increase their attention on this potentially explosive area as well.

At some point during our meeting, the chief of Shin Bet, Yuval Diskin, entered the room. Like Dagan, Diskin is a courageous man with a razor-sharp focus, especially when dealing with complex missions. Smart, precise, and devoted, Diskin is one of the best people to have ever led Shin Bet. Working with him was very special for me, even though he never stopped needling me about the superiority of the Maccabi Tel Aviv soccer team.

At the end of the meeting, I conferred with the defense minister and the IDF chief of staff to formally approve the increased intelligence operations.

The rest of that week and through the beginning of the next, I continued my routine as prime minister: meetings with foreign dignitaries, discussions on economic policy with the finance minister and his team, or with the governor of the Bank of Israel, a meeting with Palestinian Authority President Abbas, and so on.

But then, on the morning of March 13, Dagan called and asked to see me urgently. I was scheduled to tour IDF units in the south that day. A barrage of Qassam rockets that had been fired from the Gaza Strip had required a military response and I thought it was important to be there in person, to see firsthand the soldiers' exercises and to hear the commanders' assessments. I decided to stick to the agenda and meet Dagan later in the day in Jerusalem. I spent half the day with Major General Benny Gantz, who later became the IDF chief of staff, head of the Blue White Party, and alternate prime minister under a rotation agreement. I was impressed at the time by his rock-solid demeanor and the ease and precision of his presentation.

When I got back to Jerusalem, Dagan was waiting for me with his deputy, Tamir Pardo, and the Mossad's chief of intelligence Amnon Sufrin. Dagan was grim-faced. Something out of the ordinary—even for those extraordinary days—had happened. Dagan told me that the new intel had been deciphered, and the results were clear as day. A specific type of nuclear reactor, one that manufactures plutonium, was being built in the Deir al-Zour region of northeastern Syria.

While most nuclear reactors are based on uranium and can be used for both civilian and military purposes, there's only one reason to build a plutonium reactor: to make a nuclear bomb. Less than 300 miles from where we sat, such a reactor was nearing completion.

Dagan did not say a lot. There was no need. The Mossad people and I exchanged anxious looks.

A knock on the door broke the silence. "Don't come in!" I yelled. But the door opened anyway, and in walked the government spokesman, Yanki Galanti. Channel 2 News, he announced, had informed us that the state attorney's office was ordering an investigation of claims that I had rigged a tender so that my Australian friend Frank Lowy would be able to buy a stake in Bank Leumi. The channel was waiting for my comment, Galanti said.

"Tell them to go to hell," I said. Galanti, shocked, ducked out of the room. I turned back to the others and asked when the reactor would likely go online, and what, precisely, would be the consequences.

The reactor would become operational within months, they said. It was located about half a mile from the Euphrates River and if we attacked it after it was activated, the result would be a potential cataclysm affecting hundreds of thousands and possibly millions of people who lived nearby or downstream. Never in history was a "hot" reactor—uranium or plutonium—bombed, and we had no intention of being the first to do so.

Their answers drove me to a simple conclusion: The reactor had to be destroyed, and soon. From that moment forward, our daily schedules would change dramatically, with that singular aim. We agreed that as few people as possible should know about it. Dagan would update the security chiefs, while I would bring Defense Minister Peretz and Foreign Minister Livni up to speed.

Dagan left me alone in the room. I couldn't wrap my mind around how the Syrians had managed to build a nuclear reactor right under our noses, without the knowledge of any branch of our intelligence community. But this thought, along with many others, had to be put aside. Keeping a cool head now was key.

I disclosed the details of our situation to my office's inner circle. I could trust my office: During my entire tenure as prime minister, not once was anything leaked that had the potential either to harm the country or to embarrass me. That should, of course, be taken for granted—but in unruly Israel, it was no small feat.

That same evening, the state attorney directed the police to begin investigating what became known as the Bank Leumi Affair. My heart and my mind, however, were elsewhere.

———

Even at that early stage, I decided to update privately all the former prime ministers: Shimon Peres, who was now serving as deputy prime minister; Benjamin Netanyahu, who was now leader of the opposition; and Ehud Barak, who was now a private businessman. All three were stunned by the news. Netanyahu and Barak had the same response: the reactor must be destroyed before it goes online.

Peres, on the other hand, reacted a bit bizarrely.

He was very tense, and focused on technical questions: What kind of output was the reactor capable of? How exactly would the Syrians deliver a nuclear bomb? Via missiles? Perhaps, he suggested, we could strike a deal with them.

I couldn't hide my disbelief. Of all the people in the world, the idea that Shimon Peres—the former director-general of the Defense Ministry who, in the early 1960s, was behind the creation of our own nuclear project in Dimona—would suggest such a thing was astonishing. I told him that my intention to destroy the reactor was not up for negotiation.

Netanyahu asked to see me alone a few days after I had first briefed him. He urged me to act quickly. Even though Ehud Barak was neither a member of the government nor privy to the discussions surrounding the operation, it was clear Netanyahu was scared I might take some bad advice from Barak. I let him know that in terms of execution, I was leaning toward an aerial strike, but no decision had yet been made. We would have a few options prepared in advance, and at the right time we'd go with whatever made sense, both to minimize the size of the operation and to avoid a war with Syria.

It took a few weeks more of further intelligence-gathering, analysis, and confirmation before we felt absolutely sure about what we understood to be happening in Syria. The time soon came to update the Americans as well. The fact that the Syrians had apparently built the reactor with help from North Korea would be of utmost concern to the Bush administration.

In the second week of April, I sent Dagan to Washington. There he met with the National Security Adviser Stephen Hadley, Vice President Dick Cheney, and CIA Director Michael Hayden at the White House. President Bush joined halfway through the meeting.

The news astonished the Americans. Naturally, they asked to see our raw intel so they could analyze it independently. We agreed, but with the caveat that access be granted only to the most necessary individuals. The Americans did not disappoint: later on, Bush would joke that the lack of leaks from the American side was nothing short of a miracle.

No decisions were supposed to be made on Dagan's trip; that could only be done between President Bush and myself at a later date. For now, the Americans needed time to digest the information and to conduct their own analysis, only to reach the same conclusions we did. A flurry of meetings followed, both in Jerusalem and Washington. The clock was ticking, and one thing was clear to both sides: the reactor had to be destroyed.

Still, neither side offered any proposals as to how it should be done, or who would do it.

———

The question of who would act was on all our minds. On the one hand, we had never asked the Americans to fight our wars for us, and we weren't about to start now. On the other, the reactor wasn't just an Israeli problem, so it seemed reasonable that the leader of the free world take it upon itself. Either way, preventing a full-scale war with Syria was critical to everyone. Another salient point in favor of American action arose in internal discussions with my closest aides: If the Americans were to destroy the reactor, it would send a clear message to Iran about what awaited them if they continued working on their own nuclear program. I became convinced that I would need to raise the issue directly with the president.

In the meantime, there were changes on our side. Gadi Shamni was replaced in the role of IDF secretary by Major General Meir Klifi. Klifi's wisdom and patience made the transition smooth, and he made a good impression on his colleagues by, for example, arranging for breakfast at our weekly meetings.

But there was another change around that time that was far more significant. In early June 2007, Ehud Barak reentered the political arena when he won the Labor Party primary election. On the surface, having served in the past as both prime minister and IDF chief of staff, it seemed an obvious choice for Barak to replace Amir Peretz as defense minister.

But as I would quickly find out, Barak was entirely unsuited for the job.

As we continued our weekly discussions on Syria, Barak began canvassing to delay the operation. He couldn't understand what the rush was. Though as a private individual he had completely agreed with my position, suddenly as head of the Labor Party he now proposed putting the mission off until the next spring—nine months away. Everyone was taken aback. All our intel suggested the reactor would go online well before then.

"So what?" he retorted. "We'll neutralize it once it's active."

My colleagues turned pale.

At the end of the meeting, the head of the Israel Atomic Energy Commission asked me if he had even heard Barak's position correctly. Could it really be that our defense minister proposed something so awful? The nuclear contamination of the Euphrates, the horrific carnage, would be on our heads.

Don't worry, I assured him. We would destroy the reactor before it went online.

———

In mid-June 2007, I flew to the United States. No one had any idea of the real purpose of my visit. The dozens of journalists who accompanied me were convinced I was going for talks on the Palestinian issue. President Bush had, in fact, been updated on every detail about Syria by Dagan, by my chief of staff Yoram Turbowicz, and by my diplomatic adviser, Shalom Turjeman.

Since our initial meetings in Washington, the Mossad had gathered much more information regarding North Korea's involvement, including the identities of those building the reactor.

Bush welcomed me with affection. Ours was a close relationship that went back years.

Vice President Dick Cheney, despite being extremely reserved, was always open with me. He ardently supported the inclinations of both Bush and myself, and willingly fought on our behalf. I discussed Syria at length with both of them. I told Cheney that an American attack would kill two birds with one stone: Destroying the reactor would completely change the way Iran dealt with the United States and Europe. Cheney was on the same page. With Bush, however, things were more nuanced. He feared that the military would resist any American action. While the intelligence community completely accepted our findings, the Pentagon was still reeling from the Iraq War.

The president grew increasingly hesitant.

He later told me that since the Syrians had not yet developed a platform for delivering a nuclear weapon, he saw no need to act militarily, and certainly no need to involve the U.S. military. To us, however, it was clear that the Syrians were constantly and actively developing weapons systems that could later serve as a platform to deliver a nuclear bomb. In one of our conversations, I reminded the president that the United States had no intercontinental ballistic missiles when it bombed Hiroshima and Nagasaki. The lack of appropriate Syrian missiles was merely an excuse spun by his military chiefs. I knew, from various sources, that Defense Secretary Robert Gates opposed any American action and was exerting tremendous pressure on Bush not to get dragged into another war against an Arab country.

Gates' 2014 memoir, *Duty*, published after he left the post, confirmed as much. In it, he writes that he was greatly concerned about "the influence of the Israelis . . . in the White House, particularly Prime Minister Olmert."

Bush promised a quick answer about whether the United States would be willing to launch the attack themselves. The president and I were in almost daily contact for close to a month after my visit to Washington, yet no answer came.

On Friday, July 13, we spoke on the phone in what was one of the most dramatic conversations between an Israeli prime minister and an American president. Bush was friendly, as usual, but spoke with resolve. After extended discussions with senior administration officials, he had decided to reject two of the three options we had spoken about. Neither America nor Israel would attack the reactor. The only option acceptable to Washington now was diplomacy. To that end, Bush had directed Secretary of State Condoleezza Rice to fly to the Middle East within two days and hold a joint press conference with me. It would be an unprecedented diplomatic effort, he said, at the end of which Syria would be forced to destroy its nuclear reactor.

I had been sure that the president's answer would be different.

I probed Bush about the reasons behind his decision. He spoke of military constraints. But I began to suspect that the reason was more political: Bush would have to justify any military action to Congress, and the first thing he would be asked would be on what intelligence the action was based. The moment he revealed the source as being Israeli, the entire world would pounce on the United States for taking action against an Arab country because of Israel. That was the argument made in the case of Iraq, even though it had been entirely untrue.

Either way, it was clear to me that the president was trapped. "So Condi will come to you on Monday for a press briefing," he concluded.

"Excuse me, Mr. President," I said. "You know I am fond of the secretary of state, but I ask you not to send her at this time. I understand that the U.S. will not take military action, and while I respect your reasons, we will do what is necessary."

I was not asking for approval. I was simply stating the reality: You won't do it, and we get that. But we will.

Elliott Abrams, then deputy national security adviser, later told me that he and Stephen Hadley, who were listening in on the conversation, were nervous Bush would get angry at my words. "Who does this Olmert think he is?" Abrams recalled thinking to himself. "For years I have listened to the president speak with world leaders, and no one has ever had the audacity to reject a proposal outright."

When Bush put the phone down after forty-five minutes, Abrams was waiting for a furious outburst. Instead, he recalled, Bush smiled broadly and said, "I love Ehud so much. He is such a courageous man."

A moment later, Bush stunned his aides a second time. "You heard what Ehud said," he told them. "I am charging you with following Israel's every move and ensuring that no official from this administration does anything to interfere." Indeed, the help and support I received from Bush throughout the whole process was unparalleled.

Just before we got off the phone, I asked the president not to mention our conversation to anyone. "I will be buttoned up, my friend," he said.

———

Syria went back to being an exclusively Israeli problem.

Once it became clear that the Americans would play no role in the strike, we knew we now had to move quickly, while ensuring that the fallout would be minimal. I was not looking to trigger another war in the region. Neither was I seeking an Israeli "win," as some people have alleged, or attempting to reestablish the IDF's deterrence, which some argued we had lost in the Second Lebanon War the previous year. I knew these were silly claims, and that when the day came, the IDF would once again prove its strength to the world.

But the fear of war with Syria was a real one. Right around that time, the Syrians were concerning themselves—needlessly—with a possible joint offensive between the United States and Israel against the Assad regime, Iran, and Lebanon. They responded by positioning and aiming their missiles at strategic targets in Israel.

It was clear then that any plan for the reactor had to include an assessment of the chances of all-out war. Such a scenario would mean our whole country, from the Galilee to Eilat, would be in the range of missiles carrying one-ton payloads.

The defense establishment was of two minds. Some said Assad would never dare launch missiles, while others argued that he would not be able to resist the temptation of a full-scale war involving Hezbollah in Lebanon and even Hamas in the Gaza Strip.

No one was eager to enter another conflict only a year after the Second Lebanon War. But neither was the idea of Assad building a nuclear bomb exactly appealing.

I studied the situation from all angles, the risks and the odds, and after a great deal of reflection I decided, as the one who bore ultimate responsibility for the lives of our citizens, that the threat must be eliminated, and that we would deal with whatever came after.

Over time, the internal debate only intensified. We would need to prepare for the possibility of war, especially now that the Syrians, fearing an Israeli attack in the fall, had put their entire missile fleet in firing positions. No doubt they would interpret any extraordinary moves by the IDF as the beginning of an assault, and we would lose the element of surprise. On the other hand, insufficient preparation could result in unnecessary loss of lives were a war to break out. I was convinced that despite the opinions of some, the chances Assad would retaliate were relatively low. A debate also ensued as to whether or how to prepare the home front for possible retaliation. Barak, as defense minister, presented a plan that was terribly inadequate, for it would certainly tip off the Syrians and allow them to strike first. I dismissed the plan outright.

Much has been written about the disagreements between myself and Barak over the strike. Barak, again, only opposed the strike once he became defense minister. Later he claimed it was because he wanted to prevent failures of the kind he said happened in Lebanon. It's worth noting that Barak had been full of praise for how that war was conducted—that is, until the public outcry came. Then he suddenly became its most vocal critic.

I began to speed up the decisionmaking process. The circle of people who knew about the reactor grew with each day. The security cabinet was updated, and so were several other ministers who needed to know. By the time of the operation, there were some 2,500 signatories on a secrecy document. Nothing leaked.

Turbowicz prepared a public diplomacy drive to be implemented immediately after the operation, to get ahead of any potential unwanted diplomatic or military fallout. We would also update, when necessary, various world leaders and heads of state, an effort that would be divided up with the Americans.

In the days following the operation, Turbowicz and Turjeman embarked on secret visits to several European capitals and shared details of the mission with their leaders. In cases where I thought a personal meeting would help build ties with that country, I went myself. Everywhere we went, we were met with total understanding, and also outright astonishment. Foreign Minister Livni, of course, was involved from the outset. In my estimation, our multipronged outreach helped keep a lid on the operation and prevent negative repercussions.

Other than the United States, only one other country, the identity of which remains classified, was given advance warning about the actual operation. The decision to do so was not taken lightly. Traditionally, nobody other than the United States gets to hear about high-stakes missions before they are carried out. However, due to the special nature of my personal relationship with the leader of that country, and because of the extraordinary cooperation we shared with its intelligence services, I made an exception. The chief of that country's intelligence agency would later tell me that he never experienced such a level of trust from a foreign intelligence agency as he had from Israel, and for that he was grateful. His prime minister expressed his gratitude as well.

Later, in a completely different context, we received vital assistance from that same leader. He acknowledged that the decision to do so was because of the trust we had placed in him before the Syria strike.

———

One evening, President Bush called to tell me that Condoleezza Rice and Defense Secretary Gates were scheduled to visit Russia. He asked me if I would agree to their briefing Russian President Vladimir Putin about the reactor. I said I was strongly opposed. I had a special interest in talking directly to Putin about it, and also about Russia's relations with Assad. Bush promised to tell Rice and Gates not to raise the issue.

Nevertheless, I was afraid the subject might still come up. That same evening, I called Putin and told him I had to meet him urgently. He told me to come the next day. I explained that it would be impossible to organize such a visit so quickly. Unfortunately, he was scheduled to fly to Iran the day after that to meet with Supreme Leader Ayatollah Ali Khamenei.

Upon hearing that, I took the opportunity to tell him that I also wanted to discuss the ties between his country and the Islamic Republic, in particular his plans to supply Tehran with S-300 antiaircraft missiles and nuclear fuel for Iran's Bushehr nuclear power plant.

Putin explained to me at length that the fuel was solely for civilian purposes. The reactor would be under the supervision of both Russia and the International Atomic Energy Agency. Russia would also be in charge of its operational control. If, for whatever reason, there was any kind of interference in the transmission between the reactor and the Russian control station, Russia would intervene immediately and stop the reactor's operation.

I told him that our primary concern was Iran's acquisition of know-how and expertise that might then be employed for noncivilian purposes. The supply of both fuel and S-300 missiles, I explained, was a step toward Iran fulfilling its nuclear ambitions. A country that could boast this level of protection might be tempted to show aggression to other countries.

Putin promised to consider the matter. We agreed that I would fly to Moscow two days after his return from Tehran. Later I read about his meeting with Khamenei, but there was no mention of the Russians supplying either nuclear fuel or missiles to Tehran.

Bush called. He sounded elated. "Well done, my friend. You actually succeeded with Putin," he said.

Putin had called Bush to brief him on his visit to Iran and told him that despite the arms sale being the entire purpose of his visit, he had decided at this stage to postpone the deal. When Bush asked him what had changed his mind, Putin replied, "I spoke to Olmert just before I flew. He convinced me."

"Mr. President, that is not what I think happened," I said. "Putin's decision had nothing to do with my conversation with him. He decided to delay the deal because of the pressure you exerted on him, but it was much more convenient to use me as an excuse than to admit he gave in to pressure from you."

Bush was pleased with my explanation, and I was pleased with Putin's decision.

The next day I received a call from German Chancellor Angela Merkel. She asked me to help her with Putin on a sensitive issue. I was surprised. "Why do you think I can help you?" I asked.

Apparently Putin had also told Merkel that his decision to delay the deal came after speaking to me. I agreed to try and help her but added that I was not sure I would be of any use.

In his memoir, Gates recalls how he and Rice were made to wait a long time in the hallway to Putin's office. It was an episode that made headlines. When Putin finally stepped out to receive them, the former secretary of defense recalls, the Russian president "apologized, explaining that he had been on the telephone with Israeli prime minister Ehud Olmert, talking about the Iranian nuclear threat."

———

On Wednesday, August 1, 2007, I convened the defense chiefs and cabinet ministers for what was supposed to be another routine meeting on the Syrian issue. Although I detest long meetings, I asked all those present not to leave anything unsaid. Dagan complied, as did Diskin, who is usually a man of few words. Major General Ido Nehoshtan presented the position of the IDF. Nehoshtan, who was later appointed commander of the Air Force, is a man of impressive caliber. His briefing took about twenty minutes and summarized all our discussions until that point. It included assessments from the entire military establishment and the recommendations of the IDF chief of staff, who sat next to him.

But as Nehoshtan was about to present the recommendations, Barak, who was still opposed to the mission, emitted a noise that can only be described as a roar.

"Sit down, I forbid you to continue," Barak boomed.

The room fell silent. Barak's face was scarlet. "I'm in charge of the army," he bellowed. "The chief of staff and Nehoshtan are my subordinates, and I am ordering that this stop immediately."

Nehoshtan was stunned. Even though, by virtue of my authority as prime minister, I could have put a stop to Barak's antics, I restrained myself out of concern that he might later take his anger out on Nehoshtan. Instead, I calmly instructed Nehoshtan to have a seat, and that I would finish the briefing myself. I read out the recommendations myself, and Barak tried numerous times to interrupt.

"Sit still and listen," I told him in a low voice. "The prime minister is doing the talking now."

When I finished, Barak wanted to respond, but I didn't let him. I saw no need to have an argument about authority and status in the presence of senior military and defense officials. The final authority lay with me, and I was not about to allow him to abuse them.

Major General Amos Yadlin got up to speak. Yadlin, a modest man, was one of eight fighter pilots who destroyed the Osirak nuclear reactor in Iraq in 1981. It was no coincidence that he was here now, as chief of Military Intelligence. "No one will shut me up," Yadlin said. "As chief of Military Intelligence, I will say everything that needs to be said to the government." He launched into a detailed survey, at the end of which he arrived at what was by now a near consensus: We must destroy the reactor as soon as possible.

I concluded the meeting. I looked closely at the faces of my fellow ministers. Many of them were still in shock. Some, including those from Barak's own party, shook my hand. You were right all along, the situation is indeed dire, they told me.

I told them that it was fine for Barak to disagree, but that there are appropriate ways to express it.

———

During the preparations for the attack, I would often tell my cabinet that the 2006 Lebanon War was never far from my mind. On the one hand, we couldn't repeat the mistakes of Lebanon. On the other, the failures of that war—as there are in every war—should never scare us into making bad decisions. I had firsthand experience of cabinet officials who had agreed to a plan of action only to change their minds with the shifting winds of public opinion. That was not my way, not then and not ever.

None of us were looking for war. Nonetheless our discussion focused on dealing with a possible broader conflict, should it erupt. At the time, I was also engaged in talks with Turkish President Recep Tayyip Erdoğan to act as broker in negotiating a possible peace deal between Israel and Syria.

All this required tremendous discretion among everyone in the know. But there was another reason for utmost secrecy. It was my belief that it would be very difficult for the Israeli public to come to terms with a Syrian nuclear capability. As it was, the nuclear threat posed by Iran's program had already planted deep-seated existential anxieties in the Israeli collective consciousness.

I outlined the goals of the mission as follows: First and foremost, destroy the nuclear reactor, keep collateral damage to a minimum, and prevent an escalation. Second, I wanted the mission to improve our position in dealing with the Iranian threat, as well as our standing in Washington and our overall deterrence.

In a July 17 speech to the Syrian parliament some weeks before, Assad had spoken in vague terms about his country's changing destiny. The year "2007 is a fateful year," he said gravely. "Over the next few months the fate of the region and of the entire world will be cemented." He did not elaborate, but it was obvious to me that he believed that once he had a nuclear weapon, he would begin dealing with Israel in a very different manner.

We set a date for the mission for the early fall, in a month's time. Barak was still vehemently opposed, insisting we could always destroy the reactor later, after it went live. I said to him: "If you discover a small fire, should you wait for it to become a big fire before putting it out?"

One day, soon after, I walked into my office to find a letter on my desk from the defense minister. It was dated August 8—the date of the planning meeting when we had outlined the goals of the mission. In the letter, Barak declared that the briefing had been based on outdated intelligence that had been gathered before he took office as defense minister. "The Planning Directorate's document was not approved by the IDF chief of staff or the defense minister," he wrote. The presentation, he said, was little more than a "collection of slides" that had not received official approval.

I didn't know whether to laugh or cry.

Restraining myself, I replied with a letter that, at the very least, gave the respect his office commanded. I made it clear that the top echelons of the army had approved the Planning Directorate's briefing, and so it was a clear reflection of the IDF's official position and not merely a "collection of slides."

I was confident. Even if Barak did not relent, I could leave the decision to the cabinet, and an overwhelming majority would support my position. I was ready to put it off for two or three weeks, but I made it clear to Barak that the operation would take place no later than the end of the first week of September. Barak, however, was determined to stop me. I heard rumors that ministers were being called in for private meetings during which Barak would demonstrate his special talent of endlessly talking until he wore them down completely. He even told the justice minister, Danny Friedmann, that if I went ahead with the strike it would mean the end of the State of Israel. Friedmann found it hard to understand why an attack in the fall, with minimal fallout, would precipitate Israel's annihilation, while attacking an activated reactor in the spring would be acceptable. Nothing Barak said made sense, but he kept saying it.

Barak even summoned my two closest advisers, Turbowicz and Turjeman, to a meeting. They came away deeply troubled. All sense of reason, judgment, proportion, and accountability were missing from his presentation, which lasted until the early hours of the morning. Barak was known as a sophisticated man, but the things he said sometimes felt more like sophistry.

On August 31, I convened what was to be the final meeting on the matter at the prime minister's residence. Air Force Commander Eliezer Shkedi was invited to present the details of the proposed mission. Shkedi is one of the best fighter pilots in Israel's history. He is dispassionate and a consummate professional. I have always been impressed with his composure. The son of Holocaust survivors, Shkedi always remembered where he came from and was acutely aware of the burden he carried as commander of the Air Force of "the State of Israel and the Jewish people," as he put it.

Shkedi's words now would have a decisive effect on the upcoming decision. He spoke briefly and to the point, outlining the formation of his jets during their pinpoint operation, the timing, the approach and their planned escape routes. It sounded startlingly simple.

After a hard few months of deliberations, it all came down to this.

Before leaving the house, Shkedi asked to speak to me alone. "Mr. Prime Minister, I am asking you to please approve my plan," he said. "Put your trust into my pilots. They are the best in the world."

"As are you," I told him. "There is no need to worry."

———

But I was worried. Mainly about how Assad would respond. His missiles were deployed, and both his political and military standing were at an all-time high. His ties with Iran, on the one hand, and his connections to Hezbollah in Lebanon, on the other, only amplified his sense of empowerment. Syria was also enjoying a period of economic stability. Israel, meanwhile, was still reeling from the Second Lebanon War.

In the wake of that war, a narrative took hold among many Israelis—largely led by the media—that painted it as a failure. Stories were told about poor preparedness, about the failure to remove Hezbollah from the border, and so on.

Assad, too, was under the dangerous illusion that we had lost in Lebanon. He was convinced that the IDF—and, in particular, its commanders—were still licking their wounds. This made it harder to predict how he would react to the strike. Dagan doubted he would retaliate, but many disagreed with him, convinced the Syrian dictator would not be able to take so blatant an Israeli attack on the chin.

And that wasn't all. Another question troubled me, as well: How do you prepare for war without anyone noticing?

Assad, I came to understand, had long ceased listening to the old advisers who had surrounded his father, Hafez, who had ruled before him for decades. Even in the innermost circle of his government, the younger Assad had unquestioned authority.

My feeling was that as long as we didn't provoke or insult him publicly, he would begrudgingly accept Israel's action and the statement that it implied: that there were simply some threats that no sovereign government could tolerate. Instead of retaliating, he would focus on finding out how he had failed to conceal it.

Both the Mossad and Military Intelligence agreed with my assessment.

The suggestion was even made that we secretly inform Assad, by way of a third party, about the strike, either as it was happening or immediately after. We had done something similar during the Second Lebanon War when we conducted an air strike in the Bekaa Valley near the Syrian-Lebanese border. Here, too, it was suggested, such a move would make it clear to Assad that this was a targeted strike and not intended to trigger any escalation. Such messages, which were generally conveyed through people at the United Nations, had proved helpful in the past and had prevented retaliations.

This time, however, it was agreed that the best course of action would be to distance Assad as much as possible from the strike, since any kind of explicit alert might push him into a corner where he felt like he had to respond. Since so few people in Syria knew about the reactor's existence in the first place, Assad would almost certainly prefer to cover up its destruction rather than draw attention to the terrible embarrassment it would entail. Any message on our part would only serve to sharpen his sense of humiliation and raise questions in his mind about who else knew.

We decided we would act quickly and efficiently, without saying anything, neither in advance nor after the fact. It sounds easy enough, but in a country like ours it's almost impossible to believe that nothing will leak. To this day, I still can't believe we pulled it off. I never had any doubts that Shkedi and his pilots would destroy the reactor. But I always feared that the element of surprise would be lost when any one of the thousands who were in on the secret would fail to keep their mouths shut.

I will always remember a story Amos Yadlin shared with me. In June 1981, on the eve of the Shavuot holiday, eight pilots returned from the mission to destroy the Osirak nuclear reactor in Iraq and landed at a base in the south of the country. Before they went to sleep that night, they were reminded once again about the importance of keeping the operation secret. The next morning, Amos asked permission to visit his family. He stopped at the exit gate of the base to pick up a hitchhiking soldier. As the soldier seated himself, he turned to Yadlin and said: "You won't believe it, commander, but yesterday we destroyed a nuclear reactor in Iraq." Amos told me that he almost crashed the car.

———

As we were poised to take the final cabinet vote on the operation, I knew I had to get Barak on my side. Despite my estimation to the contrary, all-out war was still a real possibility, and even though Syria would suffer greatly—a war with us would, at a minimum, result in the destruction of its infrastructure and weapons systems—Israel, too, would take heavy civilian casualties. If word got out that the defense minister had fiercely opposed the operation, it could cause a nightmare. I was determined that our government show a united front, and Barak threatened that.

I summoned Major General (reserve) Amos Yaron, the former director-general of the Defense Ministry, to a meeting. Yaron, a former paratrooper who was both straight as an arrow and lacking in any personal agendas, was one of the few people in the world Barak might listen to. As with all the other missions I had tasked Yaron with in the past, he completed this one successfully. I have no idea what he said to Barak, but the result was that the defense minister turned himself around during the critical vote.

On Wednesday, September 5, 2007, the cabinet was set to vote. The discussion was blessedly brief. Even the defense minister—who the day before was still trying to maneuver to prevent the mission—understood that the die had been cast. Before the meeting, I called on Barak, Turbowicz, Turjeman, and the attorney general to help formulate a formal resolution to be voted on.

Experience had taught me that such pieces of paper are of little relevance for successful missions. They only matter when they fail. I knew that if, God forbid, something terrible happened, I would bear full responsibility.

Also, the Second Lebanon War had taught me that there were people who wouldn't hesitate to turn on me and burn me at the stake, who would completely forget everything positive that had been said before things went south. Only a year earlier, government ministers had, with unwavering conviction, called on me to deliver a violent blow to Hezbollah. Any hesitation would bring about untold danger, I was warned. More than once I reminded them that Hezbollah had the ability to target population centers in the middle of the country and that many, many people would be forced into bomb shelters. I also warned that any confrontation with the Lebanese terror group would last a long time, and that it would end with a large number of casualties. Those ministers, however, chose not to remember those conversations later. I did not want to repeat that mistake again.

As usual, Barak tried to add in all kinds of clauses, but I stopped him. We wrote a simple document that stated clearly that the prime minister, in consultation with the defense and foreign ministers, had decided on a date and method for destroying the Syrian nuclear reactor.

With the exception of Public Security Minister Avi Dichter, all the cabinet ministers voted in favor of the mission. I didn't wait around to hear the reasons for Dichter's opposition, nor did I care enough to try and change his mind. Instead, I called for another meeting at 6:00 p.m. in my office with IDF Chief of Staff Lieutenant General Gabi Ashkenazi, Mossad chief Meir Dagan, Defense Minister Barak, and Foreign Minister Livni.

At that meeting, Dagan and Ashkenazi were given the opportunity to speak first, and both recommended that the strike take place that very night, after midnight. They left the room. Barak and Livni each said they accepted the recommendation as well. I assented as well.

The trigger had been pulled.

———

Barak told us all to gather at midnight in the Pit. A fully equipped office and bedroom would be prepared for me, in case I needed to stay there for more than a few hours.

In the meantime, I invited Netanyahu to the prime minister's residence at 8:00 p.m. I told him that we would be destroying the reactor that night. He wished me success. I told Aliza that I had a long night ahead of me at the IDF headquarters in Tel Aviv, and I went to sleep for two hours. Much later on, friends of mine were shocked to learn that I'd managed to sleep at all. "You weren't too nervous?" they asked. I answered that my peace of mind resulted from the enduring trust I had in our Air Force.

At exactly midnight, we all gathered, deep underground, at the Air Force's command station in the Pit. Alongside Livni and Barak were the IDF Secretary Meir Klifi, the director-general of the Prime Minister's Office Raanan Dinur, as well as Turbowicz, Turjeman, and a few others. Since we were such a large group, Ashkenazi suggested we move to the larger hall next door, and leave Shkedi to command his pilots. A giant plasma screen showed the operation in real time. We all took our seats.

People often imagine that at times like these, everyone is unbearably tense. But sometimes reality doesn't work that way. In this case, Brigadier General Avishai Levy patiently explained the motion of the planes on the screen before casually remarking, "As we can see, they're deploying the ordnance."

Twenty minutes later, Shkedi walked into the room and said, simply: "Mr. Prime Minister, the pilots have just reported that the target was completely destroyed, as ordered."

I answered Shkedi with an embrace.

We then moved to another room to await further information. It was not yet clear whether the Syrians had understood what had happened, and if so, what their reaction would be. In the meantime, we chatted idly.

"That's it, you can now retire," Turbo quipped to me. "You've done your duty for the people of Israel."

Again, I responded with a hug.

An hour later, Syria issued a statement announcing that an attempted attack by Israel had failed, and that Israeli jets had been downed by the republic's air defenses. It was clear that Assad was choosing the quiet way out.

I felt the sudden need to take a long walk, much to the dismay of my security detail. I arrived back at my office in IDF headquarters at 3:30 a.m. I contacted the White House and was told that Bush, who was in Australia, would get back to me within the hour. When he called, I was careful with my words, even though I was sure he was on a secure line.

"Hey buddy," he said in his Texan drawl. "What's up?" I told him I was sorry for interrupting his trip but I wanted to let him know that the "thing" in Syria had been taken care of.

"That's great!" he enthused. He asked if I was expecting a response. I said that it was still too early to say for sure, but it seemed unlikely.

"If there are any problems, I want you to know that the United States will do everything to help you," he added.

I knew I would sleep well that night.

———

The day after we bombed the reactor in Deir al-Zour, barely a peep was heard about it from any Israeli sources. The international media reported on a mysterious overnight explosion in northeastern Syria. Damascus released a statement that foreign jets—likely Israeli—infiltrated Syrian airspace before being fought off by air defenses.

The following day, two jettisoned fuel tanks with Hebrew writing on them were found in separate locations in Turkey. The Turks demanded an explanation. I apologized to Erdoğan by phone, telling him that one of our planes had gone off course while on a training flight. Later I issued another public apology to the Turkish people, and soon enough the incident was forgotten. The local and foreign media continued to speculate about the incident, but we remained tight-lipped. That evening I attended an event hosted by the Kadima Party in honor of Rosh Hashana, and I was to give a speech. Journalists from every conceivable outlet were present, clinging to my every word, hoping I might let something slip about Syria. Instead I talked about pretty much everything else, just not that.

That same evening, the leader of the opposition, Netanyahu, was being interviewed on the news. The anchor asked him if he knew anything about Israeli planes that may have bombed Syria. He answered that needless to say, the matter was classified, but that after consulting with the prime minister, he had given his blessing. He added that when it comes to security matters, all parties must show a united front. I was appalled: How much more could he say short of admitting it outright?

Even then, though, we stayed silent. Our refusal to comment, coupled with the upcoming high holidays, helped push the matter out of the news cycle. And despite his slip-up, to his credit Netanyahu had known about the strike for many months and had never said a word.

Eventually, in April 2008, an official statement about the mission appeared on the CIA's website. The announcement came on the heels of a White House report submitted to Congress. Thereafter came a deluge of conflicting accounts of the mission. In the years that have passed, the Syria attack has shed much of its secrecy.

———

We made a serious effort to open peace negotiations with Syria.

I believed that the key to breaking through the walls that surrounded Bashar al-Assad rested with Turkey. I spoke about this with Recep Tayyip Erdoğan, then the prime minister of Turkey and today its president, a number of times. The first time, I asked him for a private meeting, just the two of us plus an interpreter. I was asking him to put together a delegation that might just have immense historic significance.

I wanted to make peace with Syria.

"I believe," I told him, "that you are the most appropriate person to launch a new dialogue between Israel and Syria. I know exactly what Assad wants, and you can tell him that in my name." I asked Erdoğan to tell Assad that I wanted a full peace, full diplomatic relations, open borders, trade, to cut the link between the Syrian military on the one hand and Hezbollah and Iran on the other hand, and to stop the infiltration of terrorists from Syria into Iraq, where they were attacking American soldiers. "If this can be the basis of talks," I added, "then I'm ready and willing."

The first conversation with Erdoğan was in March 2007. He responded by asking me about an entirely different topic. "Why are you wasting your time in talks with Abbas?" he said. "Abbas doesn't represent the Palestinians. You need to talk to Hamas."

I was getting dragged into an argument. I explained that Hamas could not be a partner for negotiations. Its leaders were not even willing to consider accepting the principles of the Quartet—a joint delegation of the United States, Russia, the EU, and the UN—which was the internationally agreed prerequisite for recognizing them. There was no chance I'd talk with them.

The conversation dragged on. Erdoğan forgot about Syria.

I tried again, but Erdoğan was preoccupied with Hamas. I would ask about Assad, and he would answer me about Hamas's leader, Ismail Haniyeh.

I was undeterred. I was convinced that precisely because Erdoğan was a fundamentalist Muslim, the leader of an Islamist party, Assad would be more ready to accept him than any European intermediary.

Eventually he started listening. We agreed that Erdoğan would meet with Assad in person. It had to be an intimate, heart-to-heart conversation, with Erdoğan personally endorsing me, saying I had convinced him of my determination to reach a peace agreement with the full knowledge of what Assad would expect in return.

Some time passed, and then a reply finally came.

————

Assad was ready to begin indirect talks.

Assad would send people to Ankara, I would send people of my own, and the Turks would shuttle between their hotels. We would see where things went from there.

This arrangement gave the Turks center stage, and it was important for me to know who would be representing Erdoğan. The two people he picked were his personal adviser, Ahmet Davutoğlu, and his deputy foreign minister, Feridun Sinirliouğlu. Sinirliouğlu had previously served as Turkey's ambassador to Israel. An honest man, friendly to Israel and also personally to me during his time in Tel Aviv, Davutoğlu would go on to become the prime minister of Turkey after Erdoğan became president. Then he got in trouble with Erdoğan and revealed himself quickly as an extreme Islamist. Despite this, in the context of his efforts to foster dialogue with Syria, he played a fair hand.

I appointed my two closest aides—Yoram Turbowicz and Shalom Turjeman. They were perfect for this sort of negotiation. Beyond their other strengths, Turjeman spoke fluent Arabic, which helps in any negotiation with an Arab state like Syria.

Assad sent the legal adviser to Syria's foreign ministry, Riad Daoudi. Daoudi took part in all of the preliminary talks and could be relied upon to recall everything that had been discussed, agreed to, rejected, or happened between us and the Syrians.

During all of this we continued with our preparations to destroy the nuclear reactor in Syria. The Turks clearly knew nothing about it. I wasn't worried that destroying the reactor would scuttle the talks.

From the outset, again, I assumed it was extremely unlikely that Syria would allow itself to be dragged into an all-out war with us. They would have no chance in such a war: Their forces would be crushed, Damascus would be leveled, and their missile arsenal would be eviscerated. Of course, we, too, would pay a very heavy price. At the same time, having a channel of dialogue open between us could help ease things in the aftermath of our attack on the reactor. It never occurred to me to abandon the plan to destroy it under any circumstance.

———

Turbowicz and Turjeman started flying regularly to Istanbul. Nobody knew about it. I told them to update only two other people: Uri Sagi and Itamar Rabinovich. Sagi, a reserve major general, was a serious, profound thinker who had handled negotiations with Syria during Barak's government, and I liked his approach. I figured that if the talks developed into complex direct negotiations, Sagi would undoubtedly be a senior member of the team. I wanted Turbowicz and Turjeman to hear from him early on about what had previously been discussed and to draw insight from someone who knew the other side well.

Rabinovich, a world-renowned expert on the Middle East and former Israeli ambassador to the United States, was also a veteran of contacts with Syria going as far back as the government of Yitzhak Rabin. Itamar had been Rabin's confidant. I respected—and continue to respect deeply—his experience, his amazing breadth of knowledge, and his discretion. He, too, had a lot to teach us.

———

I decided that a strict veil of secrecy had to be placed over the talks. Naturally, things started off unevenly, the meetings occasional, but each meeting required thorough preparation. This enabled Turbowicz and Turjeman to build trust with their Turkish counterparts. Without trust, I knew, there would be no progress.

I did believe it was important to update the Americans, however. Traditionally the road from Jerusalem to Damascus passed through Washington—so it was under Rabin and continuing during the governments of Peres, Netanyahu, and Barak. This time, despite my complete faith in the Bush administration, I felt that using a different go-between would be more effective. But I didn't want to leave the Americans out of the loop. That's not how you behave with your closest allies, especially given my nearly daily contacts with the administration's most senior officials.

I told Secretary of State Condoleezza Rice about my intention to negotiate with Syria, and about the connection I'd made with Erdoğan and the initial steps we had taken. I asked her to let the president know. She wasn't pleased. She said they had already understood that efforts were being made to reach out to the Syrians. They felt, however, that Assad could not be trusted.

I made it clear that I would not reach understandings with Assad without coordinating with the United States, or without a Syrian commitment to stop the flow of terrorists into Iraq. Rice asked me to update her from time to time. I assured her that I would.

At a much later stage, in one of my conversations with Bush, the president told me that he wouldn't have tried to negotiate with Assad. I explained to him why it was important to Israel. I believed—and I still believe—that peace with the Palestinians and a peace treaty with Syria would have completely changed the geopolitical map.

Bush was curious as to why I had chosen to reject the traditional Israeli position, according to which you don't pursue peace talks with more than one Arab state at the same time.

I said that many myths had been crafted to justify inaction or failure. Maybe nothing would come of this, but I wasn't looking for excuses. The myth that it would be impossible to convince the Israeli public of two parallel diplomatic agreements was not something I believed in. If the agreements were good for Israel, Israelis would support it.

Bush remained doubtful, but said to me explicitly: "If you get close to a deal, it's important that Assad knows that the road to Washington goes through Jerusalem." This was deeply encouraging.

Meanwhile, the clock was ticking. Early September arrived, and we destroyed the reactor. As we expected, the Syrians took it on the chin. I wondered whether they would pull out of the talks. Surprisingly, the opposite happened.

Sinirlioğlu and Davutoğlu asked to meet with me in early November 2007. They came to Israel and told me that the foreign minister of Syria, Walid Muallem, had invited them to Damascus and told them that Syria wanted to continue the quiet diplomacy with Israel. It was a pleasant surprise.

In the meantime, the Annapolis Peace Conference had been set for November 27 (an event I detail in the next chapter). The Americans proposed that the Syrians participate as well. I wasn't convinced that the rest of the Arab states, which had distanced themselves from Assad, would be happy about this, but I didn't interfere. In the end, Syria's deputy foreign minister—a lower-level representative than the dignitaries of the other countries—showed up, signaling that Assad didn't want to be left out.

———

The talks in Istanbul continued. Erdoğan's emissaries shuttled between the hotel where Turbo and Turjeman were staying and that of Daoudi, but it felt like they were spinning their wheels. I wanted to see progress. I felt the time had come to end the preliminary stage and to reach a formula that would allow for a public announcement about the talks, even if they were still indirect.

Until then we had managed to keep everything under wraps, but it was clear that sooner or later something would leak. At some point a reporter for Channel 2 caught a glimpse of Turbowicz and Turjeman at the airport in Istanbul. It was not hard for him to gather, and I believe he went on to report, that Israel was doing something secret in Turkey. I had also filled in Ehud Barak and Tzipi Livni, and my experience had taught me that nothing stays secret forever. I was worried that an irresponsible leak would bring the talks to a halt—that either the Syrians or the Turks would call it off. I didn't want to embarrass either of them, especially at the expense of our own national interest.

On May 15, 2008, at noon, the announcement was made simultaneously in Jerusalem, Ankara, and Damascus. It said that Israel and Syria were looking into the possibility of direct negotiations leading toward a peace deal, with the mediation of Turkey.

It was received with total surprise. Nobody in Israel (other than Barak, Livni, Sagi, and Rabinovich) had any inkling. Nothing had leaked. The surprise and the hope that followed were great. The fact that Syria had agreed to publicly acknowledge the talks was a big step to the next phase. It created a sense of commitment on Assad's part toward Turkey, Israel, the international community, and the Arab world.

———

The Syrian negotiators put their focus on the border demarcation in the area of the Sea of Galilee. They spoke explicitly about having the border run a few hundred yards east of the shoreline, north of Kibbutz Ein Gev, and that the road from the sea to the border would be under Israeli sovereignty. The worry that Syria would insist on having direct access to the Sea of Galilee proved unfounded, at least at that stage.

I presented the details to Barak and Livni. Barak was surprised and said that what Syria was proposing was infinitely better than what they had offered eight years earlier. Livni didn't seem interested in the details.

———

In the next phase, Turkey produced a list of points that, in their view, would have to form the basis for negotiation. They let both sides know that they would agree to continue mediating only if the two sides would accept these points. If either side opposed, they would pull out, without casting blame on either side.

We looked over the paper, and we were not especially troubled. There was the basis of agreement on a reasonable border, without the Syrians having access to the Sea of Galilee. Barak said that we had to respond favorably. Livni expressed shock, claimed she hadn't been updated on the details, and even sent me a letter expressing her objections. Turbowicz reminded her that her ministry's director general, Aharon Abramovitch, had been updated directly. And Barak, as always, did not pass up the opportunity to flip-flop. A few weeks later he sent me a letter saying we should reconsider our position. He now opposed the paper as well.

I read his letter carefully and decided to continue on the path we had started on.

———

As 2008 progressed, I felt we had to do something to ensure the future of the talks.

I invited the Turkish mediators to Israel and told them the indirect talks were taking too long. The time had come to change course. I had responded favorably to all of the Syrian proposals and also to the Turkish list of points, including the border. "You," I told the mediators, "can tell them that I am serious about achieving a peace deal. The rest is up to them. If they are serious, I will agree to meet with Assad in Ankara."

It was in December 2008 that Erdoğan called to tell me he had reached agreement with Assad, in accordance with the principles I had expressed to the Turkish emissaries. He then invited me to come to Ankara within a week. The understanding was that this visit would include a three-way meeting, together with Assad.

———

The Israeli Air Force jet landed in Ankara. We were received warmly at the national guest house. The atmosphere over dinner was jovial. At the end of the meal, Erdoğan suggested that he and I retire to his private study. There he told me that he would call Assad right then and there. Rooms had been reserved for all of us in a hotel in Ankara, and in the morning there would be a joint press conference with the three leaders.

Erdoğan suggested that I stay in the room as he spoke to Assad. I politely declined. He would instead talk to Assad and tell me about it afterward. I knew that Erdoğan spoke fluent Arabic and that they would be speaking in Arabic. I didn't want to be in a position that would allow someone to claim I had witnessed a conversation and given something my tacit approval, when in fact I hadn't understood what was said.

I went to the next room. The conversation went on and on. Every half hour or so, Erdoğan called me in, signaled that Assad was with him on the line, and put his hand over the mouthpiece. Clearly there were problems. I said I would wait outside. I had time.

———

At 1:30 a.m., Erdoğan told me that Walid Muallem's plane was on the tarmac at Damascus airport, waiting to take off, but Assad was adamant that at the next morning's joint press conference the announcement would be made that Israel was returning the Golan Heights to Syria.

I made it clear that this was not happening. No such understanding had been reached. I was willing to negotiate about peace. The contents of that negotiation would include the price that each side was willing to pay for it. I had been invited to Ankara under this understanding. If more time was required to convince Assad, I was just a ninety-minute flight away. Whenever Erdoğan and Assad were ready, I would happily return to Ankara.

We parted ways. I never met with Erdoğan again.

———

A fundamental question arises when comparing the Syrian nuclear threat with that of Iran. Why did I feel it was absolutely necessary to destroy the reactor, in the process flouting the opinion of the president of the United States? How is it that when the United States refused to take military action in Syria, I took up the baton, but when it came to Iran I argued that under no circumstance should Israel take the lead in attacking Tehran's nuclear infrastructure?

It should be made very clear that even after President Barack Obama concluded his nuclear deal (known as the JCPOA, or Joint Comprehensive Plan of Action) in 2015, Iran did not change its nuclear aspirations. This Iranian project has been going on for many years, and enormous resources have been invested in it. If it weren't for the regime's single-minded determination to become a nuclear power, there is no way Iran would have continued to absorb such crippling sanctions from the West.

A nuclear Iran would completely change the balance of power in the Middle East and constitute a very real threat to Israel. The tiniest military act anywhere in the region would need to be weighed against the possibility of nuclear war. I have repeatedly emphasized my position, both as prime minister and since then, that Israel cannot accept a nuclear Iran.

On this issue at least, Netanyahu and I are in complete agreement. We discussed it many times when I was in office, and I was always attentive to his thoughts and advice. Israel has for years acted both openly and in secret to combat Iran's nuclear program, and has achieved some stunning successes on this front.

Israel is not the only country to take measures against Iran. Other countries, either acting alone or in partnerships, have taken steps to stop the Islamic Republic. Many experts were convinced that by 2008 or 2009 Iran would have already built a bomb. The fact that more than a decade later it still hasn't happened is due to the courage of those leaders who have acted to stop it.

That being said, I believe that President Obama's nuclear agreement, while certainly far from optimal, was preferable to an Israeli attack on Iran. I know from personal conversations with some of his closest aides that the overwhelming advice Obama received from his intelligence chiefs was that an Israeli attack would not only fail to eliminate the nuclear threat, it might even accelerate it. At the same time, it would plunge the entire Middle East into turmoil that could have a devastating ripple effect on Europe. Obama came to the correct conclusion that negotiating with Iran was the lesser of two evils.

The indefatigable noisemaking of the Israeli leadership, characterized by the raucous, theatrical hyperbole of Netanyahu and Barak that included misleading reports to the cabinet, doomsday scenarios, wildly exaggerated timelines about an Iranian nuclear "breakout," Netanyahu's performative-theater speech at the UN, and his very public clash with President Obama that culminated in Netanyahu's 2015 speech before a joint session of Congress, no doubt backfired, increasing the Obama administration's determination to close the deal. It also harmed U.S.-Israel relations to this day.

TEN

The Promised Land

I've told you about how, in the weeks leading up to the March 2006 elections, I decided to ignore the advice of all my campaign staff and put my plans for peace with the Palestinians, and the territorial compromise this necessarily entailed, explicitly at the center of my campaign. While every candidate for prime minister before me, from Begin to Rabin and Peres to Sharon, felt a need to hide their true intentions in this area during the campaign, I believed that I owed it to the voting public to know where I stood, even at the risk of a few Knesset seats.

I was willing to withdraw unilaterally from the West Bank, just as Sharon had from Gaza. But what I really wanted was a negotiated, comprehensive peace deal with the Palestinians. And I knew that to even begin talking, official Israel would have to change its tone. We needed to stop belittling the Palestinians and complaining about previous commitments they hadn't honored. Instead, more than any prime minister before me, I tried to create an atmosphere of cooperation, mutual respect, trust, and patience. I was determined to focus on the future, not the past.

Every successful negotiator, whether in business or public affairs, knows there is no substitute for patience. Give the other side time to digest your moves. Let them come around to see things your way. Sometimes you have to make them sweat while you stay steady and calm. Eventually, the other side will wear out. If they don't, and only then, does the time come for unilateral moves.

Opponents of the 2005 disengagement from Gaza argued that by acting unilaterally, Israel had given up on any future negotiated settlement. The claim is legitimate, but it ignores the fact that in all the years since the Oslo Accords, we had been dealing with Yassir Arafat. According to our intelligence, Arafat had given up on achieving any negotiated settlement. He was the one who had taken advantage of the Oslo Accords to prepare for further bloodshed, and who had rejected Ehud Barak's generous offers and chosen instead to launch the Second Intifada.

The rise of Mahmoud Abbas as the Palestinian Authority president after Arafat's death in November 2004 created a new opportunity. He turned against the terrorist organizations and spoke out against terror. And it wasn't just lip service in English, the way it had been with Arafat. Abbas spoke out in Arabic, to his own people.

I wanted to send a clear, undeniable signal to the Palestinians that if I were elected, we could create a new future for both our peoples.

———

And so, immediately after the election, I sent a message to Abbas of friendship and the hope that we would meet soon.

He replied in a similar vein, but events got in the way of our meeting. In June, we informally saw each other, for the first time since the election, in Petra, Jordan. But it was purely symbolic, and I was interested in starting something formal and substantive. The Second Lebanon War erupted in July, and ended on August 14, and no Arab leader could get away with meeting me during a hot war. Subsequent clashes between Israel and Hamas in Gaza made it difficult for him to appear with me in public, even if he shed few tears about our hitting his archrivals. During the fall, we agreed by phone to set a meeting, but then he kept rescheduling last-minute.

Seven and a half months would pass from the time I was elected until he finally agreed to a dinner on a Saturday night, December 23, 2006, at the prime minister's residence.

From the Palestinian side, participants were to include Ahmed Qurei, one of the most powerful people in the PLO, as well as chief negotiator Saeb Erekat, and Abbas's chief of staff, Rafiq al-Husseini. From the Israeli side I invited my aides Yoram Turbowicz and Shalom Turjeman, the government's military secretary Gadi Shamni, and my spokesman Asi Shariv.

The day before the dinner, at 11:00 a.m. on Friday, I received a call from Turjeman. Erekat had called asking to set up a phone call with Abbas instead of dinner.

"Don't let him get out of it," Turbowicz implored. "Whatever happens, insist. If this meeting gets postponed, we'll never see him."

We got on the phone with Abbas.

Abbas quickly got the point, telling me he was sorry but couldn't make dinner Saturday night. He had to be in Gaza. "Let's put it off for a few days," he offered.

I kept pushing him to come to dinner. He offered various excuses, but it was clear he was just trying to get out of it. When I saw that he wouldn't budge, I said to him, "Okay, Mr. President. I understand that you have decided to embarrass me. I assume you have a good reason that you aren't sharing. But why do you insist on offending my wife?"

"Your wife?" he was surprised. "How am I offending your wife?"

I told him that from the moment I told Aliza that he would be a guest for dinner, she had been on her feet, cooking anything she thought he might like. "What do I tell her now?"

He fell silent. I could feel his discomfort. "I will come," he said. "Tomorrow at 8:00 p.m."

On Saturday evening, Turbowicz and Turjeman, accompanied by six police cars, received Abbas and his entourage in their black Mercedes limousines at the Bitunya checkpoint. They set out together for Jerusalem. When they arrived, the Palestinians saw two flags raised above the Prime Minister's Residence: One Israeli, the other Palestinian.

It was the first time the Palestinian flag had flown over the residence. Just a few years earlier, you could go to jail for raising it at all. But you can't negotiate for peace without treating the other side with mutual respect, both on the personal level and at the level of national symbols.

Once inside, they found that the table, too, was decorated with Israeli and Palestinian flags. Palestinian and Israeli photographers snapped pictures which went out to media around the world and were published even as we were still eating.

After the initial pleasantries, the first topic of discussion was the freeing of Palestinian prisoners. Abbas said it was a critical issue, touching the lives of thousands of families. We were prepared. It was clear they were talking about prisoners from his own Fatah faction, not the rivals in Hamas. I asked him how many prisoners he expected us to release.

He said 500.

I told him we would have no choice but to release 900.

This wasn't what they expected to hear. They then asked for 1,000 rifles for their security forces. I agreed. Abbas said he needed our approval to take delivery on 50 light armored personnel carriers that the Russian government had granted for law enforcement. I agreed.

I asked them how much money they needed.

"Israel always gives us less than we have coming to us," Abbas said of the taxes we collected on the Palestinian Authority's behalf as part of the Oslo Accords. For years, we had paid them in drips and drabs, leaving them dependent on our graces and giving us a point of leverage. "I have been advised to ask for 10 million shekels," he continued, "but we need 50. That's what I'm asking for."

Instead I offered him 100 million U.S. dollars, or about eight times that. "We will send you the full amount immediately, and from now on we will pay you whatever we owe."

The guests weren't sure they heard me correctly. They were stunned, baffled, and above all, they began to understand how different my government's approach to peace was from everything that came before.

"The money is yours," I said. I wanted to make clear that we would be doing things very differently under my leadership.

———

In a one-on-one meeting after dinner, Abbas and I discussed who would be heading up our negotiating teams. He chose Ahmed Qurei, and though I was skeptical about his intentions, Abbas insisted that he needed Qurei's political support for any deal. On our end I appointed Tzipi Livni. When I told Tzipi of the appointment, she was at home, sitting *shiva* for the death of her mother. She told me it was, for her, a dream come true.

The negotiations would split into two different tracks. One would address a long string of technical issues such as airspace, border controls, electromagnetic space, access to the sea, water sources, and so on, to be worked out through side agreements.

The other track concerned the basic issues. I would handle them myself directly with Abbas. I had no intention of letting anyone else touch them, and Livni was fine with that. We would update each other, I'd respond to her concerns, but I gave her no authority over them.

"Everything is on the table, including Jerusalem," I said to Abbas on that first night. "There is no subject that I refuse to discuss."

Abbas then said something I would never forget. "I need something symbolic on the subject of refugees," he said. *"I don't want to change the nature of the State of Israel."*

Those were his exact words.

We can argue about his character, his power, his honesty, his ability to deliver, or his true aims. I'm familiar with all the arguments. Nobody can erase what he said, however.

Israel, in the simple meaning of his words, is a Jewish state. He was asking us to make a symbolic gesture on the subject of refugees, because he understood that there was no chance that everyone who left in 1948, including their children and grandchildren, which started as hundreds of thousands but now went into the millions scattered in refugee camps across the Middle East, would be allowed to return to the villages they had left. No one expects Israel to erase its identity and destroy its essence.

I didn't ask him to elaborate. I told him that this would be up for discussion as well.

That first meeting had dramatic implications for two main reasons. First, it created a positive atmosphere between the two teams. It would take some time for that to turn into friendship and trust, but the first meeting laid the groundwork for genuine discussions rather than arguments, finger pointing, and unflattering leaks.

Second, both sides were given the opportunity to lay out their expectations. I had no interest in another round of posturing. I wanted to negotiate for real.

The meeting ended. The motorcade pulled away, the limousines escorted by police cars with lights flashing and sirens blaring, befitting a foreign head of state.

Later I was told that as soon as he got in the car, Abbas told his aides that a new era had begun in relations with Israel. From then on, nothing would be the same. "Olmert," he said, "genuinely wants to take this very far."

———

I proposed to Abbas that we meet every two or three weeks. He agreed. In parallel, I set up a support staff for Livni's negotiating team that included people from the relevant ministries and intelligence agencies. The team reported to me and frequently updated my aides, and we also received ongoing intelligence from Shin Bet about how the other side was responding to our proposals.

The only thing that got in the way was Abbas's frequent trips abroad. I wondered why he had to travel so often. When I asked him, he told me that while I only had to update the United States and a few European leaders, he was obligated to meet with leaders of all the Arab states that were funding him, and had to see them in person so that none of them felt slighted.

All along the way, the most important question was how much we were willing to give up: What degree of risk were we willing to take on, what we could get in exchange for that risk, and where we couldn't be flexible.

First of all, I had to spell these things out for myself.

By setting my own red lines and sticking to them, I could avoid long days of self-torture when the time came to decide on painful concessions. I knew I'd be under immense pressure—not just from the Israeli public, but above all from myself, my own long-held beliefs and aspirations.

There was very little outside pressure. Though they occasionally objected to minor developments, such as our responses to terror attacks, at no point did anyone from the Bush administration—certainly not the president—ask us to compromise on our own vital interests. The same was true for European governments. No threats, even implicit ones, of diplomatic isolation or economic consequences if we didn't compromise. We enjoyed the best possible conditions for productive negotiations. We just needed to make sure we didn't lose momentum after a strong start.

The most important next step was for me to get closer with Abbas. I was aware of his suspicions flowing from his prior relationships with Israeli leaders.

In our second meeting, I didn't dive straight in. I figured that if there were problems that could be solved at the day-to-day level—transfer of funds, onerous checkpoints that hindered the movement of ordinary Palestinians, unplanned clashes between members of their security forces and ours, the provocations and, at times, criminal behavior of settlers—he would not hesitate to raise them. Some of our people found it amusing that the Palestinians opened every meeting with a series of complaints. But what choice did they have? Were they just supposed to swallow their pride and not complain? Would we have behaved differently?

After lunch with the teams, Abbas and I retired to the study. I suggested a more personal conversation. I wanted to hear about his family, and I'd talk about mine. How could we talk about our "peoples" without talking about our own children and grandchildren?

This was unusual in Arab diplomatic culture, and certainly in the history of meetings with Israelis, but I knew it would move us forward. I heard him choke up when he spoke of Mazen, his son who died of a heart attack. It was easier when my turn came. I told him about my children and grandchildren. He said he had heard a lot about Aliza and her political opinions. We spent hours talking about things that may have seemed irrelevant, but I saw them as extremely valuable. They allowed us to create a personal connection, and then negotiate in a warm atmosphere.

The meetings followed a regular format. Lunch at the residence at around 1:00 p.m., with both teams there. From our end that usually included Tzipi Livni and her team. On the Palestinian side Qurei and

Saeb Erekat were always there, as well as some others depending on the topic. Lunch went for about an hour, and afterward just the two of us would go into our study, for at least two hours more. The teams waited outside, talked, and hammered out a press release about the meeting.

———

Meanwhile, the Arab world made sure its voice was heard.

In March 2007, the Arab League held a summit in Riyadh, the Saudi capital, and called upon the Palestinians to create a unity government that included Hamas. In their view, only through the resolution of inter-Arab conflicts could an effective response to the rising threat of Iran be mounted. We saw this as an unfortunate walking back of quiet understandings we had reached with several Arab states, including those with whom we had no formal relations. The upshot of the announcement was to legitimize Hamas, an internationally recognized terror group. I read it as casting doubt on Abbas's ability to hold on to his rule. We, too, were concerned about his ability to deliver, but we had expected the Arab League to back him rather than demanding that he join up with his most bitter enemies. Since they were the main source of his funding, he had no choice but to comply.

I expressed my disappointment and made clear to Abbas that Israel would only deal with and through the PLO. The joint delegation of the United States, Russia, the EU, and the UN—the Quartet—was not happy, either. President Bush told me explicitly that his faith in Abbas, which was anyway limited, had been shaken. Condoleezza Rice was frustrated too. The Israeli-Palestinian conflict had been her central project as secretary of state, and she hoped to reach a peace deal that had been a holy grail for every secretary of state and president since 1967. The Riyadh summit lowered the chances of it happening.

During this time, the Arab League also reaffirmed its commitment to the Arab Peace Initiative that was first proposed in February 2002 in Beirut. According to the initiative, "a just and comprehensive peace in the Middle East is the strategic option of the Arab countries." The Arab states would declare an end to the conflict with Israel and normalize relations, but demanded in exchange the complete withdrawal from all territories conquered in 1967, including the Golan Heights and eastern

Jerusalem, the establishment of a Palestinian state in the territories we evacuated, and also a "just solution to the Palestinian refugee problem."

When the Arab Peace Initiative, or API, was formally adopted by the Arab League in 2002, I didn't say anything in public. I was, at the time, the mayor of Jerusalem and not a member of government. I did share my thoughts privately with Sharon, however. API contained landmines that wouldn't allow Israel to accept it in its current formulation. But the willingness of the Arab League to commit to full peace with Israel, even under conditions Israel would never accept, was unprecedented.

Soon after the establishment of the Palestinian unity government, I received a visit from Abbas and Muhammad Dahlan.

Dahlan, one of the leading security figures among the Palestinians, was the chief of Fatah, the largest faction in the PLO, in Gaza. He told me his plans for eliminating Hamas from the strip, spelled out the forces he had at his disposal, how they were armed and deployed. He said he planned on launching a military offensive that would shatter Hamas in Gaza and open the door for a change in attitude toward Israel.

The opposite, of course, happened. In early June 2007, in a complete surprise, Hamas launched an operation to destroy Dahlan's forces. Dahlan himself was in Cairo at the time undergoing medical treatment. Hamas may well have taken advantage of his absence to get the element of surprise. Within a few days, almost nothing remained of Dahlan's military forces. Hamas opened up Dahlan's armories and found brand new weapons, wrapped in their original packaging, but none of his officers had been able to launch a significant counterattack.

Hamas showed extreme brutality, throwing Fatah members out of sixth-floor windows, crippling others by shooting them in the knees.

So much for the unity government. The entire Palestinian Authority was on the brink of collapse.

Abbas was in shock, and not just him. The Americans too. A few days later I flew to the United States on other business. The Americans, again, supported my peace moves but had doubts about Abbas's ability to deliver. Bush even said to me: "He doesn't know how to seize opportunities. He will not pass the test." Opinions about Dahlan were divided. Many thought he was corrupt and cavalier, that there was no connection between his overconfident words and his ability to conduct a tough campaign against Hamas. They were not surprised that his forces were routed.

Since I never had expectations, I was not disappointed. I always thought Hamas was ready for war against Dahlan. Shin Bet, too, had been skeptical. Dahlan, they said, was too busy dealing with his own personal finances to put in the work required to build a serious military force. At any rate, the Hamas overthrow of the strip fundamentally changed the strategic reality in the region.

Egyptian President Hosni Mubarak called me up. He was worried. He proposed a summit at Sharm El-Sheikh, on the southern tip of the Sinai Peninsula. We would ask King Abdullah of Jordan to join, as well as Abbas.

———

The format for the summit, held June 26, 2007, was straightforward: One-on-one meetings for each leader with each of the others, ending with a final meeting of the four of us together with the press. The aim was to make it clear that we had Abbas's back, that we were all cooperating in the effort to find a solution of peace in the Middle East, and would do everything to stop Hamas, including the use of force.

My conversation with Mubarak was fascinating. He was bitter that the United States had pressured Abbas to allow Hamas to participate in the elections they held in 2006: "Your friend Bush wanted Hamas to take part in the elections, because he believes in democracy. So here you go, now they have democracy."

The Egyptian president went on to discuss at length the ignorance in the Western world about the true nature of extremist groups, and complained loudly about the criticism against him for his actions against the Muslim Brotherhood. His position was understandable, and would become more so later on. The Muslim Brotherhood took advantage of the Arab Spring protests to try to overthrow Mubarak and take over Egypt. The Americans—by now it was the Obama administration— pressured Mubarak to resign, laying the groundwork for an extremist government led by Mohamed Morsi.

Mubarak was right, of course. The Morsi regime was much worse than his. The Muslim Brotherhood, like its Palestinian spinoff Hamas, is a radical jihadist group, with no interest in democratic, civil, or human rights.

———

Not every nation is ripe for democratic rule.

The traditional American position, which focuses on the universality of political rights and freedom, is of course, morally right. But when you try to force democratization, it can undermine the stability of countries like these, with the result being far worse from the perspective of rights and equality. Anyone who lives in a real democracy can't publicly support a regime that tramples on human rights and equality before the law. At the same time—how do we make sure that getting rid of one nondemocratic regime won't bring another one, possibly far more violent and dangerous?

I can still see the images of Mubarak in his iron cage, standing trial while lying down, accused of corruption and opening fire on civilians. Some people felt satisfaction, since he had been similarly brutal toward his own rivals, and the charges he now faced may have had more than a bit of truth to them. But anyone who treats a former president this way won't have much regard for democratic principles. The Morsi regime was fundamentalist and extreme, and could easily have become a major sponsor of terror in the region.

Fortunately for the region and the world, the overthrow was later followed by a military coup. Morsi was deposed after only thirteen months in the wake of massive protests. The new regime under Abdel Fattah al-Sisi is not all that different from Mubarak's. Al-Sisi is certainly not the democratic leader that Bush and Obama may have wanted. Washington, too, learned that the attempt to bring Western democracy to a country like Egypt could end in catastrophe. You have to accept al-Sisi and hope that he leads responsibly. So far, so good.

———

My meeting with Abbas at Sharm el-Sheikh was no less depressing than the one with Mubarak.

As we began, he opened a folder and handed me a ten-page document. On every page was a photograph, along with the name of the man in the picture. These people, he told me, had conspired to kill him. He was on his way to Gaza a few days earlier when he got word from his security chief that a half-ton bomb had been discovered under a bridge along the planned route. He was forced to turn back.

He was already shaken by the events of the previous month: The murder of dozens of Fatah people in Gaza, the maiming of dozens more, and now this. "These people deserve to die," he said. I couldn't tell whether he was asking me to take action or just sharing the danger he was in. It was clear the Palestinian Authority was in distress, and that he needed my help to bring order, strengthen his forces and prevent the infiltration of Hamas in the West Bank.

At the end, each of us gave a speech. We all tried to bolster Abbas's standing. I emphasized that Israel was committed to improving the quality of life of the residents of the West Bank, and that we would do everything to strengthen the new government, without Hamas, including transferring tax funds we had collected on their behalf.

I also spoke about the residents of Gaza. I said that I knew that many of them were suffering under Hamas and exposed whenever we retaliated against Hamas terrorism. I knew the time would soon come that Israel would have to launch a ground assault in Gaza. Hamas's overthrow of the strip made that time draw nearer. Later, in December 2008, in the waning months of my term as prime minister, that day would finally arrive.

———

I made clear to Abbas in our meetings that I accepted the principle of returning to the 1967 borders. Implementing it, however, would require some adjustments.

The majority of Israeli West Bank settlers lived in three main blocs—two of them, Gush Etzion and Maaleh Adumim, abutting Jerusalem and the third around the city of Ariel. In these blocs, hundreds of thousands of Israeli citizens had made their lives over the four decades that had passed since 1967. People were born there and were buried there. In addition to housing, there were factories, farms, shopping centers, community centers, and more. Uprooting the twenty-one small communities of Gaza had been a national trauma and led to months of civil unrest. Evacuating whole cities was simply impossible.

And so, while Sharon was still prime minister in 2004, the idea had arisen of "land swaps." An agreement with the Palestinians would include annexation of these blocs, and in exchange Israel would give over land from within its borders. President Bush had expressed his support for the idea in a letter to Sharon and it became part of the U.S. plan.

I told Abbas that such swaps should, in my view, be made on a one-to-one basis. He accepted this. The question was: What land would we offer him in exchange?

We also talked about Jerusalem. Abbas's real political difficulty came from the fact—almost unknown in the West—that most of the Palestinians in the neighborhoods and villages that had been annexed to Jerusalem were not, and today still are not, interested in being cut off from the Israeli capital or from Israel in general. Living in a unified Jerusalem under Israeli rule gave them freedom of movement in Israel as well as significant benefits, including access to jobs, Israel's National Insurance, healthcare, public education, and more. According to polls, a majority of Jerusalem's Palestinians oppose any solution that would disconnect them from Israel—yet there can never be a two-state solution without a hard border that includes these neighborhoods as part of the Palestinian state.

And then there was the most sensitive issue: The Old City, or more specifically, the "Holy Basin" that includes the Temple Mount, the Western Wall, and the Church of the Holy Sepulchre. We had to find a way to avoid either side having supremacy over this land, but still to ensure absolute freedom of movement and worship.

I had some fairly radical ideas percolating in my mind. But it was still 2007, and I thought it was too early to say them.

———

Meanwhile, Condoleezza Rice decided to inject energy into the talks by calling for a summit in the United States. By October, we found ourselves preparing for the Annapolis Peace Conference, to be held at the U.S. Naval Academy in Maryland the following month.

My goal at the summit would be to showcase Israel as a country that wanted peace and was ready to prove it on the world stage. Amos Oz, the famous novelist and a good friend, suggested I find a way to say things that no Israeli prime minister had ever said before—specifically with respect to Palestinian refugees. Of course, he said, there was no way to give in to Arab demands of a "right of return" for the millions of descendants of those who had left their homes in 1948. We couldn't bring them back—but perhaps we could show some empathy for their plight?

The more he talked, the more his words sunk in. I asked him if he would draft a speech for me. What he sent me was more of an outline. He didn't want to put words in my mouth.

So I wrote it myself. Of course, I had speechwriters on staff. But something told me this speech had to be entirely my own.

———

The talks continued leading up to Annapolis, under the framework of what was known as the "road map." Originally approved in 2003 under Sharon and pushed hard by President Bush, the road map defined the stages of the negotiation, with the understanding that each stage would begin only after each previous stage had been fully implemented.

As prime minister, however, I wanted quickly to get to the core issues, including Jerusalem, borders, refugees, and security arrangements. Having patience in negotiations was one thing, but having artificially imposed delays was quite another. At the same time, I didn't want to break the framework of the road map. I was concerned that the Palestinians would use it as a way of getting out of their commitments. So over and over again, whenever we spoke with the Americans about the negotiations, I made it clear that any understanding between Israel and the Palestinians were subject "to the full implementation of the road map."

In the first stage of the road map, the Palestinians would be allowed to open offices in eastern Jerusalem—a clear precedent that would prejudice the talks toward dividing the city. At the same time, that phase also included a complete halt to acts of terrorism. In the past, the Palestinians had allowed terror attacks to happen as a way of increasing leverage during negotiations. I wasn't having any of it. And so, during the negotiations, even when we talked about numerous final-status issues, I insisted on sticking to every provision of the road map. The phrase "subject to the full implementation of the road map" became a refrain in all our discussions.

President Bush, by the way, agreed with me. To make this abundantly clear, he would always throw in, "Everything is subject to the full implementation of the road map." Then he would look at me and say, "Okay?" and then move on to the next topic.

———

Another issue was settlement construction.

Anyone claiming that President Obama turned American policy against Israel is mistaken. Bush and Rice were no less critical of construction in the territories.

I had no intention of allowing widespread building on the other side of the pre-1967 border known as the Green Line, but I felt it necessary to let off some steam from time to time, allowing a limited degree of construction, mainly within the settlement blocs that would anyway remain under Israeli control and really did not undermine any future deal. I had quite a few discussions about this with Rice, Bush, and of course with Abbas. I made my position clear.

Bush and I agreed that each time I wanted to allow some construction, I would update both the Americans and the Palestinians in advance. Rice requested, and I agreed, that even in such cases, construction would only take place next to existing structures within the blocs, and not on new tracts of land any more than absolutely necessary. In practice, we found the right balance: Every few months we would approve the construction of a few dozen housing units within the blocs. State Department officials voiced their disappointment. Palestinians protested. But the talks kept going.

In one of our discussions with the Palestinian team, Qurei complained about the construction. I explained my approach, and told him it was fine with me if every time we built, they protested, as long as it didn't get in the way of the talks. Qurei kept insisting.

I finally looked him in the eye and said, "If we don't build, we cannot continue purchasing Palestinian cement."

He took a breath, looked back at me, and said, "Fine, just don't go overboard."

He wasn't just a politician. He also was the owner of a cement company.

———

The Annapolis Peace Conference was held on a single day, November 27, 2007. It began with a photo op in which President Bush, Abbas, and I appeared together. That was followed by speeches, including Foreign Minister Livni and Defense Minister Barak, whom I'd asked to join. It was important for me to demonstrate unity within my government behind the peace efforts. They were followed by speeches by European foreign ministers, representatives of the Palestinian Authority, and Condoleezza Rice. The night before, Rice had hosted a reception at the State Department for all the guests.

For me, as an Israeli, it was deeply moving. So many countries, so many VIPs, the fawning media, without anyone denouncing or accusing Israel. No resolutions of condemnation. No need to defend ourselves. All we got was respect. It was a gratifying moment.

Before the public ceremony, the three of us, together with our teams, met in the office of the commander of the Naval Academy. We needed to agree in advance on the wording of a final statement of the conference. As usual in cases like these, each side has certain sensitivities, and a minor disagreement over a word or phrase can threaten the entire effort.

President Bush sat at the head of the table and ran the meeting with impressive efficiency. His critics would say that he didn't fully grasp international affairs—as they did about Ronald Reagan a generation earlier. That was completely untrue. He displayed a grasp of every detail, raised the key issues that the negotiation turned on, analyzed each of them, and often came up with the best way to phrase the closing statement. At one point Livni and Qurei left the room together with Rice to work out a phrasing, and came back in a few minutes later. Abbas, Erekat, and I also left, talked, smoothed a few wrinkles, and came back into the room. Bush summarized the meeting. We all signed the document.

For me, the most important achievement was the agreement that we'd wrap up negotiations within a year. I would end up holding about 20 meetings with Abbas, and Livni met repeatedly with Qurei. But we still needed this public declaration to give ourselves a tailwind to try and close before the end of Bush's term. I didn't want the most serious peace talks in history to cross the finish line after he and Rice were out of office.

———

The three of us—Bush, Abbas, and myself—walked across the plaza leading from the Naval Academy headquarters to Memorial Hall, where we would address the world.

We chatted as we walked. Three men, three different worlds, three different dreams. At that moment, we were united in the powerful desire that this day would not be just another trivial moment in the history of our peoples. Dignitaries and journalists waited for us to speak. Just a few days earlier, Americans had celebrated the Thanksgiving holiday. Now it was our turn to give thanks.

Bush gave the opening address. He began by thanking the many guests and then reiterated the dream of two states for two peoples. He read out the joint statement and added thoughts of his own. He explicitly referred to Israel as the "homeland for the Jewish people." I hadn't insisted that this phrase appear in the wording of the joint statement. The fact that the president said it in his speech gave indirect expression to the American position on the issue of refugees as well—for it implicitly ruled out the possibility of millions of Palestinians ever relocating to Israel. I was satisfied.

Abbas spoke next. He talked about the historical significance of the conference, and especially about the Arab Peace Initiative. Even though it wasn't a detailed diplomatic plan, he said, it was nonetheless a strategic milestone signifying a fundamental and courageous shift in the region. He also mentioned the problem of refugees, repeated the demand to halt construction in the settlements, and said that the time had come for a peace agreement based on Israeli withdrawal, including in Jerusalem.

Most important, the speech lacked any of the moral approbations we had come to expect. He ended with a passionate call to the Israeli people, and repeated his rejection of terrorism and his desire for real peace. Given the incredible pressures he was under, especially during the period leading up to the conference, I felt it exceeded all expectations.

In my speech, I decided to emphasize my positive approach to the Arab Peace Initiative. Since Israel's founding in 1948, no Israeli prime minister had expressed understanding for the suffering of Palestinian refugees. According to the Arab claims, thousands of Palestinian families were driven from their homes and lands and lost their property. Certainly there were more than a few such cases, even if Israelis are reluctant to admit it. Our official response was always one of denial, noting that there were also Arab leaders who called for Arab residents to flee until they could return as victors. Tens of thousands heeded their call.

But the end of conflict will not be based on the return of all their descendants to Israel. The world has changed. The Middle East has changed. Jews can never return to the countries they were expelled from, forced to leave behind their memories and property. And the Jewish refugees who came to Israel vastly outnumbered the Palestinian refugees of the same era.

So any such "right of return"—such as that voiced in United Nations General Assembly Resolution 194 in 1948—is a nonstarter. But that doesn't mean we can't recognize the suffering of both Jews and Arabs who became refugees. It is even reasonable to speak of reparations. The money can come from nations of the world who want to be part of bringing a solution of justice and peace.

In my first meeting with Abbas, he told me that most of the refugees would not choose to exercise their right of return. They don't want to live either in Israel or in a Palestinian state, and would be satisfied with reparations. I later raised this with Bush and Rice. It was clear that the United States would need to be the main donor to an international fund to help the victims of dispossession from the conflict. That's an appropriate solution. Recognition of suffering is not the same as accepting blame. It is, rather, a sign of goodwill and of a willingness to start a new page of history.

President Bush told me explicitly that if and when we reached a deal, the United States would be willing to take in 100,000 refugees. It was a dramatic statement. We agreed to keep that card up our sleeve and pull it out at the appropriate time.

————

When I returned from Annapolis I decided to try to build a consensus around a definition of Israel's minimum security needs.

There still wasn't a detailed agreement, but it was clear that it would be based on a territorial withdrawal based on the 1967 borders, with land swaps. On that assumption, I wanted us to define our basic security needs, and then get the Americans to agree. We could make peace with the Palestinian Authority. But our security would require an understanding with Washington. The United States was still the only power that could have an impact on Israel's survival.

I directed Defense Minister Barak to have the IDF put together a document delineating the principles that would be the basis for an internal discussion, after getting feedback from our National Security Council. The process took a few weeks. In the end, Barak produced a paper that had been approved by all the key security bodies as well as the IDF chief of staff. The main points:

1. A Palestinian state has to be demilitarized. It could have law enforcement, a police force, appropriately armed, but no more than that. (The Palestinians were prepared to accept this, and said so repeatedly in our talks.)

2. The Palestinian state could not enter into alliances or military treaties with any country that had no relations with Israel.

3. Israel would continue to have warning stations on mountaintops in the Palestinian state (to identify threats coming mainly from Syria or Lebanon).

4. A military force would divide between the Palestinian state and the kingdom of Jordan (the document did not explicitly say it had to be an Israeli force). I knew this demand would be a nonstarter for the Palestinians.

5. The IDF would be able to cross the border with Palestine in the event that a foreign army moved forces near the border with Jordan.

6. Israel would control all airspace and electromagnetic frequencies.

7. The Palestinian state would have no airport of its own.

8. Israel would have the right to defend itself against terrorism. This right would not be constrained by any territorial limitations.

When Bush visited Israel in May 2008, I asked Barak to present the list of minimal security requirements. It was important to me that Barak do it. My experience told me that even though it had been prepared by the IDF under his direction, went through a whole process of review, and was approved by all the relevant bodies, including the National Security Council—none of this guaranteed that Barak would support it in the future. Only by having him present it to the president of the United States would he have to commit to its principles as the basis for a peace agreement.

The conversation with Bush focused on a few points. The right of the IDF to cross the border in the case of a military threat raised some eyebrows. In the end, an agreement was reached. The paper would be phrased as a formal document and forwarded to the Americans as an agreed-upon text. The agreement was only between Israel and the United States, but it was clear that it would have to be the basis for security arrangements with the Palestinians.

———

Gradually I settled on the core ingredients of a peace deal that I would present to Abbas. My plan was to give him a fully developed plan, leaving little room for further negotiation. At a certain point in any negotiation, you need to set your eyes on an endpoint and stick to it, or else the haggling will go on forever.

Frankly, I spent more time negotiating with myself than with him. Our meetings, which continued frequently, often went for hours into minor issues that were not central to the conflict. A large part of these were addressed between Livni and Qurei, but Abbas really liked getting distracted by them.

For example, in one of our meetings Abbas decided that it was crucial that we evacuate the city of Ariel. I told him the chance of that happening was close to zero, but I could agree to narrow the strip of land leading there from the Green Line, and to build either overpasses or tunnels to allow Palestinians to cross that strip.

Abbas said that he couldn't budge on it, and accused me of holding onto Ariel in order to keep control of the mountain aquifer it sat on.

I laughed.

"Why are you laughing?" he asked.

I told him that I was willing to sign, then and there, that the aquifer would remain under Palestinian control. He looked at me, baffled. I explained.

"Israel," I told him, "is about to build desalination plants on a massive scale. The plan that I submitted to the government speaks of building five new plants that could produce more than 19 billion gallons of drinkable water." I added that the new reverse-osmosis technology would permanently solve Israel's water shortage. "We also have no problem building one or two plants that will provide all the water the Palestinians will need. We'll build them on the coast, one opposite Samaria and one opposite Hebron, they will be under absolute control of the Palestinians, and the water will be delivered via underground pipes. You can have the mountain aquifer too. Anything else?"

Abbas never again raised the issue of water. Livni and Qurei kept talking about it, and I'm sure they prepared well-phrased working papers, but it became a trivial point in the talks.

Reality changes, conditions change, and perspectives change entirely as a result. I thought back to the bloody battles we'd had with Syria in the 1950s, trying to prevent it from controlling the sources of the Jordan River. For many decades, we in Israel had been exceptionally sensitive to the water level in the Sea of Galilee. Every morning, the news would report on any rise or fall of a centimeter or two, compared it to previous years, and the man in charge of measuring it had his own regular spot on morning radio.

That era was over. It doesn't mean we will cavalierly give away control of water resources. But it means that it's a lot easier to compromise in the context of a peace agreement. And it's not just true for water: The range of areas where we can't give an inch because of existential danger has considerably narrowed as we have gotten stronger, wealthier, and more technologically advanced over time.

———

During the first half of 2008, I put together a framework for a deal. I knew exactly how far I was willing to go, and that now was the time. I decided to share the plan with Condoleezza Rice. Her reaction to it, I figured, would be a good litmus test as to the chances of getting Abbas on board.

She was scheduled to visit Israel in early May. I sent her word that I'd want a one-on-one meeting.

On a Saturday night, May 3, 2008, Condi came for dinner. The weather that evening was wonderful. Jerusalem evenings in the late spring are amazing. A cool breeze blew, but it wasn't too chilly, either. Ideal for sitting out on the patio outside the guest room in the prime minister's residence. The staff set a table for two. We chatted about all sorts of things. Then I charged forward.

I had been holding in a great deal of what I wanted to tell her. I started to list the main points. I talked about 1967 borders with land swaps. I said we would annex about 6 percent of the territory and give them the same amount of land from within Israel. I said we would be able to take a few thousand Palestinian refugees, not based on any "right of return" or family unification, but on an individual, humanitarian basis. Israel would have veto rights over any specific cases. I felt that 1,000 refugees per year for five years made sense as a symbolic gesture. I talked about creating an international fund for reparations to anyone who had lost their homes in the conflict, and this would include Jews who were displaced and dispossessed from Arab countries as well as Palestinians who were forced or chose to leave their homes in what became Israel.

I was apparently quite worked up, because at some point I realized that neither of us had touched our food. Condi later said that whenever the staff came near the table, I waved them off.

I got to the subject of Jerusalem. I explained that the city would no longer be a patchwork of unrelated neighborhoods. We would withdraw from all the Arab parts. The Jewish parts, including those built after the Six Day War, would all remain under Israeli sovereignty.

As for the Holy Basin, neither side would have absolute sovereignty. Instead we would establish, through a detailed UN Security Council resolution, a mechanism that would grant five states—Saudi Arabia, Jordan, the United States, Israel, and Palestine—legal authority over the area. Freedom of movement and worship would be absolutely guaranteed for members of all religions. The rights of residents of the Holy Basin would be preserved by a joint trust of the five states.

I kept on talking, not letting her get a word in. I spoke quickly, a storm of words. It was the first time I had ever revealed what had been boiling inside for a long time. It was clear from that moment that things had now left my control, and had become a part of the diplomatic process that would determine the fate of the entire Middle East.

Rice probably knew in advance that my proposals would go much farther than anything she had ever heard from Ariel Sharon. But what she heard that evening on the patio of the prime minister's residence nonetheless surprised her. I think we finished the uneaten meal with a quick cup of espresso.

In her memoir, Rice says that she went back to her hotel, and when she reported the conversation to Welch and Abrams, she didn't mention my proposals about Jerusalem. She trusted them immensely, but was afraid that any slip of the tongue could cause me irreparable political damage.

She then set to meet with Abbas, to tell him about my ideas.

His reaction was cold. Abbas asked her how he was supposed to tell four million Palestinian refugees they'd never be going back.

I wasn't troubled by his reaction. There was plenty of time to talk it through. I recalled what he had said early on, that he had no desire to change the nature of Israel. He clearly never really believed that all the refugees would move to Israel.

The central tragedy of this conflict was, and continues to be, that the Palestinians are not ready to give up publicly on the "right of return," while there is not a single sober Israeli who would consider allowing it.

It looks like an impossible impasse, but it's really just a psychological hurdle. We can find a way past it.

The truth is, I was prepared to take as many as 15,000 refugees, if he had demanded it.

———

I knew I was running on borrowed time. Different forces were working around the clock to undermine me.

Some of them were inside my own party, especially Tzipi Livni. She had seen how easily I slid into the position of prime minister. As I had been for Sharon, she now was deputy prime minister.

In her memoir, Condoleezza Rice wrote that "Tzipi Livni urged me (and, I believe, Abbas) not to enshrine the Olmert proposal. 'He has no standing in Israel,' she said." Behind my back, Livni did her best to actively undermine Abbas's will to move forward to a peace deal. There's no other way to put it.

Meanwhile, a media-hungry state comptroller was willing to do anything, including things that struck me as quite illegal, to bring me down. At the same time, an obsessive state attorney, an uninhibited, unbridled self-appointed purist, apparently had made it his life's mission to indict me. They were being helped by an attorney general who saw my justice minister, the renowned legal scholar Danny Friedmann, as an enemy of the rule of law. They teamed up with a string of sitting and retired judges, all of whom wanted my head.

And then there were my political rivals on the right, backed by infinite financial resources from abroad.

The investigations grew more intense as the peace talks advanced. Leaks followed leaks, new cases arose every few weeks. Just days after my dinner with Rice, the press reported a new one, a serious charge of bribery in what became known as the Talansky Affair, in which I was accused of accepting illicit campaign contributions in cash from a New York businessman. After many months of steady progress with the Palestinians, this one report undermined me sharply and ultimately had a decisive effect on the course of events. Abbas's attention was turned towards those self-serving souls who told him not to sign any deals with a prime minister who wouldn't be able to deliver. Abbas must have worried that to do so would undercut his own leverage in the future if he were to agree to my terms, only to have them reneged on by whoever succeeded me.

The Americans were troubled as well. I became a much weaker prime minister in their eyes. Bush and Rice agreed that so long as I was in office, I would be the only address in Israel. I knew they hoped I would survive the crisis, but there was nothing they could do to help. It was true that a large part of the campaign against me was being funded by Americans living in Las Vegas, Chicago, and Miami Beach, pouring millions into stopping the peace process. But neither the president nor the secretary of state were in a position to intervene.

I decided to do everything I could to block out the noise and push forward.

———

I put a lot of time into the question of land swaps. We had agreed on the principle, but now I needed to figure out exactly how much land we would keep, and which land we would offer in return.

The settlement blocs—Gush Etzion, Maaleh Adumim, and Ariel— were heavily populated not just by settlers but by Palestinians as well. As much as 6.5 percent of the West Bank could easily be annexed. But when we looked at the maps, it was clear we would be hard pressed to come up with that much territory to give in exchange.

Of course, we could offer areas in the desert south of the Gaza Strip or in the Judaean desert. But the Palestinians weren't interested in inarable land. What you give us, they said, needs to be of equal value to what you're taking. And we knew their argument would enjoy international support.

This would turn out to be an exceptionally difficult circle to square. And so, we looked for ways to scale back the amount of land we would annex. How much of the West Bank did we really need?

Meeting followed meeting through the summer, but at some point you need to cut your losses. I came up with the principles of a peace deal and a final plan to propose. It wasn't put in writing. We did, however, draw up a map that included the most critical places to annex, as well as land we would be willing to exchange for it. We offered small areas dispersed around their borders—up north near Beit Shean, tracking along the Green Line to the south of Afula, West toward Netanya, and some of the ridges overlooking Jerusalem in the Nataf area, and down south to Lachish, as well as widening the Gaza Strip.

In the end, I proposed that we'd take 6.3 percent, and offered 5.8 percent in return. We would also dig a 25-mile tunnel connecting the Gaza Strip with the West Bank in the Judean hills, or alternatively build an elevated highway. Either way, this would make up for the final 0.5 percent.

———

Summer turned to fall, and my fateful meeting with Abbas was set for September 16, 2008. Most of it was just the two of us, in the study at the prime minister's residence. After nearly two years of talks, I finally presented my plan, which included a formal end to the conflict.

The core principles included:

1. The territorial solution would be based on the 1967 borders, with land swaps. I showed the map I'd prepared, and went over it with him.

2. Lands that were considered demilitarized zones on June 4, 1967, would be divided evenly.

3. Regarding Jerusalem: The Jewish neighborhoods built after 1967 would remain in Israeli sovereignty, and would be included in the 6.3 percent of annexed territory.

4. The Arab neighborhoods that were currently part of municipal Jerusalem, but most of which were not part of Jerusalem before 1967, would be detached from the city, fall under Palestinian sovereignty, and could be used as the capital of the Palestinian state.

5. The Holy Basin would be placed under the trusteeship of the five states (Saudi Arabia, Jordan, the United States, Israel, and Palestine). It would have authority in all areas under the auspices of the UN Security Council. There would be no limitations placed on worship or movement in the Holy Basin.

6. Refugees: Israel would be willing to take in a symbolic number of refugees that would be agreed upon. This would not be based on UN General Assembly Resolution 194, and there would be no "right of return" or unification of families. The agreement would specify that it was based on the Arab Peace Initiative, and that both sides recognized the suffering of the Arab and Jewish refugees.

7. The two sides would work, together with international bodies, to set up an international fund to provide generous reparations to Palestinians and Israelis who had been harmed by the conflict.

8. The Palestinian state would control a part of the Dead Sea in proportion with its part of the coastline.

9. There would not be free movement between the Palestinian state and Jordan. An agreed-upon international force would be stationed in the Jordan Valley on both sides of the Jordan River. I also listed the other security needs, though he was already familiar with them from his conversations with Rice, who confirmed that the United States supported them.

I spoke for half an hour without taking a breath. Abbas took notes. When I was done, he asked if he could hold on to the map.

"Mr. President," I said, "I can certainly give you a copy of this map, on one condition: That you initial it, and I keep the signed copy. I'm frankly worried that if I give you a copy of it without proof of your approval, there will come a time in the future when you'll want to restart talks, and you'll use the map as the starting point of negotiations.

"The map is mine," I added. "And it's my final offer. If you want it, sign it."

I knew that the biggest struggle for both of us would come after we initialed an agreement and then had to sell it to our respective constituents. So I proposed that we both sign, and then go straight to a special meeting of the UN Security Council in New York to present it. I had no doubt that such a dramatic presentation would win the unanimous support of the council. I told him that the next step after that would be a session of the UN General Assembly, which was already scheduled to meet in New York, present the deal there, and get the support from the majority of the nations on earth. Then we would present it together before a joint session of Congress and then at the European Parliament.

As a final move, we would invite world leaders to the double-capital city of Jerusalem, and there, in the presence of Bush and Putin and dozens of other heads of state, we would announce that both countries would hold elections within three months.

All these theatrical moves would create enormous momentum for selling it to our respective electorates.

After that, we would need to agree on a timetable for implementation. We would have to remove tens of thousands of Israelis from their homes outside the blocs, mostly into the blocs themselves. There was enough room for them, and many would anyway choose to move within the Green Line.

––––––––

I believed this was a winning formula.

Abbas said he would need to hold intensive internal discussions about the map. He proposed sending a map expert, along with Saeb Erekat, to meet with my expert and Shalom Turjeman to talk through the details so that he could develop an informed opinion. Erekat and Turjeman were waiting in the next room, so we brought them in and told them to meet the following day, together with the experts.

Abbas then grew quiet for a bit.

"This is serious," he suddenly said. "We have never gotten an offer as serious as this one. I need a few days to think it over before getting back to you—after I've heard the expert opinion about the map."

The room went silent for a long while. We had reached the end of the meeting. The entire time, I had felt something I had never felt in the two years we had been talking. There had been times of sluggishness, moments of levity, joy and hope, arguments and exhausting discussions, and digressions into trivial issues. But not now.

Now the atmosphere was heavy. I couldn't pretend to be in a good mood. Over the years I had made plenty of life-or-death decisions, but I had never felt such a weight on my shoulders.

I felt the weight of thousands of years of Jewish history.

I had been mayor of Jerusalem and knew it better than almost anyone. I loved it and still love it with all my heart, its Jewish and Arab neighborhoods alike. For years I had been one of the biggest spokesmen for the "eternal, unified capital of Israel and the Jewish people." I had stood before every kind of audience and spoke of Jerusalem passionately, with a deep sense of responsibility. Until I understood the enormity of my error, that in fact municipal Jerusalem was a patchwork of neighborhoods, many of which could—in fact must—be separated and made part of the future Palestinian state.

Now, at the moment of truth, after days and months of torturing myself, thoughts of everything that had come before, what Jerusalem had meant, and still meant, for us, for generations of Jews who had prayed for the return "to Thy city Jerusalem with great mercy." I thought of the millions of Jews who prayed to the Holy One three times a day, over many centuries, that God would "Dwell in Jerusalem Thy city as Thou have spoken, and prepare the throne of David Thy servant"—prayers unlike those of any other people on earth—and now I was speaking in the name of the State of Israel and the Jewish people.

Never in my life did I face a moment as difficult as this one.

———

Thirteen years have passed, and Abbas still hasn't gotten back to us.

The noise surrounding the criminal investigations reached a fever pitch. In the summer, the state attorney indicted me regarding alleged crimes that were both trivial and false, and for which I would ultimately be exonerated. Nonetheless, I had long declared my intention to resign if indicted, despite being under no legal obligation to do so. On July 30, 2008, I announced that I would not run for the leadership of Kadima in the upcoming September primary elections, and would resign from office once a new leader was chosen. In September, Tzipi Livni handily won the primaries and I announced my resignation, though I nonetheless remained in office as a caretaker until a new prime minister, Benjamin Netanyahu, was sworn in in March 2009, after general elections. A year and a half would ultimately pass between Annapolis and the end of my term.

We were inches away. I was within a hair's breadth of fulfilling the dreams of millions of Israelis who longed for peace. I had seen the Promised Land, but was not allowed to enter.

Perhaps Livni believed that if she won the election, she'd be able to take credit for the peace agreement I had spent years crafting. But she didn't win the election.

I have no doubt that if the next prime minister had been determined to follow the trail I had blazed, Abbas would have signed. He might have haggled a bit more, but he would have signed. But that's not what happened. The man who followed me in office was much more of a talker than a doer. He followed a single principle: Survival. Israel's survival in its present format, but mostly, his own political survival.

Perhaps I moved too fast, and in doing so, I fell into the traps my rivals had set for me.

I tried with all my strength, without ulterior motives, to bring peace between us and our permanent neighbors, the Palestinians. I did so out of a belief, which has only grown stronger with time, that we have no alternative. That peace is the key to the next stage in our people's history.

Will I get to see that day? I don't know, but I will always know that I did everything in my power to make it come. With or without me, it will come.

ELEVEN

There's More than One Way to Assassinate a Prime Minister

It may be hard to imagine, but almost the entire period of my term as prime minister—from the election campaign of March 2006, through the Second Lebanon War in the summer of 2006, through the peace talks with the Palestinians that began late in 2006 and ramped up after the Annapolis conference in late 2007, through the operation against the Syrian nuclear reactor in September 2007 and the battle in Gaza in early 2009, and through all the vast yet ordinary coalition politics and policy implementation that any prime minister has to deal with—all of this took place against the steady drumbeat of criminal investigations.

They didn't all come at once. To the contrary, there was an almost methodical continuity to the process—a cascade of accusations and interrogations, one following another like clockwork. It was as though an entire assembly line had suddenly emerged to manufacture more and more cases, to overwhelm me with investigations, regardless of their actual merit.

They began just a few weeks after I took office in early 2006 and never stopped. They continued after my first indictments prompted me to announce my intention to resign in March 2008. They continued after I formally resigned in the wake of the Kadima Party primary in September 2008, and after the general election of February 2009, in which Tzipi Livni led Kadima to 28 seats, the most of any party, but failed to form a government. They continued after finally I left office, with the creation of a new government under Benjamin Netanyahu in March. They continued even when it was clear I was heading for prison, foreclosing any possibility of a political comeback.

The great majority of these accusations came to nothing. Police investigations were closed due to lack of evidence. Others went to trial and ended in acquittal. There were appeals, too: Not only my own appeals when a hostile judge convicted me unjustly, but also the prosecutors appealed my acquittals, because that's something the Israeli system allows. Every accusation, rumor, media report, and investigation, every trial and every appeal, required assessment, responses, legal consultations, research to disprove them, a media strategy, and a constant burden on my time and financial resources.

In the end, two minor counts ended in conviction, and on February 15, 2016, I surrendered myself to Maasiyahu Prison, to begin what would, after further legal wrangling, turn out to be a sixteen-month sentence. It was during my time in prison that the majority of this book was first drafted in longhand.

Those two convictions that ended my political career were, I regret to say, every bit as preposterous as the countless other accusations I had to deal with.

———

I understand that the moment you choose a life of public service as an elected official, you take into account that there will always be people who want your head. Every appointment you make, every tender you award, almost every decision creates potential enemies who may spend years looking for payback. Others are ideological opponents, people so virulently opposed to the policies they believe you will implement, that they will to stop at nothing to prevent it. Still others are troubled souls, who try to make themselves important or wealthy, or get themselves out of trouble, by trying to destroy you.

By the time I became prime minister, I had been in public life for more than three decades, and had seen my share of courtrooms. I had no shortage of enemies.

But from the moment I entered the Prime Minister's Office, things entered a wholly different dimension. What happened to me was, simply, a prolonged and ultimately successful campaign of political assassination. A decision on the part of a broad range of interested parties to remove me from power and make sure I never returned.

It is important to understand the forces that combined to bring me down. Not just because I feel the need to clear my name and set the record straight—I have already done so at much greater length and detail in the original Hebrew version of this book. But more important, because my story brings into relief some of the vulnerabilities inherent in the democratic system, and the pitfalls that any elected official can face if they don't fall in line with entrenched interests and opponents with infinite means. My story is a cautionary tale that shows just how fragile democracy—not just Israeli democracy, but any democracy—can be against the interests of power and money.

In my case, there were two broad forces that came together in an unholy alliance.

One may be called the "legal puritan camp," and it included prosecutors, police investigators, judges, the attorney general, and the state comptroller's office. Israel is a small country, and many people from this camp know each other personally and build their careers through the network. This camp, as a whole, decided early on that I was one of the bad guys who had to be targeted with every tool at their disposal, along with a number of tools that were blatantly illegal. The legal camp was, to a large degree, fueled by a constant stream of misinformation, so-called "evidence" and "tips" that came from somewhere else.

The second camp comprised my political rivals on the right, led by the leader of the opposition at the time, Benjamin Netanyahu. Driven by a nationalist ideology, they saw Ariel Sharon as having betrayed the national camp when he implemented the disengagement from Gaza, and saw me as potentially doing something much worse in attempting to reach a peace agreement with the Palestinians that included territorial concessions.

Behind this second camp stood almost infinite sources of funding, mostly from the United States, and especially from the billionaire Sheldon Adelson. These sources paid for demonstrations, publicity, private investigators who tried to dig up dirt, and, in all likelihood, a few things that were far worse. Taken together, they built a narrative that attacked me from every angle—painting my leadership as corrupt, the Lebanon war as a failure, and my peace efforts as dangerous.

And alongside these two forces, there was, of course, the media. Israeli journalism often leaves much to be desired when it comes to fact checking or sourcing of claims. It is often sensational, especially about the rumored malfeasance of politicians. In my case, journalists became both the suppliers of material to trigger investigations as well as recipients of leaks from prosecutors and police. One pseudo-journalist, the blogger Yoav Yitzhak, provided a constant flow of rumors and documents to the state comptroller, who then passed them to the state attorney, who passed them to the police. At the same time, Adelson launched the *Israel Hayom* newspaper and turned it into a permanent fixture in the campaign to bring me down from the right. All the while, news media on the left, especially *Haaretz* newspaper, became a willing mouthpiece of the legal puritan camp.

I managed, apparently, to awaken more than one sleeping dragon when I entered the Prime Minister's Office.

———

The first of these investigations became public on March 7, 2006—two months after I assumed office as acting prime minister, and just two weeks before the general elections that would put me into office for the first time as an elected prime minister.

It concerned the sale of our home on November 29 Street in the Katamon neighborhood of Jerusalem to the well-known American-Jewish philanthropist S. Daniel Abraham. Someone worked extremely hard digging up every detail about the apartment, the original purchase price, the sale price, the precise specifications. According to the complaint filed by Yoav Yitzhak with State Comptroller Micha Lindenstrauss, I had sold the apartment well above its market value, taking the unusual profit as an illicit tax-free gift from a philanthropic friend.

Lindenstrauss, it should be emphasized, was an unworthy choice for the job. A former chief justice of the Haifa District Court, he was known among the judicial community as an insufferable media hound who knew no limits. I was one of the few members of Knesset who voted against his candidacy, and he decided never to let me forget it.

Having received Yitzhak's complaint about the apartment, Lindenstrauss immediately opened an investigation. Quickly he discovered that the entire sale had been conducted under the auspices of an authorized, independent, and capable assessor, who determined that the value was fair-market, and that the process was unimpeachable. Lindenstrauss closed the investigation, but not before breathless media reports surrounding it began to set the tone for years to come.

Only a few days passed before I heard from Lindenstrauss again. This time, Yitzhak had filed another complaint, saying that because I continued to live in the same apartment, but was now paying rent to Abraham, that perhaps that constituted some kind of illegal activity. Again, the media jumped all over it, the state comptroller launched an investigation, and once again found that the rent I paid was entirely reasonable in the current market.

Not long after that, I discovered that a third investigation was under way—again, someone had fed Yoav Yitzhak information, and he had turned around and given it to Lindenstrauss, who then leaked it to the media, in violation of the law. This concerned a house that Aliza and I had decided to purchase on Cremieux Sreet, in Jerusalem's German Colony. This time, the claim centered around the contractor who was renovating the house for us, and it was argued that I had received a massive discount on the renovation in exchange for getting permits for other projects expedited in City Hall. Again, the complaints went nowhere, but it took them months to close the case, after Lindenstrauss passed it to the attorney general, who ordered a police inquiry that found insufficient evidence of a crime. It was, all, of course, accompanied by a prolonged campaign of targeted leaks to the media, which turned into countless headlines.

These cases, which took up a fair amount of oxygen throughout 2006—the year I became prime minister, won an election, led the country through the Second Lebanon War, and initiated peace negotiations with the Palestinians. But they were trivial compared with what 2007 had in store for me.

In January 2007, it was announced that I was under police investigation in what became known as the Bank Leumi Affair, which I mentioned earlier. According to this one, during my tenure as finance minister I allegedly tampered with a tender for the sale of part of Israel's oldest bank, attempting to tilt it in favor of the Australian real estate tycoon Frank Lowy, who was a personal friend of mine. Mishael Heshin, the retired Supreme Court justice known for his overblown pronouncements, declared it to be the "biggest corruption scandal in the history of the State of Israel."

This case, which wasn't closed until late in 2008, began with a request from Citibank in New York to purchase 5 percent of the bank on behalf of an anonymous client. They actually made the request twice, and both times, the buyer backed out at the last minute. That buyer, it later turned out, was Lowy. But I had no idea of his identity at the time, and the sale had been approved by both the professionals in the ministry as well as the prime minister and the governor of the Bank of Israel. Later on, we decided to offer a much bigger slice of Bank Leumi for sale, attempting to sell 10 percent of the bank with the option of an additional 10 percent down the road. The tender went better than expected, and the shares in the bank were sold for a premium against its stock market valuation.

Lowy wasn't involved in the larger tender. And yet, somehow, a criminal investigation was opened, with the claim that Lowy had paid me hundreds of thousands of dollars to tilt it in his favor. It was a bizarre case, involving dozens of hours of police questioning and countless front-page headlines, despite being essentially made up. They questioned Lowy as well. Eventually the case was closed: There was, simply, no evidence that anything resembling the claim had ever happened.

Ordinary citizens who have been falsely accused of crimes often experience it as something traumatic. Even after their name is cleared, the pain and humiliation stays with them. As prime minister and a career politician, I didn't experience it the same way. I understood that being hunted is part of the cost of admission. At the same time, there was something deeply troubling, not to mention exhausting, of having a legal sword constantly dangling over my head.

There was the case where I was investigated for helping business associates of my former law partner, Uri Messer, gain access to government funding for investments while I was minister of trade. Another involved a claim that I had improperly awarded members of the Likud Party with various political appointments. There was the case where I was investigated regarding a modest personal loan I'd received seventeen years earlier and had never paid back. (The man who lent me the money didn't mind, but I quickly repaid it as soon as it became a legal question.) They even opened a criminal investigation surrounding the value of a collection of fountain pens I had been accumulating over a period of decades, and whether I had received them as illicit gifts.

It seemed that nothing could stem the tide of investigations. As every litigator knows, when your case is not very good, one common tactic is simply to flood the field with complaints, frivolous countersuits, and endless motions. If you overwhelm the other side's resources, you can get what you want, such as a settlement much more favorable to your client than anything a court would rule.

Throughout my term as prime minister, this was the main strategy used against me: To flood me with endless, frivolous investigations without any regard to what would hold up in court—all in the hope that either something would stick, or that eventually I would collapse under the pressure. Because a few judges were in on this campaign, it would often take years of appeals before I successfully cleared my name.

The two biggest cases that emerged over the course of 2008 were precisely of this nature. The Rishon Tours Affair, where I was accused of double-billing nonprofit organizations that were reimbursing expenses for some of my trips abroad; and the Talansky Affair, where I was accused of receiving hundreds of thousands of dollars in illegal campaign contributions, handed me by an New York businessman in cash-stuffed envelopes—these became the biggest scandals in Israeli media of 2008.

In these cases, I was actually indicted for the first time. And because unlike Benjamin Netanyahu, I believed it proper for a prime minister to resign upon indictment even if the law didn't require it, they resulted in my leaving office—even though I would end up being exonerated in the key charges in both of them.

A final case that began in 2008 and continued for years after involved bribes I allegedly took from a developer in Jerusalem to allow him to build an apartment complex on the site of the old Holyland Hotel. Bribes had in fact been given, it turned out, though not to me. Again I was cleared of the main charge, but a bizarre spinoff from the case, involving money given to my estranged brother Yossi, would haunt me for years to come.

In the vast majority of these cases, the charges led to nothing. But every one of them was accompanied by news reports based on leaks. Together they built a narrative that someone wanted to create. The headlines could never be erased.

Now, one can argue that in many of these cases, the police were just doing their job. There was a suspicion, it was investigated, and when the misunderstanding was cleared up, it was closed. What's so bad about that?

But when literally more than a dozen such investigations are undertaken against a sitting prime minister over a period of a year and a half, and each one is leaked to the media to great fanfare, there is something clearly fishy going on. It seems much more like a coordinated campaign. Somebody was paying to dig up all these initial suspicions, to find the slightest pretext to open an investigation and maybe even find something that can bring a prime minister down. The system was clearly being used for political ends.

Simply put, I had a contract put out on me.

―――――

A central part of what makes such a campaign possible is money. The more you have, the easier it is, through both legal and illegal means, to achieve your desired outcome.

The political right in Israel, led by Netanyahu and funded principally by Adelson, took advantage of a legal system that was, for reasons of its own, all too willing to be deployed as a political tool. The forces on the right believed that my attempts to achieve peace with the Palestinians were "bad for the Jews" and had to be stopped at all costs. So they didn't just pay for public demonstrations of the reservists after the Second Lebanon War or the public outcry around the Winograd Report. They also funded private investigators, paying people to deliver evidence to prosecutors.

On February 17, 2008, Israel's Channel 2 television reported on a well-funded operation undertaken by both Israelis and right-wing American activists. They were paying, it turned out, for private investigators to scour the earth for incriminating evidence against me. These private investigators met with business people, contractors, anyone who may have dealt with me over the years. In one recorded conversation, a private investigator (PI) is speaking with a businessman who had dealings with the municipality when I was mayor of Jerusalem.

> PI: At first this might be hard for you, but think about it carefully. You don't have to give me an answer right now, but if you're interested, the return will be very very nice. . . . A number of top international people are behind this. The situation today is that he [Olmert] is bad for the Jews. You know it as well as I do, that he's very bad for the Jews. And there's a group that has taken this upon themselves. Extremely wealthy people. World-class, I'm telling you. Good Jews. I was sent to handle this issue, and to try to bring down that guy. How do you do that? The pot is extremely large.
>
> Businessman: I, actually, am not so interested in the pot so much as the ideology.
>
> PI: You're a better man than I imagined. I wanted to interest you in both—the pot and the ideology. I'm trying to find material in all sorts of places, saying that Olmert took bribes, that he embezzled or did other things . . .
>
> Businessman: How much are we talking about?
>
> PI: If we do good work, a million dollars.
>
> Businessman: What is considered "good work"?
>
> PI: If we can bring something that the prosecutors or the police or the media or somebody looks at it and says, "With this we can bring him down," then Olmert is finished.

It might be argued that there's nothing wrong with paying someone who digs up evidence to convict a criminal. Evidence is evidence, after all, right? My answer to that is that it reflects a significant distortion of the process of justice when you're offering a million dollars for incriminating information. Especially when you consider how easy it is for that kind of money to be applied not only to finding evidence but to fabricating it, or to buying witness testimony—and even more so when the money is coming from the backers of the leader of the opposition.

And the biggest backer of them all was Sheldon Adelson.

———

Sheldon Adelson was a businessman from Boston who moved to Las Vegas in the 1980s and made tens of billions of dollars through casinos both there and in Macao, an island in the Pacific belonging to China. A strong supporter of Israel, and married to an Israeli woman, he aligned himself with the pro-settlement, nationalist political right in Israel.

I got to know him a bit when I was mayor of Jerusalem. He would bring delegations of pro-Israel members of Congress, especially Republicans, to Israel on his private plane. As a member of Likud who constantly spoke, back then, about the eternal unity of Jerusalem, I appealed to Sheldon. He saw me as a kindred spirit.

That changed when I supported Ariel Sharon's disengagement plan, and grew much worse when Kadima broke off from Likud. Once I became prime minister and made my own vision of a peace agreement with the Palestinians clear to the public, Adelson decided to start putting his vast capital behind Netanyahu's efforts to replace me.

In all of Israel's history, there was never so aggressive or brutal an intervention by a single individual, a noncitizen in a foreign country, in our democratic electoral process—or, quite possibly, that of any democratic country.

Adelson, a brash, unreservedly aggressive man who passed away in early 2021, was of the far right. Years before he involved himself heavily in American politics, he was effectively Netanyahu's boss. He was the main backer of Bibi's supporting organizations, including the One Israel Fund, a pro-settlement activist organization, as well as the Adelson Institute at the Shalem Center, which paid the salaries of pro-Netanyahu political players on the right, such as Moshe Yaalon, the former IDF chief of staff who would later serve as Netanyahu's defense minister.

Adelson also supported major public campaigns against my government. Demonstrations always look like they're an expression of grass-roots anger, but there are always bills to be paid by someone with deep pockets and a fat wallet: Organizers, banners, buses, PR—somebody is behind all of it.

When protests were held across the country in advance of publication of the second Winograd Commission report in January 2008, they called explicitly for my resignation over the handling of the Second Lebanon War. One of the key organizers was Uzi Dayan, a former major-general and nephew of Moshe Dayan.

Uzi and I had been friends. He had long believed in a peace process with the Palestinians, even if his proposals weren't as far-reaching as mine. He had launched a Center-Left political party called Tafnit that tried, but failed, to cross the electoral threshold to get into the Knesset. More than once, he came to me asking to be put onto the Kadima list.

But money talks.

As soon as he started getting funding from Adelson, Uzi changed. Not only did he lead the protests against me, he then took his Tafnit group and merged it into Netanyahu's Likud. Suddenly he became a right-winger. Eventually, he even made it into the Knesset as a member of the Likud Party.

The protests Uzi led were funded and organized by a web of Adelson-backed bodies. In 2009, after Netanyahu became prime minister, I received a copy of an internal strategic document, called "Go Home," that provided detailed plans about the campaign, with the express goal to "create public and political pressure to cause the prime minister to resign." It included a wide range of public protests from both left and right, coordinated activities from a broad range of NGOs, cultural figures, and public intellectuals, as well as a website and campaign-style "war room." It included paying for email lists, field workers and legal experts. Uzi's name is mentioned. So is the involvement of Adelson's *Israel Hayom* newspaper. And it included a budget of more than $100,000.

Adelson lost that battle, but he won the war. This may sound speculative, but I am convinced it is probably *only* because of Adelson's success in bringing me down that he fully came to believe in the power he could have to influence politics, and then started investing heavily in the Republican Party in the United States. He would end up pouring hundreds of millions of dollars into presidential campaigns of Republicans—including Newt Gingrich, Mitt Romney, and Donald Trump. He became, without peer, the biggest donor to Republican candidates in America.

I was, it seems, his test case.

———

Why am I so sure that Sheldon Adelson wasn't just a simple, right-wing pro-Israel philanthropist, like so many others? How do I know he made a strategic decision to intervene in Israel's democratic process, to bring me down and replace me with Netanyahu no matter what it cost him?

There's no need to look for a smoking gun. It's already there. It's called *Israel Hayom*.

Adelson launched the newspaper in July 2007. It was distributed free of charge, handed out on street corners, newsstands, and at bus stops. In theory it was a for-profit company, making its money through ad revenue. But it didn't turn a profit, instead relying on the constant infusion of tens of millions of dollars each year from Adelson himself.

When he launched the paper, he spent good money hiring away top-level journalists who all happened to be hostile to me. Some of these were notable left-wingers—like Motti Gilat, who left *Yediot Aharonot* to work for the paper, or Dan Margalit, the editor of the *Maariv* newspaper. Their politics didn't matter. The only thing that counted was that they all despised me and what I stood for. One study showed that during the 2009 election, for every *Israel Hayom* article critical of Likud, dozens were published attacking Kadima.

I once saw Adelson at an event and asked him bluntly why *Israel Hayom* was so unremittingly hostile to me. He looked down and just mumbled, "I can't read Hebrew."

Israel Hayom grew quickly, fueled by Adelson's largesse, and would eventually overtake *Maariv* and *Yediot* to become Israel's highest-circulation daily paper, losing hundreds of millions of dollars in the process.

For all I know, it's still operating at a loss. What I have trouble understanding, however, is why launching an entire newspaper for the sole purpose of attacking one political candidate and supporting another is even legal: Why isn't it an obvious, illicit campaign contribution? And I'm asking this as someone who was prosecuted for allegedly having much smaller amounts given to my political campaigns, despite no actual records of this taking place, through extremely generous interpretations of what constitutes a campaign gift.

Adelson's campaign didn't just hurt me, however. I have no doubt that it caused irreparable damage to the State of Israel. One of the main pillars of Israel's success in the world is the belief that our country has immense influence on American governments, regardless of which party is in power in Washington. That the support for Israel is bipartisan. But the partnership between Adelson and Netanyahu severely undermined this bipartisan support—expressing itself in the latter's irresponsible behavior towards President Obama and his Secretary of State John Kerry, and his fawning support for President Trump. The last decade has seen tremendous erosion of support for Israel in the Democratic Party, and this is potentially disastrous for Israel.

Adelson once even had the *chutzpah* to tell a major world leader, while I was in office, that I was a "traitor" to Israel because of my peace efforts, and had to be removed.

I don't think Adelson's statement had much of an effect on that particular world leader. No matter how many billions of dollars a man has, there is nothing that makes it reasonable to call the elected leader of a foreign country, who has spent decades of his life struggling for the good of his country, and who has embarked on the most ambitious effort in its history to resolve an endless blood-soaked conflict, a "traitor."

Sheldon Adelson died on January 11, 2021, just five days after President Trump, whom he had supported heavily, encouraged a violent insurrection that stormed Capitol Hill and forever damaged the fabric of America's democracy. His unfortunate legacy lives on, both in the United States and in Israel.

———

During the months that passed between the announcement of my resignation in September 2008 and my leaving office in March 2009, I was in some sense a lame duck: The resignation was, for many people, a resolution, a culmination of a long struggle, and while the legal challenges continued for years, the media grew less interested over time.

Yet I was still prime minister during that period. Perhaps I no longer had the political clout to bring the Palestinians into a peace agreement, but I still was responsible for the fate of my country.

When the Hamas terrorists in Gaza decided to escalate their rockets in our south, the decisions as to how to respond still rested on my shoulders.

Throughout 2008, Hamas increased its rocket fire. Towns like Sderot, Netivot, and Ofakim, kibbutzim in the south, and many other communities found themselves heading to bomb shelters with increasing frequency. The damaged cause by the Qassam rockets was far less than the panic and media coverage would suggest, but I couldn't ignore the ongoing trauma, the fear parents had about sending kids out to play or taking them for a drive.

No country can, and no country should, accept such a reality. All the more so as we could see how, over time, the range of their missiles grew, including longer-range Grad missiles that started reaching our larger cities—Ashkelon, Ashdod, and Beersheva. Meanwhile, closer to Gaza, Qassams and mortars were fired at local communities on an almost daily basis.

We clearly had no choice but to make an aggressive military move, changing the calculus. So long as Hamas and Islamic Jihad kept launching rockets, and our response stayed limited to artillery fire, they could keep shooting at us. But while Gaza's leadership had no problem tolerating the suffering of their own population, we couldn't.

In April and May of 2008, the IDF put together a plan for a more fundamental treatment of the threat of rockets from Gaza. This was, again, the most difficult period of my term as prime minister. The Talansky Affair had just erupted. And along the way, I also discovered that Ehud Barak, my defense minister, had been conducting back-channel talks with the office of Omar Suleiman, the chief of Egyptian intelligence and Mubarak's right-hand man. Amos Gilad was going back and forth to Cairo, and I had no idea.

I would soon learn why.

Barak was secretly negotiating with Hamas over a *hudna*, a prolonged cease-fire. I confronted him about it, and he hemmed and hawed. Meanwhile, the mood in the security cabinet was belligerent. Avi Dichter pushed hard for a massive military operation as soon as possible.

I was concerned about the timing. I was flooded at that time with headlines surrounding the investigations—Talansky, Rishon Tours, and so on. I was sure that challenging Hamas at that moment would look like a deliberate effort on my part to take attention away from the scandals, and the damage to the country would be far greater than any advantage of striking now. I didn't have confidence in Barak's secret negotiations, but I decided to wait on any military move until the timing felt better. In the end, Barak and Suleiman reached some kind of a deal, and it was approved by the cabinet.

The *hudna* didn't last long. Hamas had no interest in stopping the terror, and the attacks quickly resumed. I wasn't surprised.

I knew that I could not leave the Prime Minister's Office without putting an end to Hamas' provocations. We would have to strike them hard.

"A volley of Grad and Qassam rockets has landed on Ashkelon, Ashdod, and Beersheva." That was the update we received in the middle of a meeting of the security cabinet in late December 2008. Within a three-hour period, 80 rockets had been launched. Hundreds of thousands of residents had taken to shelters. It was clear that the moment of decision had come. I had held back for months, but couldn't any longer. We didn't have any Iron Dome yet back then, and every rocket was a catastrophe waiting to happen. We would need to retaliate now, and hard.

At 10:00 a.m. on December 27, I gave the green light. More than one hundred aircraft took part in the assault that had been carefully planned for months. It lasted only thirty minutes, but they were among the most painful minutes the Gaza Strip has ever seen. Yet our aircraft achieved a remarkable degree of precision, targeting individual Hamas commanders, avoiding civilian casualties wherever possible.

Even then, the timing was not easy. We were weeks away from elections. It would be easy for people to claim that a lame-duck prime minister, who wasn't running and wouldn't have to live with the consequences, shouldn't be making such decisions. On the other hand, if I had been running for office, the same people would have claimed it was an election ploy.

Hamas leaders responded as they always do, declaring that there had been a massacre of civilians and forcing the journalists stationed in Gaza to echo the claims. Meanwhile, they kept firing the rockets at our cities and towns. The IDF began moving tanks and ground troops in, with the initial aim of cutting the strip in two, between northern and southern sectors. The result of the ground operation was that terrorists left their bunkers and took flight, which exposed them to attacks from the air.

After twenty-three days of fighting, the results were significant: We had killed many hundreds of Hamas operatives, significantly degraded their rocket-firing capability, and done our best to limit civilian casualties. Most important from my perspective, we had limited the casualties on our own side, both military and civilian. Nearly a thousand Hamas terrorists were killed in the operation, with only about two hundred casualties to Gaza civilians and only a handful to Israeli troops and civilians.

I was not satisfied by the outcome, however. I believed a more significant ground operation would have had a decisive and permanent effect on Hamas's ability and desire to harass our civilians with rocket fire. But Barak, who had repeatedly misled me and the cabinet, had been working hard to get the IDF on board with his opposition to continued conflict, and they suddenly reversed their position of just a few days before, and warned me that a massive involvement of ground troops and reserves would last months and result in hundreds of soldiers dead. I no longer had the political clout that I once had, and had to settle for whatever results we had already achieved. On January 14, 2009, eighteen days after we launched what became known as Operation Cast Lead, we decided to stop. We took the gains, but the opportunity to land a final, irreversible blow on Hamas was missed.

I was actively undermined by my defense minister, just as I had been by my foreign minister during the late stages of the peace talks with Abbas. We could have destroyed the sources of Hamas's power, weakened the foundations of Hamas's rule over the strip, and invited an international force to help change the reality in our south for many years to come.

But politics got in the way.

Hamas back then was much weaker than it is today. It didn't yet have attack tunnels, guided missiles, or drones supplied by Iran. It was on the verge of collapse, and we chose to pass up on a real opportunity to finish if off and free the Palestinian population in Gaza from the rule of a brutal Islamist dictatorship that continues to bring new devastation on its population every few years.

Six years later, Netanyahu's government launched Operation Protective Edge.

It was completely different. By that point, Hamas had started building its extensive system of tunnels, and for fifty days our ground units fiddled around the edges of the strip but never really went in. Over the weeks of fighting, we lost 74 people in that operation—more, I believe, than we would have lost if we had finished the job in 2009. The achievements of Protective Edge were minimal. Yes, we dumped thousands of tons of explosives on multistory buildings, regardless of their strategic importance. At the end of the day, however, we didn't destroy Hamas's military capabilities, and the international response was sharp, leading to claims of war crimes and an inquiry of the International Criminal Court.

In 2021, Hamas launched an unprecedented number of rockets at Israeli citizens, against a backdrop of riots in Jerusalem and among Israeli Arabs in many cities. Millions of Israelis, including residents of Tel Aviv and Jerusalem, had to seek shelter. The IDF's brief operation in Gaza, called Guardians of the Wall, included eleven days of intensive precision bombing without sending in ground forces. It was justified, necessary, and far better executed than 2014. It will hopefully buy some quiet for our residents.

But it did not solve the fundamental questions—and if anything, it brought into stark relief the immense challenges facing Israel's relations with the Palestinians, with Israel's own Arab citizens, with the Americans, and in its own internal political conundrum. Some people may claim that Netanyahu was eager for something, anything, that would take attention away from his own legal problems and prevent the creation of an alternative government in the thick of a political deadlock.

I have no doubt that our failure to take care of Hamas, once and for all, in 2009—and all the suffering and pain on both sides of the border that we have seen in the years since then—can be traced to the extreme campaign of political defamation that had been launched against me by Netanyahu and Adelson from the moment I entered office.

If not for that, the Middle East would look very different than it does today.

———

I have been asked many times how it is possible that I, of all people, ended up being put through this particular wringer. People who have gotten to know me over the years, whether socially or professionally, know me as a man of my word, an efficient manager and decisive leader, and as someone deeply passionate about the fate of my country both at the historical, geostrategic level and in the daily quality of life of every citizen.

There are, it seems, different kinds of politicians.

All successful political actors, of course, need to understand the different pieces of the puzzle. You need to build coalitions. You need to appeal to voters. You need to understand policy. You need to offer a vision, to offer hope. And, when given the opportunity to hold office, you need to do a good job.

Part of politics requires political calculations, of course. You have not only to understand what motivates people, but also build alliances, predict reactions, control the narrative. Above all, you need to win elections.

Some politicians, however, have an additional feature that perhaps I have always lacked: A certain compulsion to destroy one's rivals. To treat them not as opponents but as enemies. To spend countless hours plotting, digging up dirt, lying, doing anything you have to in order to win a zero-sum game.

I cared about policy. And I cared about *how* things were run—about the efficient and proper functioning of government. For me, all the politics—campaigning, coalition-building, media, and so on—all of it was just a means to an end, and not an especially gratifying part of the job.

So, when faced with the challenges that eventually brought me down, I knew that I was facing a highly sophisticated, infinitely funded, complex, and unscrupulous adversary. But I also knew that I had to put limits on the demands it could make on both my time and my mental energy. Because at every moment, my foremost responsibility was to carry out my duties as prime minister of the State of Israel—an incredibly difficult job, but one that I believed I could do well, and thereby serve my country in the best way possible. I wasn't about to let myself be overwhelmed.

In the end, however, the forces at play overwhelmed me. I doubt whether any prime minister would have been able to withstand them.

Yet despite it all, I remain optimistic. My story perhaps gives me as much reason as any man alive to be a pessimist—and yet, despite everything I have gone through, I remain hopeful about the future of my country, and the future of democracy.

TWELVE

Towards a Better Israel and a Hopeful Middle East

In early April 2009, Shimon Peres, who was now Israel's president, hosted a special gathering to mark the transition between the outgoing government, which I led, and the incoming government of Benjamin Netanyahu.

Peres was experienced in putting together meetings of this sort. If in the past he had been one of the central political players in the country, now he had taken on a new role, that of a founding father, the adult in the room, a man with more experience in Israeli national life than anyone. By that point, he was the last person from his generation, the generation that declared independence in 1948 and built the foundations of the country, who remained in Israeli public life. I saw on his face how well the role suited him: At long last, he was getting the honor he had always felt was due him, towering over all these upstarts who had taken over the podium of our public life. But no one could take away that which was uniquely his: the vision, the accumulated wisdom, the unwavering faith in our collective future.

For me it was a sad moment. This was not the way I had wanted my time as prime minister to end. On this occasion, I tried to sum up briefly my term in office. Today, more than twelve years later, I have a broader perspective, especially in light of what has happened in the intervening years: The mistakes Israel has since made, and both the external conflicts and the internal crisis we now find ourselves in, which we have no choice but to solve and resolve if we want to get back on the amazing path that has been the history of Israel.

In the seventy-three years that have passed since 1948, the most incredible part of the story has been that of the massive ingathering of the Jewish people from almost every corner of the planet. In 1948, Israel was home to 650,000 Jews. As of Independence Day 2021, close to 8 million Jews have made Israel their home. For the first time in thousands of years, the Land of Israel hosts the largest Jewish community in the world. They even came, as my own family can attest, from China.

Millions came. Many of them felt like strangers in a strange land when they arrived, but with time, they became an integral part of the new society that was created in Israel. America holds itself up for its multicultural melting pot, yet it is tiny Israel that has been forged, perhaps more than any country on earth, from nationalities from literally every part of the globe.

In this wondrous Israeli mosaic, unprecedented in the history of nations, there are communities of white Jews from Europe and the Americas, Jews who came from Muslim lands, black Jews from Ethiopia, and so many others whose background is a special mixture of descendants of different religions, races, and cultures, all alien to each other.

And all of them—or at least the great majority—now speak Hebrew. The same language that King David wrote his psalms in, thousands of years ago. It is the most magnificent poetry ever written.

This, too, is unprecedented. Never in human history has a language spoken thousands of years ago been preserved, lost, resurrected, and turned into a modern-day tongue the way Hebrew has.

At the same time, alongside the unique, unbelievable return of the Jewish people to their historic homeland, there are also other people who live here—and have for centuries. They haven't gone anywhere. They, the Arabs, most of them Sunni Muslims, some of them Christians, live in towns and neighborhoods across our country, and many of them have never fully accepted the Jewish dominance that brought about the creation of the state.

We have survived so many crises, overcome so many obstacles, handled so many profound threats to our lives over the decades. But we have never successfully integrated the Arab citizens of Israel with true equality for all. Nor have we built a relationship built on trust, acceptance, and conciliation with the Palestinian population—most of which has lived under Israeli military occupation since 1967.

It should be clear, of course, that the conflict with the Arab nations began with their own unwillingness to accept, from the outset, the creation of Israel as a Jewish state in a region that is mostly Muslim.

From the moment the UN voted for the establishment of the Jewish state in November 1947, the majority of Arab states refused to accept Israel as a legitimate neighbor or build close relations with it. This "great refusal" brought round after round of military conflict, terrorism, and immense bloodshed, and left behind enduring mutual resentment, much of which remains today.

But thanks to visionary leaders like Menachem Begin, Anwar Sadat, and King Hussein of Jordan, and only after horrific wars and loss of life, we have benefited from peace with Egypt and Jordan, the two Arab states that share our longest borders.

And yet—we still have the conflict with the Palestinians. The occupation is an open wound, both for them and for us. It demands a solution that will require significant, painful, unprecedented concessions: first of all from our side, but also from theirs. I have no problem saying we have to go first, because if we don't, no solution will ever come.

In 2008, I conducted intensive negotiations with Mahmoud Abbas, president of the Palestinian Authority. We were very close to reaching a deal that would have enabled the establishment of a Palestinian state based on the 1967 borders, though not identical to them; that recognized of the Arab parts of Jerusalem that Palestinians claim as their own; and that redefined the Holy Basin in Jerusalem, which contains the sacred sites of the three great monotheistic religions, as an international zone under no country's sovereignty but open to people of all faiths. We agreed to solve the problem of Arab refugees from 1948 in the framework of the Arab Peace Initiative, which was proposed by

Saudi Arabia and endorsed by the Arab League in Beirut in 2002 and in Riyadh in 2007.

As I have written, it should have been clear from the outset that Israel could never, under any circumstances, recognize a "right of return" for Palestinians who, as a result of the war that had been waged against Israel since the moment of its independence, became refugees. The entire logic behind creating a Palestinian state was to allow any Palestinian to live within its borders, and to drop any additional territorial claims—just as Israel had done, and would continue to do, for Jews. To finally end a conflict that began with competing claims to the land.

The suffering of the Palestinian refugees, just like that of hundreds of thousands of Jews who were dispossessed and forced to flee the Arab and Muslim countries they lived in, required an appropriate solution. I proposed the creation of a generously endowed international fund that would offer compensation to both Palestinian and Jewish refugees who had lost their homes in the conflict. I spoke about this with Abbas. As for Palestinians "returning" into Israel, he made it explicitly clear that he had no intention of changing the character of Israel—though he did want to see some kind of symbolic recognition of their aspirations.

We were on the verge of signing a historic agreement. President George W. Bush and Secretary of State Condoleezza Rice supported and encouraged us. But just as we were about to close the deal, Abbas declined to sign.

He knows he made a historic error. It is an error that will forever tarnish his reputation as it continues to inflict pain and anguish on the people he was supposed to serve.

Thirteen years have since passed. We are still occupying, the Palestinian governments—both in Gaza and in the West Bank—still deny their own people the freedom they deserve, the Palestinians still cannot exercise their right of self-determination, and the bitterness and anger continue to boil over. The Palestinians continue to blame Israel publicly, but they condemn their own leaders privately.

We cannot let the Palestinian leadership off the hook. They were given the chance to fulfill their own dream, and they failed to find the courage.

But the real question, from Israel's perspective, is not about who's to blame. Our nation's supreme interest is to reach a final-status agreement and end the conflict. To close a deal with those Palestinians willing and able to reconcile with Israel. They won't be found in Gaza, which is now ruled by a terror organization. But Israel has a critical interest in reaching a peace deal with the Palestinians in the West Bank.

Unfortunately, Israel's leaders in the last decade haven't been able to muster the strength to get the negotiations back on track, to restart a dialogue that can lead to achieving the dream shared by both nations, the dream of peace and conciliation.

In the last decade, the Israeli government has preferred to weaken the Palestinian Authority, to ignore its president, Mahmoud Abbas, and to carry on a sordid affair with the leaders of Hamas. The idea that indefinitely putting off the question of how to end the conflict with the Palestinian Authority somehow serves Israel's interests is a dangerous illusion. There is nothing more urgent for the future of Israel's identity and international standing than peace with the Palestinians. The further it is delayed, the more damage will be done to Israel's global position—which will have negative consequences for every Israeli.

Even now, as the international community has watched the period of boundless American support that Israel enjoyed under President Trump come to an end, there is increased concern being voiced about Israel's continued occupation of the West Bank.

We are not talking just about a few companies refusing to sell their products to West Bank settlers, but also an increasing hostility toward Israel on campuses across North America and Europe. Some describe this is an expression of anti-Semitism, which must be vigorously opposed. And it is true that anti-Semitism often disguises itself as opposition to the occupation. The boycott, divestment, sanctions (BDS) movement is definitely something to fight against with every tool at Israel's disposal. This movement, under the pretext of calling for boycotts to end the occupation, in fact rejects Israel's right to exist. There is no room for compromise with its demands.

But many students across North America and Europe, many movements committed to defending human rights, and many leaders of countries around the world are driven not by hatred of Israel, but rather by a revulsion against what looks like a pattern of arrogance and dismissal on the part of the Israeli government toward the rights of the Palestinian people, and of Israel's refusal to work as hard as it can to reach an agreement based on a two-state solution.

The years of the Trump administration did little to build the trust needed to reach a peace agreement with the Palestinians. President Trump's "Deal of the Century" was a nonstarter. And while he deserves credit for facilitating Israeli agreements with the UAE and other Middle Eastern countries, Trump never really cared about the Middle East. For him, Israel was nothing more than a tool for appealing to his own electoral base, especially among evangelical Christians, whose agenda has nothing to do with Israel's future as a Jewish and democratic state. Trump is gone, and so is the peace plan he trumpeted.

The two terms of President Obama, with his two secretaries of state, Hillary Clinton and John Kerry, were wasted years. I do not accept the attacks on Obama often voiced both in Israel and in the diaspora, especially in the United States. Barack Obama was, in fact, a great friend of Israel. He wanted with every fiber of his being to end the conflict between us and the Palestinians. The criticism against him was laced with arrogance, both from the leaders of American Jewry and especially from Israel's government.

Many of us remember the infamous meeting between Obama and Netanyahu at the White House in May 2011. Netanyahu sat before the president, wagged his finger at him, and presumed to school the president on Middle East history. Obama was an amazing student at Harvard Law School, where he graduated magna cum laude. He was a senator and the nation's first African American president, and there he was now, being asked to take lessons from the Israeli prime minister. It was a humiliating moment that had a direct impact on relations between the two leaders for the entire eight years of Obama's presidency.

That meeting reminded me of something I was told by a close friend of President Bill Clinton, after the latter's first meeting with Netanyahu at the White House in the late 1990s. I was part of Netanyahu's entourage during that trip, and after they had a long one-on-one meeting, Clinton hosted a luncheon for us together with Treasury Secretary Bob Rubin and CIA director John Deutsch—both of them Jews with strong ties to Israel—along with a few of their aides. Clinton looked sullen during lunch. The next day, Clinton's friend said to me that the president had told him that when he sat with Netanyahu in the Oval Office, it wasn't clear who was the leader of a global superpower and who was merely the leader of a client state.

When Obama visited Israel as a presidential candidate in 2008, I hosted him and some his advisers at a dinner at the prime minister's residence. He said at the time that one does not have to be a member of Likud to be a friend of Israel. He truly was committed to Israel's welfare, just as he was to that of the American Jewish community. Ben Rhodes, at the time deputy national security adviser for strategic communications, wrote in his book *The World As It Is* that in one of his conversations with Obama, the president told him that they were very similar. Rhodes had grown up among pro-Israel Jews in Brooklyn. "Me too," Obama told him. "I came out of the Jewish community in Chicago. I'm basically a liberal Jew."

Those were the words of a man who felt a deep respect for the Jewish community that had warmly supported him throughout his career. I never had any doubts about this. We did a grave injustice to one of the sharpest, most fascinating, and influential leaders of the twenty-first century. This president, whom so many accused of being distanced from Israel, funded Israel's Iron Dome system, even during the worst period of the financial crisis, and despite the slashing of the U.S. defense budget.

Obama, like his two secretaries of state, very much wanted to pursue Middle East peace. Israel didn't really cooperate. Hillary Clinton, who knew Netanyahu well from the years of the Clinton administration, gave up quickly on trying to push Israel toward peace. John Kerry, one of Israel's greatest friends in America, refused to do the same. To accuse Clinton, Kerry, and Obama of hostility to Israel reflects ingratitude and ignorance. When it came to peace, however, Netanyahu never was willing to make a bold move, especially one that he felt would put his coalition at risk, in order to address the State of Israel's greatest need.

———

Netanyahu's dependency on his coalition partners was matched only by his dependency on supporters and donors abroad.

The most important of these, again, was Sheldon Adelson, the Las Vegas casino king. Adelson was an offensive, aggressive man whose worldview was simplistic and hollow. He was not satisfied with just getting me out of office. He truly believed that only by actually evicting the Palestinians from the West Bank would we solve our problems. No less alarmingly, Adelson also pushed for attacking Iran with nuclear weapons to eliminate their nuclear program.

Every Jew, especially one who gives so much to Israel, has a right to express his or her opinions about the Jewish state. But Adelson didn't just speak his mind. He spent hundreds of millions of dollars of his own money to influence political outcomes in the country over many years. If you didn't agree with Sheldon 100 percent, he cut you off. And as Netanyahu was completely dependent on Adelson's largesse, there was no chance the prime minister would ever pursue policies that contradicted the casino mogul's far-right agenda.

I remember one of the most humiliating moments in this context, when Adelson brought a delegation of wealthy American Jews in 2012, together with the Republican presidential nominee, Mitt Romney. Romney is a good man and a longtime friend of Israel. Adelson, with Netanyahu's help, held a fundraiser for Romney in Jerusalem and raised many millions of dollars for the campaign. Transforming Jerusalem into a fundraising hub for a U.S. presidential candidate was an unbelievably irresponsible move on Netanyahu's part that did permanent damage to the bipartisan nature of U.S. support for Israel that had begun with Democratic President Truman's recognition in 1948.

But while Adelson succeeded in buying decisive influence in Israeli politics, he was ultimately less successful in the United States. Romney, of course, lost the election. Adelson, alongside his very generous gifts to a broad range of worthy institutions like Yad Vashem and Birthright Israel, could have just been seen as a distraction or an American problem when it came to Israeli politics. But the combination of his extreme views on the most important issues facing Israel's future with Netanyahu's almost absolute dependence on him created an intolerable problem for my country.

———

Do we, in 2021, really have to accept, as so many have, that there is no longer any chance of solving the Palestinian problem through the establishment of a Palestinian state alongside the State of Israel?

I, for one, have not given up hope. Because there is no alternative.

But time doesn't stand still. What would have been easy to execute thirty or forty years ago, what was much harder but still possible in 2008 when I put my own peace proposal on the table, could become impossible in another ten years.

When the West Bank becomes home to a million Jewish settlers, an Israeli withdrawal will be impossible.

Today, it is still possible to resettle the great majority of the settlers into settlement blocs that take up only a tiny part of the territory, to turn the Arab neighborhoods of Jerusalem into part of the Palestinian capital, and to create a new sovereign state based on the 1967 borders, with adjustments through land swaps on a one-to-one basis.

It is still possible to reach agreement on the problem of refugees, in the framework of the Arab Peace Initiative (though without accepting a Palestinian "right of return," but rather on humanitarian grounds) such that a small number of Palestinians will be allowed to move to the State of Israel.

It is still possible to reach understandings about the Holy Basin that will respect freedom of religion and the connection of each religion to their own holy sites, without giving any country exclusive sovereignty over it.

Such a plan requires courage and vision.

Will Israel's new generation of leaders—Naftali Bennett, Yair Lapid, Benny Gantz, or others who may yet follow—see the need to move forward, urgently, on peace? Will the governments of the coming decade be brave enough, bold enough, and imaginative enough to take these crucial steps?

I wish I could tell you with confidence that they will. But I am far from certain. The new coalition is, at best, a marriage of convenience. The ideological gaps among the different parties are too wide to bridge, especially on this subject. The parliamentary majority they have built thus far is far too slim and fragile.

These facts cannot be ignored. But the new leadership that today makes up the governing coalition represents a fresh, honest approach that gives us hope.

I believe that this government, if it manages to stay in power for most of its term, might surprise us with a pragmatic approach that will clear the air with the Palestinian leadership.

There may be no choice but to go to yet another election—one that will focus specifically on the issue of peace with the Palestinians and the nature of Israel moving forward. Courageous leaders might seek a national mandate for moving forward.

The coming period will prove critical. Israel will have to confront the failures of the last decade.

Israel must lay a new foundation for its relations with its neighbors, one that will defuse the hostility that comes from endless occupation and the denial of the right of self-determination to another people.

We have to end the occupation of the territories, where we are spending billions each year in infrastructure projects for settlers who will one day be uprooted in order to make room for a future Palestinian state.

We have to stop subsidizing the settlements, giving them major allocations, tax breaks, and other support at the expense of hundreds of thousands of residents who live in poverty, who suffer from a lack of proper infrastructure, pollution, overcrowding, and environmental decay.

The IDF needs to be smaller and smarter and, as a result, to take up a reduced portion of our national expenditure. Israel's defense budget has been built in recent years mainly on panic and fear. Israel, however, is no longer threatened to a degree that justifies spending so many tens of billions of dollars on defense. I am not suggesting that the IDF needs to be weakened, God forbid. I know very well that this army, even at a smaller size, will be strong enough to withstand any future threat.

Israel also needs to prepare itself strategically for the new reality. Most important, it must prevent Iran from becoming a nuclear power that also actively destabilizes Israel's neighbors, including Syria, Lebanon, and others.

Iran is a pressing issue for both Israelis and its friends around the world. The possibility, even a distant one, that Iran could become a nuclear power, is intolerable. The consequences, unimaginable. The regime in Iran is fundamentalist, expansionist, and aggressive. Even without nuclear capabilities, they are a security threat not just to their immediate neighbors or the wider region but to every democratic state globally.

Israel and its friends around the world—especially the United States—must shoulder the burden of preventing even a limited nuclearization of Iran.

It is important to emphasize that the question is not whether Iran would actually try to use its nuclear capability to destroy Israel. Its extremist leaders like to boast about destroying the "Zionist entity," but in practice they know enough to restrain themselves, and to hold their fire in response to the humiliating setbacks that so often happen in their nuclear program.

Israel's problem, rather, is the possibility that at some point in the future, the conflicts in the Middle East will take place under the cloud of an Iranian nuclear capability. The influence it would have over the region, not just as a distant possibility but as an immediate threat, could be catastrophic.

A nuclear Iran would also create an insane nuclear arms race across the Middle East and, in all likelihood, beyond it. It would affect our whole way of life, even if the weapons were never used. We can never allow such a development, and it is clear that the State of Israel, under any government, will need to be willing to act with full force to prevent it.

During my term as prime minister, we took a great many steps against Iran in every corner of the world—including inside Iran, including at its enrichment facilities that are the centerpiece of their program to build a nuclear bomb, as well as at other sensitive facilities. Sometimes those actions did real damage, and we had good reason to believe that the Iranians were deeply frustrated by them. We refrained from talking about them publicly at the time, and for obvious reasons I will not go into details even today.

My approach here was different from Netanyahu's. I believed that Israel should not be the one to lead the international effort against a nuclear Iran. I said at the time that this responsibility fell first of all on the great powers and especially the United States, Russia, China, Britain, Germany, and France. President Bush felt as I did, and also launched initiatives, including UN Security Council resolutions, to impose a system of international economic sanctions on the Islamic Republic.

Netanyahu, on the other hand, typically used the Iranian nuclear threat politically, as a way of whipping up fear in the Israeli public and making his voters increasingly dependent on his leadership.

Netanyahu felt that Israel should destroy Iran's nuclear facilities through a military strike. Many in Israel disagreed, especially the leaders of our defense and intelligence agencies. The IDF chief of staff at the time, Lieutenant General Gabi Ashkenazi, said repeatedly and wisely that such a strike would push off Iran's nuclearization for a short time, but risked helping the regime publicly justify the program. The director of the Mossad, Meir Dagan—who had been personally responsible for coordinating all our operations against the Iranian threat—warned against any irresponsible military adventures that could end up doing far more harm than good to Israeli national and global interests.

The rationale behind an Israeli military strike was that it would hopefully force America to intervene and, at the end of the day, bring about the destruction of all of Iran's nuclear facilities. The idea amounted to a crazy high wire act. The Obama White House warned Netanyahu against such a move, and emphasized that it was committed to reaching an agreement with Iran that would prevent the kind of spiraling conflict that would likely result from an Israeli attack.

President Obama, meanwhile, assembled a broad international framework that did, in the end, reach a deal with Iran. Israel, in whose leadership Obama lost faith, wasn't invited to join the negotiations or even to get updated on its details.

When the deal was reached, a furious cry was heard from Israel's leaders. They took every advantage of the situation, mostly to try and paint the administration, both to the Israeli public and to American Jews, as hostile to Israel.

I spoke with everyone in Israel who was involved in dealing with Iran at the professional level, both on the operational side and with nuclear experts. All of them, without exception, thought the Iran deal was far from ideal, that there were quite a few problems that needed to be addressed. But at the same time, all of them felt this deal was good for Israel, certainly better than what prevailed beforehand. The Iran deal, they said, did not harm Israel, and in practice it pushed off the Iranian nuclear threat by quite a few years. President Trump, however, came into office having promised to cancel the deal. When he kept his promise, he gave Iran the excuse to restart its intensive enrichment efforts. Trump brought nothing positive to the table, and instead undid all the good that the Iran deal had brought.

President Biden has renewed talks with Iran, and all the indicators are that the Iran deal will be renewed. Biden is right to do so. Netanyahu and his vocal supporters, as well as some evangelists who long for Trump's return, will howl in protest. But the people familiar with these issues in Israel will be grateful to the president.

We have reached the point where it is better to deal with this issue quietly and to put an end to the parade of threats in which Israel has played the dominant role. I trust President Biden and his team to preserve and protect Israel's security. He proved himself over his decades in the Senate, as well as in his term as vice president.

Israel has many urgent problems that demand the full attention of its leaders. We are better off sharing responsibility for this particular problem with the world powers, especially the United States.

———

The Iranian nuclear threat is the most obvious of these problems, and it sits at the heart of Israel's security concerns. But it is not the only threat. Hezbollah, with Iran's backing, has amassed an enormous arsenal or missiles capable of reaching almost every strategic target in Israel. The Second Lebanon War created the deterrence that prevented Hezbollah from provoking Israel during the last fifteen years. But we should not dismiss the threat of a terror group with tens of thousands of missiles and an extremist, fundamentalist leadership that has no qualms about using them against our civilian population.

Even though Syria has been greatly weakened in the last decade due to its ongoing civil war, we cannot ignore the constant infiltration of aggressive Iranian forces in the country. The Syrian military, moreover, is well equipped, backed by Iran and enjoys the support of Russia. Syria, too, is an enemy state that refuses to accept the existence of Israel and must be deterred through appropriate measures.

The Gaza Strip is controlled by Hamas, an extremist terror organization that absolutely refuses to accept the existence of Israel. This group has been responsible, for many years now, for the ongoing rocket fire that threatens the lives of hundreds of thousands of Israeli civilians. The international criticism of Israeli aerial assaults in Gaza is largely unfounded. What would any other country do if hundreds of thousands of its citizens were targeted by thousands of rockets over so many years?

I do not believe there is any possibility of a political arrangement with Hamas. Israel has no choice but to defend itself against a terror organization that actively targets our civilians.

Alongside the necessary military actions, Israel should also find ways to offer residents of the Gaza Strip an improvement in the conditions of their lives. Israel has to assist in building a deep-water port in Gaza, to loosen the blockade, and to allow a broader infusion of goods and services, including the possibility of employment in Israel.

In the face of almost constant conflict with the terror group that runs Gaza, there is no easy solution. What I am proposing will require the massive investment of resources and manpower to oversee it. That responsibility rests on Israel's shoulders. It also fits our national interests.

All these challenges that Israel faces do not add up to an existential threat. The country's strategic posture in the third decade of the twenty-first century is completely different from what it was during its early years. Israel is now much stronger than all its enemies combined. Its military is more modern, better equipped, and savvier than all the armies and terror groups it has to contend with.

We have to preserve our military edge, however. The United States, our greatest ally, has committed itself to doing just that—and has come through consistently, for decades.

We are strong enough not only to defend ourselves, but also to channel our efforts and resources into other crucial areas, and to improve our quality of life and that of our neighbors.

Israel also needs to rebuild its relationship with the Jewish diaspora.

In the past, the support of American Jews was one of the foundations of Israel's power. Around the world, Israel's friends and enemies alike understood that American Jewry's staunch support of Israel was an important pillar of Israel's strength.

Yet the government over the last decade created a deep rift between Israel and significant parts of the Jewish community in America, as well as in Europe and in other Western countries.

The dominance of the Haredi parties in Israeli politics, and their brutal rejection of Conservative and Reform Jews, have caused many Diaspora Jews to disengage from Israel.

American synagogues and Jewish community organizations used to wave Israel's flag proudly and with conviction. But when Israel effectively tells Reform and Conservative Jews that it doesn't recognize their Jewish identity, it is turning its back on the core of global Jewry. This is potentially catastrophic.

We have no choice but to change the relationship between Israel's political establishment and the institutions of the non-Orthodox Jewish world, institutions that represent the beating heart and chosen path of the Jewish diaspora.

This will require a courageous, historic decision—one that must be taken before we wake up to find that these Jewish communities, which in the past rallied global opinion behind Israel and invested billions of desperately-needed dollars to help build the Jewish state, no longer see themselves as sharing in our collective fate.

There are additional challenges facing Israel in the decade ahead. Israel's educational system was once a model of success. Our schools, especially our public schools, formed the basis of our scientific, technological, social, and military achievements, turning the country as a whole into a powerhouse success story.

Strengthening our country depends on redirecting some of the resources currently spent on defense into education, which has been starved of funding for years, measurably hindering the achievements of our students.

There are also economic gaps that cannot be justified. The percentage of our population that lives below the poverty line is greater than that of most countries in the OECD. To reduce the gap, we need to invest massively in education, healthcare, welfare, and infrastructure. Israel has become more overcrowded than most European countries. Our roads can't handle the hundreds of thousands of cars driving on them each day. This has a dramatic effect on the quality of life of many of our residents, and results in wasted resources that could be spent on things that are really important.

The large part of our country in the south is made up of mostly uninhabited desert waiting for initiative, for innovation, for the creative imagination of Israelis who can turn it into a paradise. David Ben-Gurion, our first prime minister, imagined an Israel that settled the Negev and made it bloom. He himself chose to live in a remote kibbutz, Sdeh Boker, in Israel's south.

Israel today has the tools and the resources to make Ben-Gurion's dream come true, to develop the southern half of our country. But for this to happen, we will have to completely upend our national priorities as reflected in the allocation of our resources.

We need to leave the West Bank to the Palestinians, who are sick of being ruled by us, and instead to build up the Negev. To bring hundreds of thousands of people looking for the opportunity to prosper in a secure environment, in conditions that will allow for the quality of life they are today denied.

Israel is recognized around the world as the start-up nation, and justifiably so. No other nation, whether of Israel's size or even among many larger, wealthier ones, has been as successful in developing new technologies that affect almost every aspect of our lives. The innovations in agriculture are incredible. In fruit and vegetable farming, Israeli technology increases yields to a stunning degree, growing healthy, flavorful produce in quantities unknown in the past. The same is true for dairy farming. Dozens of innovative Israeli dairy farms have served as a model to bring massive increases in milk production in China and other countries.

The development of desalination and wastewater technology in Israel has completely solved Israel's endemic water shortage, and has also become a vital resource for many other countries that today might otherwise be facing unprecedented water shortages.

Israel is a global leader, as well, in a wide range of computer-based technologies, including chip development, artificial intelligence, autonomous vehicles, unmanned aerial vehicles of different sizes and capabilities, and of course the most sophisticated cybersecurity firms in the world.

Nor does Israeli creative success end with technological innovation. Indeed, Israelis excel in almost every creative field, including music, the arts, science, and medicine. The quality of Israeli doctors and the level of its medical research are among the best in the world. It should come as no surprise that Israel's healthcare providers knew how to efficiently deliver both care and vaccines—at least when compared with most other countries—in the face of the horrific COVID-19 pandemic.

Young Israelis excel in their innovation, their creative imagination, and their immense energy. It is no coincidence that these young people have turned Israel into a global leader in technological innovation. We have the most talented, dynamic human talent in the world. If we give them a path to prosperity, they will preserve our planet.

The State of Israel is infused with talented, creative, visionary people. I believe, with all my heart, that they will know, when the time comes, how to overcome the crisis of our recent years, and will lead the country to a new era of prosperity, achievement, and success.

Acknowledgments

This book was written, almost in its entirety, by longhand in Hebrew in Cellblock 10 at Maasiyahu Penitentiary, on many hundreds of pages filling dozens of yellow legal pads, over a seven-month period from early March through September of 2016.

Every Sunday during that time, my attorney Eli Zohar brought me fresh legal pads and Pilot pens. At the end of each visit, he took the pages I had filled the previous week, chapter by chapter, to a typist at Yedioth Books, which published the book in Hebrew.

By late 2016, I had written what turned out to be more than 1,200 typed pages in Hebrew. I read through them all, adding and trimming, expanding and editing. The pages were then reviewed by both the book's editor and the military censor. More than a year went by before it finally appeared in its original, full Hebrew edition in 2018.

Many people took part in this immense undertaking. I have mentioned Eli Zohar, who passed away in 2020, and I will forever be grateful for his dedication. Eli, in addition to being an excellent attorney, was first of all a supportive, wise friend.

Shalom Turjeman and Yaakov Galanti accompanied me for many years—in both my public positions and my private business. Their help was critical during the writing of this book and ever since.

Rachael Risby Raz is a friend and former assistant whose loyalty and dedication were, and still are, a source of great pride. She is an exceptional human being.

I am also deeply grateful to my other assistants—Hagar Yahav, who was an outstanding supporter above and beyond the call of duty, as well as Sharon Katz.

Sharon Tzur has been a friend and adviser for more than twenty years. Had it not been for her dedication, encouragement, resourcefulness, and unlimited energy, I doubt this book would ever have seen the light of day. I cannot thank her enough.

Frank Luntz, known worldwide as a leading pollster and international political consultant, is also a friend. During my time as prime minister, he helped me craft my address before a joint session of Congress in Washington, probably the most important speech I ever delivered in English. Then and since, I never stopped gaining from his wisdom and friendship. Frank contributed his time and wisdom in advance of the book's English-language publication, reading through the manuscript and offering crucial insights throughout.

David Hazony not only translated this book into English, but also offered his enormous experience in adapting the original Hebrew version into an English edition that hopefully may appeal to readers outside of Israel.

Peter and Amy Bernstein, my dedicated literary agents, have guided me through the labyrinth of publishing a book in America. Their vast experience and knowledge made its publication possible.

It is both an honor and a source of enduring satisfaction for this book to appear through the Brookings Institution Press. I am deeply grateful to my editor, Bill Finan, for his support, encouragement, and sage advice.

S. Daniel Abraham has been a crucial friend and supporter over decades. Few private individuals have dedicated as much of their time and personal resources into advancing the cause of peace in the Middle East as he has. Above all, he has stood by me in the most difficult periods of my life, and I am eternally grateful for his friendship.

Finally, I cannot conclude without thanking my loved ones—above all Aliza, my beloved wife, as well as my wonderful children, Shula, Michal, Dana, Shaul and Ariel, their charming life-partners, and all our grandchildren—Hilel, Roni, Alma, Ido, Naama, Itamar, Amalia, Amitai, Avigail, Daniel, Yotam, and Miriam. Your love and dedication are a source of infinite joy.

Index

Abbas, Mahmoud: Annapolis Peace Conference (2007) and, 283–87; Bush (G.W.) and, 165; Hamas and, 276; Olmert's negotiations with, 198, 233, 270–71, 294–98, 314, 320–22; Olmert's presentation of his plan to (September 16, 2008), 294–96, 321; as Palestinian Authority president, 101, 270; Rice's presentation of Olmert's ideas to, 291–92; Sharm El-Sheikh summit (2007), 278–81; Sharon and, 165. *See also* Palestinians, negotiations with

Abbas, Mazen, 275

Abdullah (king of Jordan), 165

Abdullah II (Jordan), 191, 278

Abraham, S. Daniel, 96, 302–03

Abramovitch, Aharon, 265

Abrams, Elliott, 169–70, 172, 222, 245, 291

Abrams, Rachel, 169

Abu Nidal, 71

Accusations against Olmert, 1–4, 299–317; Adelson's role in, 302, 306–10; Bank Leumi Affair (2007), 240–41, 304; convictions ending political career, 2, 300; enemies as part of public life, 300–301; fountain pen collection of Olmert and, 305; funding behind, 306–08; "Go Home" document on forcing prime minister to resign, 309; Holyland

Hotel Affair acquittal, 1–2, 4, 5, 9–10, 306; indictment causing resignation as prime minister, 2, 300, 305; lack of evidence and acquittals, 300, 304; legal puritan camp targeting Olmert, 301, 302; media role in, 302–06; Olmert's position weakened in dealing with Hamas and PLA, 292, 297–98, 315–16; personal loan Olmert received and, 305; political rivals targeting Olmert, 301, 306; prison sentence, 2–3, 25, 300; on purchase of Olmert's home in Jerusalem, 303; Rishon Tours Affair acquittal, 22, 305, 313; on sale of Olmert's apartment to Abraham, 302–03; tactic of endless frivolous suits and associated costs, 305; Talansky Affair (2008), 292, 305, 312, 313; Yossi Olmert's receipt of money from Olmert and, 3–4, 306

Adam, Udi, 216

Adelson, Sheldon, 302, 306–11, 316, 325

Adelson Institute at Shalem Center, 308

Adler, Reuven, 166, 176, 194

Al-Aqsa Mosque. *See* Temple Mount

Alef, Degania, 61

Allon, Yigal, 184

Al-Manar TV station (Beirut), 210, 213

Altalena (ship), 29, 30, 35

Altman, Aryeh, 41